Realizing the University

in an age of supercomplexity

SRHE and Open University Press Imprint
General Editor: Heather Eggins

Current titles include:

Catherine Bargh *et al.*: *Governing Universities*
Ronald Barnett: *Improving Higher Education*
Ronald Barnett: *The Idea of Higher Education*
Ronald Barnett: *The Limits of Competence*
Ronald Barnett: *Higher Education*
Ronald Barnett: *Realizing the University in an age of supercomplexity*
Neville Bennett *et al.*: *Skills Development in Higher Education and Employment*
John Biggs: *Teaching for Quality Learning at University*
David Boud *et al.* (eds): *Using Experience for Learning*
Etienne Bourgeois *et al.*: *The Adult University*
Tom Bourner *et al.* (eds): *New Directions in Professional Higher Education*
John Brennan *et al.* (eds): *What Kind of University?*
Angela Brew (ed.): *Directions in Staff Development*
Anne Brockbank and Ian McGill: *Facilitating Reflective Learning in Higher Education*
Stephen Brookfield and Stephen Preskill: *Discussion as a Way of Teaching*
Ann Brooks: *Academic Women*
Sally Brown and Angela Glasner (eds): *Assessment Matters in Higher Education*
John Cowan: *On Becoming an Innovative University Teacher*
Heather Eggins (ed.): *Women as Leaders and Managers in Higher Education*
Gillian Evans: *Calling Academia to Account*
David Farnham (ed.): *Managing Academic Staff in Changing University Systems*
Sinclair Goodlad: *The Quest for Quality*
Harry Gray (ed.): *Universities and the Creation of Wealth*
Norman Jackson and Helen Lund (eds): *Benchmarking for Higher Education*
Mary Lea and Barry Stierer (eds): *Student Writing in Higher Education*
Elaine Martin: *Changing Academic Work*
David Palfreyman and David Warner (eds): *Higher Education and the Law*
John Pratt: *The Polytechnic Experiment*
Craig Prichard: *Making Managers in Universities and Colleges*
Michael Prosser and Keith Trigwell: *Understanding Learning and Teaching*
Stephen Rowland: *The Enquiring University Teacher*
Yoni Ryan & Ortrun Zuber-Skerritt (eds): *Supervising Postgraduates from Non-English
    Speaking Backgrounds*
Maggi Savin-Baden: *Problem-based Learning in Higher Education: Untold Stories*
Peter Scott (ed.): *The Globalization of Higher Education*
Peter Scott: *The Meanings of Mass Higher Education*
Anthony Smith and Frank Webster (eds): *The Postmodern University?*
Imogen Taylor: *Developing Learning in Professional Education*
Peter G. Taylor: *Making Sense of Academic Life*
Susan Toohey: *Designing Courses for Higher Education*
Paul R. Trowler: *Academics Responding to Change*
David Warner and Elaine Crosthwaite (eds): *Human Resource Management in
    Higher and Further Education*
David Warner and Charles Leonard: *The Income Generation Handbook*
    (Second Edition)
David Warner and David Palfreyman (eds): *Higher Education Management*
Graham Webb: *Understanding Staff Development*
Diana Woodward and Karen Ross: *Managing Equal Opportunities in Higher Education*

Realizing the University

in an age of supercomplexity

Ronald Barnett

The Society for Research into Higher Education
& Open University Press

Published by SRHE and
Open University Press
Celtic Court
22 Ballmoor
Buckingham
MK18 1XW

email: enquiries@openup.co.uk
world wide web: http://www.openup.co.uk

and
325 Chestnut Street
Philadelphia, PA 19106, USA

First published 2000

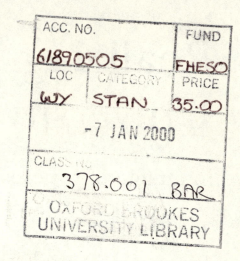
A catalogue record of this book is available from the British Library

ISBN 0 335 20248 9 (pbk)   0 335 20249 7 (hbk)

Library of Congress Cataloging-in-Publication Data
Barnett, Ronald, 1947–
    Realizing the university in an age of supercomplexity / Ronald
Barnett.
        p.   cm.
    Includes bibliographical references and index.
    ISBN 0–335–20249–7 (hbk). – ISBN 0–335–20248–9 (pbk)
    1. Education, Higher – Aims and objectives.   2. Universities and
colleges – Philosophy.   3. Postmodernism and education.   I. Title.
LB2322.2.B37   1999
378′.01–DC21   99–24212
                                                           CIP

Typeset by Graphicraft Limited, Hong Kong
Printed in Great Britain by St Edmundsbury Press,
Bury St Edmunds, Suffolk

For Gerald Collier

Contents

Acknowledgements   x

Introduction   1

Part 1: The End is Nigh   9
  1 Death and Resurrection   11
  2 The End of Enlightenment?   23
  3 The Ends of Knowledge   35
  4 The Fading Constellations   47

Part 2: Supercomplexity and the University   59
  5 The Constellation of Fragility   61
  6 Supercomplexity: the New Universal   72
  7 The Conflict of the Faculties   84

Part 3: Reframing the University   97
  8 Conditions of the University   99
  9 A Suitable Ethos   111

Part 4: Realizing the University   125
10 Constructing the University   127
11 Research in a Supercomplex World   140
12 Teaching for a Supercomplex World   153

Conclusions   166

Notes   173
Bibliography   183
Index   193
The Society for Research into Higher Education   201

He could not himself have said what he lacked. His deepest wish seemed this: that he should grow into a good, trusty scholar, soon to be received into the novitiate, and so live on to the end, as a quiet, devout brother of the cloister. He believed that his whole faculties and strength were centred in these simple, peaceful aims, and had no thought nor knowledge of other strivings. How strange and hard it seemed to him, therefore, that even this, his fair and quiet purpose, should be so difficult of achievement.

(Herman Hesse, *Narziss and Goldmund,* Penguin edition, 1971: 19)

Acknowledgements

My thanks go to Kelly Coate, Gerard Delanty, Steve Fuller, Oliver Fulton, Gunther Kress, David Telford, David Watson and Frank Webster, all of whom read and commented on the entire manuscript. I hope that each of them will see something of their comments reflected in the final text. David Telford also provided bibliographic assistance.

I thank John Skelton at the Open University Press for his continuing support and patience. Such support from a publisher is invaluable in combating the loneliness of the long-distance writer.

As always with my writing efforts, Upma Barnett has given me enormous support, not only through giving the text the benefits of her professional editor's eye but in the wider support and patience that she has continued to lend to my scholarly work. For much of the time we communicate at a distance, across the ends of our living-room, as I work on successive manuscripts. Without that support, it would be difficult to sustain my intellectual energies.

Introduction

Paradise lost or paradise regained?

A largely unvoiced problem lies before the Western university. It is, as we may term it, the problem of responsibility. Can we any longer speak of 'responsibility' in relation to the university? Is there a single large responsibility or a connected set of responsibilities with which the university might be identified? There are certainly grave difficulties attached to deploying the notion of responsibility in relation to the university, but I believe that they can be overcome.

Three difficulties in particular await us. Firstly, the notion of responsibility in relation to the university has its place within an accepted value background; for example, that the pursuit of knowledge is a good thing or that social justice is worth striving for. However, in an era that has difficulty with large ideas, no such value position can be held with any sense of security.

Secondly, value positions assume that their objects are attainable. For instance, the belief that the pursuit of knowledge is a good thing entails the further belief that knowledge is attainable. Unfortunately, such large goals turn out always to be out of our reach. But if it transpires that such goals are unattainable in any straightforward sense, then any set of responsibilities founded on any such belief is in trouble.

Lastly, the notion of responsibility in this context takes it as read that the university is a proper and an effective vehicle for realizing those values. However, amid the uncertainties of 'the global age' on the one hand and the constraints of 'the evaluative state' on the other, this more instrumental assumption is also in jeopardy. It is not at all clear that the university any more has the space and the autonomy to deliver *any* set of goals.

Values, goals and instruments: as we look at them more closely, all the conceptual and operational underpinnings of the university crumble. On any serious examination of the foundations of the university, the thought must loom that paradise lost is a proper reading of the situation before us. I do not, however, believe that such a pessimistic outlook is necessary. The university is wanted more than ever, has more resources than ever and even has more friends than ever. We should not cave into the gloom merchants too readily.

I contend that, without flinching, we can talk of responsibility in the context of the university; and I shall try to show what those responsibilities are in this book. Paradise regained may now always be beyond us. But some kind of value position may be within reach, even if it is inevitably uneasy. The problem of responsibility in the university can be solved *and* yield a positive outcome.

Old ruins or new foundations?

> We have to recognize that the University is a *ruined institution*, while thinking what it means to dwell in those ruins without recourse to romantic nostalgia.
>
> (Readings, 1996: 169, author's emphasis)

Readings has it half right. The University *is* a ruined institution, but we do not have to dwell in its ruins. We can construct a *new* University. In doing so, we should certainly eschew 'romantic nostalgia'. However, it just may be that the construction of the very kind of University that is fitting for the contemporary world might have to draw to some extent on earlier ideas of the University, even while abandoning most of those conceptual foundations.

If we are going to construct a new University, both as idea and as a set of practices, we need to have an understanding of the challenges that are besetting institutions that would go under the title of 'University'. For Readings, the modern University 'has had three ideas: the Kantian concept of reason, the Humboldtian idea of culture, and now the techno-bureaucratic notion of excellence' (ibid.: 14). It is in this third conception that the University loses its way, for the idea of excellence 'has no *content*; it is hence neither true nor false, neither ignorant nor self-conscious' (ibid.: 13). I agree with this diagnosis, but I believe that there is an even larger problematic at work. It is a problematic that requires that the assault on the traditions of the Western University be formulated more broadly than Readings allows; but it is a problematic that, at the same time, opens up new responsibilities and new possibilities for the University. Identifying that problematic, both in its challenges and in its opportunities, constitutes one of the tasks ahead of us in this book.

One way of putting these opening remarks is to proclaim that, in the contemporary era, the university lacks foundations. In a rare moment of uplift, the arch anti-foundationalist, Jacques Derrida, declared:

> We live in a world where the foundation of a new law – in particular a new university law – is necessary. To call it necessary is to say . . . that one has to take responsibility, a new kind of responsibility, and that this new foundation is on the way, and irresistibly so.
>
> (Derrida, 1992: 30)

What is this new foundation to be? And what kind of responsibility does one have to take? Derrida doesn't say. He does suggest that the 'new foundation will negotiate a compromise with the traditional law', but that's it. Again, as to what kind of a compromise is available, Derrida is silent.

Foundation, responsibility and negotiation: these terms suggest that the university is in trouble but that all is not lost. Any set of ideas and hopes – 'the traditional law' – with which the university might have been associated has been dealt a severe blow. A new settlement might just be within our grasp. I agree with all this. However, Derrida left us in the dark on these crucial matters – of foundation, responsibility and negotiation. In this book, I provide answers to each of these three challenges. Firstly, the foundations of the Western university have been undermined but new foundations can be inserted. Secondly, we can no longer use the language of 'responsibility' without pausing but, as we shall see, such language is possible; indeed, necessary (to use, again, one of Derrida's terms). Lastly, certain problematic features of the condition of the university cannot be brushed aside but a negotiation is possible that even does some justice to the value background of the Western university. Foundation, responsibility and negotiation: all are available. Securing these prizes is the triple task ahead of us.

If we keep for the moment to the architectural imagery of ruins and foundations, we can say that we are in an earthquake zone. 'The big one' may be just around the corner. Certainly, tremors will be felt from time to time. Accordingly, any new foundations that we put in will have to be built on a recognition of continuing unsteadiness. Conceptual, experiential and operational flexibility have to be allowed for. The building will shake; the hope is that it will not fall down.

Hazard notices

In the argument to come, a number of clarifications and distinctions should be borne in mind. They constitute, as it were, a set of notices of potential hazards on the journey ahead.

Postmodern or post-modern?

The argument to come hinges on a fundamental distinction between postmodernity and postmodernism. A new world order is upon us. Partly as a result of globalization, partly as a result of the information technology revolution and partly as a result of other forms of change, we have to reckon with societal and global dislocations that challenge the progress towards modernity. For convenience, I refer in what follows to the post-modern society or post-modern world. The hyphen is deliberate: the stress is on the prefix. We are into a new world order. I take this to be the case.

With it, too, goes postmodernity, that set of conditions characteristic of this post-modern order. Here, post-modern and postmodernity are descriptive and neutral terms. They are attempts to capture something of the flavour of the constituents of the emerging era.

On the other hand, there has been much talk of the postmodern and, with it, of postmodernism. These terms are largely value terms. They refer to hopes and values: they proclaim a new world order. They herald it: they put it up in neon lights. The fragmentation, the lack of foundations and the openness to human affairs that these terms are intended to convey are enthusiastically endorsed. The uses of these terms purport to be describing the world but, in fact, are engaged on the task of transforming it. They do believe that the end of modernity is nigh and, more significantly, they also believe 'and not before time'. This value-laden view is one that I contend with in this book. In it, I believe, lies an abdication of responsibility for the university. But in it, too, lies an annexation of the university to the domin-ant interests of the day. In short, behind postmodernism and talk of the postmodern lies a philosophy that I repudiate.

Accordingly, throughout this book, I use the terms 'post-modern' and 'postmodern' to convey this set of distinctions. 'The post-modern university' is used quite deliberately to mark out the conditions of the university as I see them. I am neither in favour of the post-modern university nor against it, for the reason that such responses are inappropriate. I am simply trying to capture some of the context in which the contemporary university has to be understood. The categories of the postmodern and postmodernism, on the other hand, invite value positions and I hope that I shall make clear that they are dangerous roads down which to go. They offer a cul-de-sac leading to a set of gangsters who do not have gentle motives in mind.

I consider this distinction between the post-modern as a sociological description and the postmodern as a philosophical position to be funda-mental. Unfortunately, some err in conflating the two and lead us into a double jeopardy.

On essentialism

Comments on my previous books on higher education have suggested that in my arguments lies a streak of essentialism. Some support it; others reject it.

In what follows, I tackle the matter head-on. The argument that I make rests explicitly on an acknowledgement that any straightforward essentialist argument is simply not a serious runner. The suggestion that there could be a single idea or set of ideas to carry us forward in placing and in develop-ing our universities in the twenty-first century is clearly going to be prob-lematic. We shall look at and reject in turn a number of possible claimants as 'the story' of the post-modern university. But the more general argument is even more insistent: the sheer complexity of national systems of higher education speak against *any* unifying story. Mass higher education and its resulting diversity – even if muted – puts an end to all that.

But, as I hope to show, that is not necessarily the end of the story. The question still remains a fair one: even amid the loss of any unifying narrative, indeed even amid conflicting narratives, how might we place the university? Can we talk seriously about the university having any set of responsibilities? I hope to show that we can.

On the university

Commonly in this book, I talk of 'the university'. The term 'universities' appears much less often. Even phrases such as 'the university sector' or 'the university system' are much less in evidence. There are likely to be three reactions to this terminology. On the one hand, talk of 'the university' simply fails to acknowledge the considerable diversity that exists in any mass system of higher education. Secondly, it presumes just what has been denied, that it makes sense to talk as such of 'the university'. It implies that there is a common set of ideas for which all universities stand. It begs just what is in question. Thirdly, it pretends that there is some continuity over time in the identity of universities. No 'detraditionalization' here is the message.

In fact, I presume none of these things. I address each of these issues in this book. Certainly, I begin by using this terminology and hold to it. I do so because I wish precisely to determine:

1. whether we can identify a general view as to the place of the university in the contemporary era;

and, if we can:

2. whether that general view has any continuity with what might be said to be the Western idea of the University.

In the past, there was less squeamishness about deploying such terminology. Many authors did so, building over time an extensive literature on 'The University'. Newman, Ortega y Gasset, Jaspers and Moberly would be held to be among the representatives of that genre. Even Kerr, speaking in the context of the mass and differentiated situation of the USA, resorted to the terminology. In using that terminology, I do not mean that this book should be seen as standing in that line; indeed, part of the argument here is that we have to abandon much of the conceptual and epistemological heritage of the idea of the Western university. Nevertheless, I want to place on the table the possibility not just that it makes sense to hang onto some portion of the Western idea of the University, but that universities (plural) are being asked to do so by the wider world.

This is the extraordinary possibility before us: that just at the moment when there are calls for demonstrable performativity and when the university's traditions are under assault both conceptually and operationally, there arises a wide plea for the university to retain something of its heritage. That will form one plank of the argument to come.

A supercomplex world

We now live in a world subject to infinite interpretability. It is this world for which universities are having to prepare their students; and it is this world in which research is conducted. On the one hand, as individuals, whether as members of organizations in the workplace or whether as citizens making choices in the public domain, we are besieged by multiple interpretations of our actions and, *pari passu*, the knowledge frames that we bring to bear within those actions. On the other hand, research is now a plastic activity, conducted in many different sites beyond the university and taking a multitude of differing forms. At the same time, the products of research are themselves subject to rival commentaries from various quarters.

This is a situation, I shall argue, of *supercomplexity*. This term will be pivotal in the explorations to come and it would, therefore, perhaps be helpful to say a little about the idea here.

A situation of complexity exists where one is faced with a surfeit of data, knowledge or theoretical frames *within* one's immediate situation. A doctor is faced with innumerable new drugs appearing on the market, or is aware of new forms of surgery or new instrumentation. Simply keeping abreast of the field may appear to be nigh-on impossible. This is a situation of *complexity*. But, in addition to these cognitive and operational challenges, the doctor is also increasingly faced with challenges to his or her own self-understanding. Working in an environment more subject to managerial disciplines, doctors are having to understand themselves as consumers of resources and as having to give a public account of their activities to their employing organization. At the same time, patients are presenting with increasing claims emerging from a heightened sense of their rights within a reordered professional–client relationship. They may wish to have access to their medical records, to play a part in determining the hospital to which and the consultant to whom they are being referred and to be active in deciding any interventions to be used. They may even come with suggestions as to the kinds of treatment that they wish to have and which may – on ethical or other grounds – seem of dubious validity.

In short, professional life is increasingly becoming a matter not just of handling overwhelming data and theories *within* a given frame of reference (a situation of complexity) but also a matter of handling multiple frames of understanding, of action and of self-identity. The fundamental frameworks by which we might understand the world are multiplying and are often in conflict. Of the multiplication of frameworks, there shall be no end.

It is this multiplication of frameworks that I term *supercomplexity*. It increasingly characterizes the world in which we all live. Working out its operational, cognitive and pedagogical implications for the university constitute much of the challenge ahead.

Plan

In Part 1 (Chapters 1 to 4), I show how the current candidates for supplying foundations for the university are inadequate to the task; in Part 2 (Chapters 5 to 7), I turn to depicting the new context – largely, one of supercomplexity – within which we have to understand the university; in Part 3 (Chapters 8 and 9), I move to establishing the conditions of what it is to be a 'university' in the context of supercomplexity; and in the concluding Part (Chapters 10 to 12), I show the implications of the general argument for management and leadership in the university, for research and for teaching.

The press of professional life hardly allows for the close reading of books these days. The books accumulate on the shelves, to be read 'one day'. For those in this familiar position, an abbreviated reading of the book is available via Chapters 6 (where I develop the key concept of supercomplexity), 8 (where I lay out the conditions of the university) and 10, 11 and 12 (where I illuminate the general argument by attending to the key activities of the university). Perhaps, one day, some moments of leisure will allow that fuller reading.

Part 1

The End is Nigh

1

Death and Resurrection

Introduction

The Western university is at an end. But a new university can arise. We have
to put aside some familiar and even much-cherished notions of the university so that we can move on and develop a new idea of the university. There
should be no difficulty about this process. But, of course, there will be.
Familiar notions with which we have cloaked ourselves in living out the
university are not easily abandoned. The future that beckons, however, is
not just a new order. It is an order with new possibilities which may even
turn out to do justice of a kind to traditional values.

Resurrection is possible only through death; the death is *required*. A new
kind of university is possible which disavows its predecessor; and, yet, we will
still justifiably be able to call it a university.[1] The old lives on in the new.
That is the story to be told and the claim to be argued.

This seems illogical straight away. On the one hand, a disavowal of the
old to make way for the new. On the other hand, the old living on amid the
new. Yet that apparent double think is precisely the story to be told here. Of
course, both positions have to be justified and they have to be justified
together.

Eyebrows will have been raised at these opening statements. Firstly, it will
be felt that the language of death and resurrection is just hyperbole.[2] Higher
education flourishes across the world, desired by diverse and growing constituencies.[3] The students can often hardly find room to sit down, whether
in the library, the computer room or the lecture theatre. Talk of death in
these circumstances is not just exaggerated; it is entirely inappropriate.

Secondly, the suggestion that the old can live amid the new is indicative
that the argument to come has not shrugged off the old after all. Despite
the surface talk of death and resurrection, there lurks underneath, it seems,
an *a priori* unwillingness to jettison the old stories so as properly to conduct
the last rites. The bold talk of death is betrayed by an unwillingness to let
go. Whether this reluctance to let go, this apparent allegiance to familiar

stories, is a sign of an outworn personal attachment or, more fundamentally, is an indication that traditional justifications are (for reasons yet to be
explained) of continuing resonance, talk of death while the past is living on
is, at best, problematic.

These certainly are challenges to the argument to be made here. Higher
education, in many ways, flourishes as never before; and traditional justifications for the university may continue to have resonance. Both considerations
will have to form features of the argument to come, even alongside the
central points of the argument, namely that the university as we have understood it is at an end and that we need to find a new way of understanding
the university.

Paradoxically, the university – as idea – is in difficulty partly *because of* its
new flourishing as an institution. However, we are not bereft of an institution that we can properly call a 'university'. Radically reframed, we can
continue – and with a straight face – to use the term 'university' precisely
because there will be resonances with *some* of its traditional connotations. In
the family, the new generations succeed the old, but they continue to bear
the family name. So too with the university. We are at a point where the old
has now to be laid, certainly with dignity, to rest. The new awaits; but so
does its formation, its definition and its character. Much lies ahead.

Sacred and profane

A bishop without a cathedral is termed a suffragan bishop. Office, institution and city: ideally, all were found together. A city possessed its cathedral
which, in turn, possessed its bishop. In mediaeval times, the town had made
it when it saw its cathedral taking shape above the roofs. If it could not have
a cathedral, at least let it possess a fine church. No matter how small the
town or village, there lay its status. Such universities as existed were generally a thorough nuisance and were better avoided; or, if they showed signs
of emerging, were better driven out beyond the city walls, even if a few
skulls had to be broken in the process.[4]

Subsequently, more secular entities claimed attention for demonstrations
of local superiority. In Great Britain, the Victorian railway stations came to
take ecclesiastical form, with high sweeping arches and buttresses under
which rituals were solemnly conducted and in which the different social
classes knew and took their places. More recently, the vigour of a town has
come to be marked by its shopping centre and, in particular, its supermarket. These, too, have taken on churchly appearances, with pointed roofs
reaching into the sky and dominating the local architecture.

Now, however, a new wave of local demand is apparent. Every town
wants a university of its own. This is the new symbol of local status and
energy. In the university are multiple signs to the world with which any
town would wish to align itself. Knowledge and power, production and consumption, economic renewal and social equity, responsiveness and tradition:

all these messages – rival as they may be – and many more are conveyed by the presence in the town's midst of a university. As the twenty-first century arrives, a town has become more than a mere town if it can point to its university; and, if it has one, the pointing will be done with some pride.

This is an astonishing but little remarked-on turn of events. It is astonishing in a number of ways. Firstly, the university has come back into the town. In the UK, in the last wave of their formation in the 1960s, universities were banished to 'greenfield' sites.[5] Their geography spoke of their other-worldliness; now, their inner-city presences speak loudly on behalf of their new and general validity. Secondly, as with the shopping centres, they are now centres of consumption, albeit knowledge consumption, in addition to their being centres of knowledge production and cultural enhancement (Scott, 1995). Thirdly, they are now sites of mass involvement.[6] Again, not everyone yet has economic access to shopping centres but they are centres of mass participation. So it is, if to a slightly lesser exent, with the university. Almost everyone wishes to and now can identify with the university, even if its access remains stubbornly beyond the reach of many.

As a result, and lastly, being cut off from the university is now felt to be being cut off from one of the significant cultural resources of society. In the church or cathedral, one engaged in a shared experience in which one was granted access to a different level of being above and beyond; so it is now with the university. Through membership of the university, one is now – in a significant sense – a member of the modern society, given access to some-what mysterious forms of understanding. Where there was once the church, now there is the university.

The contemporary university, accordingly, is a new embodiment of both church and supermarket, of otherness and of commodities easily to be accessed and consumed. In it are combined, if uneasily, both the sacred and the profane. In these circumstances, talk of the death of the university must appear a little premature, to say the least. It is wanted more than ever before; it is enjoyed – if that is the word – more than ever before; and it is more active, visibly so, and in many more ways than ever before.

One of the key concepts developed by Pierre Bourdieu is that of 'habitus' (1998). A complex concept, it connotes the individual as configured by a nexus of cultural predispositions, of symbolic orderings and of value positions. Raising that concept to the institutional level, we can say that the university as such is finding a new *habitus*, a new location in society, a new ordering of its perceived value, and a new register of meaning and understanding across its now enlarged audience. Indeed, through its repositioning (Coffield and Williamson, 1997), the university has managed to generate new audiences and even new customers for its services. The university lives with a renewed sense of its purposes and value in its new *habitus*. There is, surely, no end in sight here. There are all the signs of renewed vigour and expectation. Far from being in sight, the death of the university is the very opposite of the situation before us.

Wider and wider

In a recent paper, Robert Cowen speaks of 'the attenuated university' (Cowen, 1996). Perhaps this is a more fruitful line of analysis. If the university is not dead, perhaps it is now diminished in some important ways. Perhaps it is 'attenuated'.

The argument Cowen makes is that, in its contemporary situation, the university is circumscribed in all kinds of way: the state has boxed it in through its intrusive evaluative procedures; the world of work has subtly and indirectly brought about a shift in emphasis of the purposes of higher education, such that knowledge is no longer 'its own end' (as Newman urged (1976 edn)) but is now to be judged for the 'performative' competencies that it yields; the development of a quasi-market has further reduced the autonomy enjoyed by universities as institutions; and the arrival of 'the new public management' in the university has brought managerial disciplines which have further curtailed the freedoms enjoyed by academics.[7] More may now be hoped of or even demanded from the mass university than ever before; but these very demands, framed as they are from within certain value positions and for certain ends, limit the university to follow its own predilections. We are faced, accordingly, with 'the attenuated university'.

The argument may be beguiling but it doesn't quite work. At least, ever since Clark Kerr (1972 edn) introduced us to the idea of the 'multiversity' in the 1960s, we have had to recognize the growing multiplicity of roles that the university is taking on itself. Partly, this expansion of roles is due to the development of the 'knowledge society' external to the academy (Stehr, 1994) but, partly, it is an indirect consequence of the proliferation of knowledges *within* the university itself (Gokulsing and Da Costa, 1997). Of course, these two forms – external knowledges/internal knowledges – so interrelate that no clear boundary can be observed between them. As a result, knowledge is often now a carrier for extramural interests, whether of a practical or a self-actualizing form. Within the academy, epistemology is rivalled by techne and ontology: knowing about the world is compounded by practice in the world and life-world becoming.[8]

Against this background, talk of the 'attenuated university' has to be heavily nuanced if it is to be a serious runner. The diversity of activities in research and consultancy, the expanding scope of what it is to be an academic, and the widening range of students and their courses are all testimony in the other direction. To the modern university, there appear to be no limits. The modern university stretches out here and there, amoeba-like, wherever it can find a response and, sometimes still, even where it cannot.

Certainly, there are signs of attenuation and in two forms: substantively and procedurally. Substantively, there is the prospect that knowing, even in the academy, from here on has to pay its way, in whatever form. We run here into Lyotard's (1984) 'performativity' thesis (a thesis which will gnaw away under this text). This remains a radical, even subversive thesis. At its extreme, truth values are themselves sabotaged, changed from disinterestedness to pragmatic use and exchange value. We do not even have to invoke the growing presence of consultancy among academics' services. Signs of this performativity are to be found in both research, for example, through the drive towards research which will yield patents and technology transfer; and teaching, for example, in the commodification of teaching, such that it becomes an alienable thing in itself, being literally packaged for students in handouts and learning packs. In both domains, the knowing activity is at least coloured if not transformed by its exchange value.

Procedurally, too, we see signs of possible attenuation. Externally and internally, across the world, academics have come to be more managed (whether well or ill is another matter). In the 'audit society' (Power, 1997), their activities are subject to external and internal evaluation, their work is more open to scrutiny, and the extent and the pattern of their work is subject to monitoring processes. Many of these audit exercises are directed at the so-called quality of the university's activities but many now are also focused on its financial basis. Activities have normally to be solvent: there is little room for the loss leader in the modern academy.

Some of this is accountability *post facto*, after the event; but some, for example through peer observation of teaching, is real-time evaluation. What was private has now become public, both in the academy and even beyond. There are no hiding places.

More, the monitoring – for some, now become surveillance – often contains discreet nudges to take the activity under scrutiny in this direction or that. Research is analyzed more for its impact; teaching is subtly encouraged to embed transferable skills in the courses offered. Under these circumstances, academic freedom is – it can reasonably be argued – 'attenuated'.[9] But, against the background of the widening options of what it is to be a university, and the new spaces now opening up in which to be an academic, 'attenuation' has to be a curious notion at best. It has its place in a sense that things are not what they were; we no longer have the space to be the kind of assured institution and determinate social actors that we once enjoyed.

Despite the telling points to which the idea of 'attenuation' leads, it cannot be a strong concept in understanding the modern university. It is a useful corrective in curbing the tendencies sometimes apparent today to believe that the university – in an information-technology age and in a postmodern, post-Fordist and global era – has no boundaries to its activities, its purposes and its configuration. But the dominant ideas around which we understand the modern university have to contain centrally the theme of openness rather than closure. Surveillance and performativity may suggest closure; but globalization, postmodernity and post-Fordism point with even more force to openness, a lessening of boundaries, an opening of spaces and diversity. It is these ideas that supply a more insightful view because they speak to the wider picture. Surveillance and performativity are qualifiers, although important qualifiers, to the general picture; they are not in themselves the general picture. That has to be one of widening, not narrowing; of opening, not closing; and of opportunities, not denial.

Far from being the attenuated university, we have here the arrival of the expanding university.

Beating the bounds

In the mediaeval ceremony of beating the bounds, the people of a parish would process around its boundary, stopping at intermediate points literally to beat its boundary. The ceremony doubtless imparted a sense of community to the parishioners but it was only made possible because it was clear where the boundaries of the parish lay.

In the mediaeval university, too, it was clear where its boundaries lay. The walls of its emerging colleges or other communities and its quadrangles looked inwards, keeping out the wider world. Now, the boundaries between the university and the world are not just porous but have collapsed altogether. The possible arrival of the virtual university only vivifies this tendency; it does not herald it.

As the boundaries between the university and the wider world have collapsed, so its moral challenges have changed. For the modern university, connectivity between its units *and* the wider society displaces the challenge of connectivity *among* its units. The idea of academic community fades both empirically and morally. If the challenge to the modern university is that of establishing connections with the wider world, it can largely forget about the difficulties of establishing a common language and a set of values within it. Attention turns from within to without.

The premodern university, even as the disciplines were taking shape in the nineteenth century, contained an internal moral order built around a sense of equivalent-but-different. It was, in Durkheimian language, a mechanical solidarity in which the university betokened a unity of activity, in which its separate elements were similar in their ideologies and practices and so constituted a larger unified community.

The modern multiversity, by contrast, was characterized by such a striking division of labour that one's identity was formed more in the individual units than through membership of the whole clan. This disaggregation of function created at best a kind of organic solidarity, a sense of the distinct but separate contribution that each unit or activity was making to the whole entity. Community was now at an end except at a meta-level of collective understanding. The multiversity was, accordingly, a hybrid on the course of moral development followed by the university. Even as it was reaching out to the world in manifold ways, it retained a sense of itself as a corporate activity. Beckoning, however, was a conception of the university as a company, albeit one with international connections in which its many product lines and activities were developed. The bounds could no longer be beaten with any ease, but the university could at least delude itself that, in its managed state, it possessed a unity that could be projected towards the wider world.

The dissolving university

The post-modern university, by contrast with its premodern and modern counterparts, has no centre, no boundaries and no obvious moral order. Both *in extenso* and virtually, it is located globally.[10] Its research, its activities and its conversations are conducted across the world, aided by the Internet. But it also retains its local interests and networks. The university, accordingly, is a striking example of the phenomenon of glocalization (Scott, 1995), that heady and tense admixture of the global and the local in the same set of activities.

Clearly, we have gone beyond the university-as-ivory-tower; but even more modern notions which seek to convey the linkages and relationships of the university in and to its wider society fall short of the mark. For example, notions of responsiveness, accountability and the university as one site of knowledge production among many in society: all these fall short of the mark because they retain a sense of the separateness of the university from the wider society. Notions such as these fail to capture the interpenetration of the university with its wider society. In the sciences, in medicine and in the technological fields, and in the professions more generally, the university is situated *in* society, both having extensive links with business, industry and the professions and being engaged in starting up its own enterprises so as to gain from the commercial exploitation of its knowledge capacities.

The post-modern university makes its own luck in this world. For the first time, at least, it has the space to do so. The knowledge society has need of knowledge and so the university now has new opportunities opened to it to harness and make available its knowledge capacities to potential knowledge users.

A metaphor of knowledge supplier and user has to be combated. In the process of making its knowledge wares available to potential users, the character of that knowledge is affected. Knowledge cannot be 'its own end' here; it has to have use value, a value as perceived by the user. Knowledge has to work; it has to be in-work. Work can be policy creation as much as it can be industrial processes; it can be the manipulation of genetic material and it can be the formation of new means of electronic communication. Activities such as these can and are conducted both in universities and outwith universities; and, increasingly, in settings that involve conglomerates of actors from the university, commercial and consultancy domains.

We have no proper understanding of this new knowledge production, taking on, as it does, so many different forms. The work of Gibbons and his associates (1994) offered a start, but it was also unhelpful in setting up a too polarized dichotomy of knowledge production as between Knowledge 1, essentially theoretical knowledge inside the university sector, and Knowledge 2, essentially knowledge-in-use produced outside the university. The problem is threefold, as I have just hinted.

Firstly, knowledges are intermingling. Increasingly, theoretical knowledge – for example, in biotechnology and in informatics – is produced within a context of its potential use, if not its actual use. Secondly, the university is increasingly engaged in the production *and* the exploitation of knowledge-in-use. Thirdly, through this intermingling of interests and activities between universities and the wider world, forms of knowledge are themselves broadening. We have many knowledges and give value to them. To Knowledge 1 and Knowledge 2, we need to add several other forms of knowledge now being recognized, especially in the health-related professions but also more widely. Communicative understanding, practical wisdom, action learning and critical self-knowledge are just some of the claimants for a form of Knowledge with a capital 'K'.

The point of this excursion into knowledge production is to underscore the larger point about the dissolving university. The university has dissolved in a double sense. Firstly, we can no longer understand the university as a unity in itself: it has dissolved into segments, many of which in turn are interpolated into the wider society. Secondly, Knowledge has dissolved into knowledges. The inner sense of there being available a single story of its knowing efforts – captured under such descriptions as objective knowledge or propositional knowledge *or anything else* – can no longer seriously be entertained. Now we are faced with knowledges, plural, sustained through different complexes of *knowledge processes.*

Henry VIII accomplished his dissolution of the monasteries with physical force. No such brute force has been necessary on this occasion: the current dissolution of the academies is being accomplished by the academies themselves.

Dissolution is, of course, a reading of postmodernity. In the postmodern age, there are no global stories which offer a unifying account of a complex of activities found across and now central to society. The single term 'university' does duty for a complex of knowledge processes, value orientations and communicative activities. In this situation, the very term '*university*' appears to be a misnomer. On the one hand, there are no general descriptions – so it must seem – which can embrace the knowledge processes that go under its name. On the other hand, as its knowledge segments take up differing relations with and serve contrasting purposes towards the wider world, so the hope of there being a single knowledge community becomes a remote if not vain prospect. The category of the postmodern points to the intractability of universal understandings; and for the university, now the postmodern university, that has to be a matter that demands attention. In what sense, if at all, can the dissolved university retain a sense of unity of process, self-understanding, communicative powers and purposes? With the dissolution of the academy, all these implicit self-understandings appear to be threatened.

The Internet is but the sharpest symbol of this boundary-less situation in which the university finds itself. The university, *qua* institution, does not simply use the Internet as an information medium; it is a key institution in developing the Internet for conversational purposes, conversations that extend the university's epistemological character.[11] The Internet even extends postmodernity. In the Internet, we see exemplified the compression of time and space with which we are familiar in the postmodern story. But the possibility also arises that the Internet is changing the character of those conversations. The sheer proliferation of billions of 'messages' and their increasing commercialization into 'data' serve to change truth-oriented dialogue into data acquisition processes. As a result, the will towards mutual understanding – for which the university has stood – is jeopardized. The medium *is* the message.

The power and the glory

That the university is now – *proactively*, in the jargon – becoming a player directly in the wider world; that in many, if not most, fields there are no clear boundaries between the university and the wider world; and that the university is seeking to extend its activities, very often across the world: little, if any, of this has been systematically studied. How might we understand the nature of these forms of enmeshment of the university in the wider world, especially given that different interests and ideologies will be evident in different areas of inquiry and practice?

The immediate possibilities have to be matters of the power and the glory: through its new efforts in the wider world, the university seeks to extend or gain new powers and to win some glory for itself. The university needs to have no undue modesty in admitting as much. But one or two qualifications are in order.

The power and the glory are different prizes and each has its separate attractions. A university may choose to host a major debate or perhaps an event for the region or even overseas which consumes time and money; it may set up bursaries, whether at undergraduate or postgraduate level; and it may offer visiting professorships to senior executives, in both the private and the public sectors. It does these things because it wishes to advance its name and to position itself with greater clarity in all the different markets and constituencies with which it associates itself. It looks to be held in a positive regard. When a company seeks new management, the intangibles of the goodwill it has generated are often more valuable than the more tangible assets: so it is with the post-modern university. Influencing the right kind of people is the way to get on in this business; making connections is the name of this game.[12]

The university seeks glory for itself and, nowadays, glories in its own achievements. Its press officer makes sure of that. Its achievements are, to a significant degree, symbolic. *Par excellence*, the university attracts attention and wins favour for what it is, what it does and what it stands for. It survives because people believe in it. The university lives in a symbolic world partly of its own making but partly also because its symbols resonate with values and hopes in the wider society. In a mass higher education system, this symbolic ordering is unevenly distributed across institutions. It is easier for some universities to win some glory for themselves than others.

But power also has its attractions and it is available in different forms. One form of power arises out of size. Gaining a critical mass of staff in particular fields of inquiry, acquiring larger numbers of students than one's competitors, and procuring a high research rating: these achievements advance one's market position within the global higher education market. In this market, intellectual capital and financial capital go hand in hand: the post-modern university will be intent on furthering its intellectual networks, linking them with commercial sites which, in turn, generate financial capital. These linkages help to advance the university's cultural capital as a carrier of significant meanings and values, whether locally, nationally or internationally. To them that hath shall be given is a commonly remarked summary of this situation; but the ways in which power is rewarded three times over – intellectually, financially and culturally – is less well understood.

Now you see it . . .

The contemporary university is dissolving into the wider world. Its client base, its income streams and its activities: all these components underscore the dissolution of boundaries between the university and that wider world. We do not have to turn to overt commerce–university linkages for evidence of the disappearance of boundaries. Full-time students are increasingly in work (and often on the campus itself) and are less open for socialization into an academic culture. Separately, research councils look for extramural 'impact' from the projects they sponsor. In short, the areas of purity are vanishing: research and teaching, even in their apparently purest moments, are now mixtures and accommodate to interests beyond the disciplines.

This is a post-modern university. In an earlier study (Barnett, 1992), I commented on how recently the university had moved from a premodern to a modern state; postmodernity lay in front of it. It is still true that there are pockets bearing the scars of this painful transition; and pockets where even that transition has not yet been fully accomplished. Our inward smiles at Dr Piercemuller and Professor Lapping (not to mention Maureen) betray our inward acknowledgement that the weekly cameos speak of experiences too close to home.[13] In many departments, in some universities, modernity remains an unaccomplished project.

But the university is a matter of successive strata being laid down, even if earlier strata have not fully settled. The new strata are taking the university beyond modernism; it is, therefore, increasingly post-modern in character. Modernity likes things to be orderly, measured (literally), fully calculable, uniform and rule-governed. Of audit, evaluation and assessment, there shall be no end. And so on to standards, profiling and subject 'benchmarking'.[14] But postmodernity won't be put back into that bottle:

the genie has now escaped. Multiple standards, multiple purposes, multiple knowledges and multiple consumers; and that's the case for just a single university.

This post-modern university is a distributed university, taking up the agendas and discourses of its many clients, regionally and nationally and probably internationally. It is a multinational concern, stretching out to and accommodating its manifold audiences.

It is a virtual university, too. But its virtuality lies not in its use of the Internet; the Internet just accentuates its virtuality. *That* lies in its loss of a defining centre. Its widening communicative capacities, its engaging with multiple audiences and centres of power, exert centripetal forces on its own constitution (Scott, 1995). This post-modern university lives and breathes, it acts with increasing influence in the world, but it exists nowhere in particular. Probably in no university – despite the best endeavours of some university press officers – does there exist a complete inventory of the intellectual capital of any one university. Such an office inventory would have to include a listing of all the knowledge networks to which its staff were connected. In turn, those connections would criss-cross, in an infinite array of linkages, proliferating even as the multidimensional model was being newly created in the office.

In this, its post-modern realization, the university lacks specificity; it is a set of possibilities, to be realized or not partly through the fortune presented by the external world. And hence the positioning: we never know what will turn up in this world, so let's be ready for it when it comes.

Here, then, we have a glimpse of a new way of understanding the university: no longer a site of knowledge as such but, rather, a site of knowledge possibilities. The association of the university with Knowledge – with a capital 'K' – has to be abandoned. Instead, we should think of the university as engaged in *knowledge processes* in different *knowledge settings*, exploiting *knowledge possibilities*. Some of these processes and some of these settings will, it is to be hoped, yield capital of some kind: to the attractiveness of intellectual capital has been added financial and symbolic capital. Overseas students bring additional income but they also offer the prospect, however remote, of later influence in far-away commercial or even governmental settings.

We should, therefore, lay to rest, although certainly with dignity, the notions of the university that speak of knowledge and truth and of disciplines, and that hold to a secure sense of the university retaining a separateness from the wider world, the better to understand it. The university is now becoming an active player in the epistemological openings in that wider world. It may be that a new unifying story will become available to us but, for now, let us not cling to unifying notions which served another age. The age now beckoning is one of varied opportunities, of multiple clients, activities and networks, pursued through manifold and even conflicting discourses. This is an elusive university, not easily captured in any kind of linguistic or symbolic text. Now you see it, now you don't.

Conclusion

A brave new world beckons for the university; it is not one for the faint-hearted. The university may have no clear legitimizing purpose, no definite role, no obvious responsibilities and no secure values. Never mind: all kinds of new opportunities are opening up and will continue to do so if the university can position itself cleverly. The university is dead; long live the university.

This, then, is the position in which the modern or, rather, the post-modern university finds itself. All is there for the taking or for the making. This has to be the conclusion of our opening explorations. Two sets of reflections on this conclusion may be worthwhile, but they have to take the form of questions at this juncture (to be addressed in due course).

Firstly, the observation that 'all is there for the taking or for the making'. This may be the vice-chancellor's dream and dreams, as we know, are easily disappointed. But, whether disappointment is on the cards or not, how do we make sense of that claim? Is the post-modern university to be under-stood in the language of taking and making? Is that its value basis? Is it just a matter of seizing the main chance? Or can we justifiably identify a wider value base to guide its activities in this new age?

Secondly, that the university is no longer to be understood in terms of the category of Knowledge but rather in terms of shifting and proliferating processes and domains of knowing suggests that we can hang on to the category of knowledge after all; we just need to be a bit more subtle about it. Knowledge has come to be understood as outcome whereas we are now faced with engagement in and negotiation of continuing and messy pro-cesses of inquiry where even the rules of the knowing game have to be renegotiated.

Rather than speaking of knowledge, then, with all its metaphysical sense of arrival, of finality and of a secure sense of proceeding, we had better speak of more fuzzy and softer notions such as inquiry, learning and ques-tioning. We can and should dispense with the notion of knowledge; and with it, too, the notion of truth. We can jettison both terms from our post-modern university. Or so it seems.

2

The End of Enlightenment?

And let there be light

Deep down, the university still holds to a belief in its role as a site of reason in society. And not just any old reason: reason for a better world is still embedded deeply in the university's self-understanding. But that story has taken a new twist. Markets, information technology, the lure of patents and technology transfer, and the multiplication of society's economic capital: all these – and many other features – signal the insertion of the university *into* the values and activities of the wider world. The university is no longer separate from the wider world: it recognizes the claims of that wider world upon it and it falls in with the shifting sands of knowing and being in that world. Reason for a better world is now recast. The university happily places itself under the banners of the knowledge society, the information society and the learning society. Somewhat uneasily, it also acknowledges that it has to be part of the audit society, the enterprise society and even the modern society.

'And gladly wolde he lerne and gladly teche' (Robinson, 1957: 20, 1308): Chaucer's description of the clerk of Oxenford spoke of two things: a sense that teaching and learning were indivisible and that they were worthwhile in themselves. Now, both values are in jeopardy. On the one hand, there are tendencies towards a segregation of academic labour which would split apart teaching and research. On the other hand, teaching, research and scholarship now *have* to have an end beyond themselves. They are not recognized as valuable in themselves. In the UK, even the claims for a new Humanities and Arts Research Council had to be couched in the discourse of performativity: the idea could be taken seriously only if the links between humanities and arts on the one hand and economic regeneration on the other were made explicit and given overriding attention. And its proposed home was none other than the Office for Science and Technology,[1] a bizarre juxtaposition but one that even its most ardent supporters might be prepared to tolerate for the greater status that that home was likely to bring.

But still, for all the 'living in the real world' that has now come to the university, albeit reluctantly, the university still harbours within itself a sense that it remains a site of disinterested reason; and should continue to do so. Knowledge remains its own end.

Put on the spot, however, the university finds difficulty in elaborating this inner sense. How give substance to the ineffable? It's a real problem. But the university refuses to countenance a state of affairs in which it is just giving to society and the economy what they are calling for. The university could not accept a situation in which it was just a dependent variable, simply responding to its external environment. The Western university harbours jealously the hope that it has some leverage of its own,[2] that it is an independent variable amid the complex conditions that work to shape and situate it today.

The university has come into the centre of society because society now gives high marks to Knowledge, the very entity on which the university has built its self-understanding. But there is a tension here because the forms of knowing now prized by the wider society continually challenge definitions of knowledge held within the academy. The university pats itself on the back, even though it knows that the forms of knowing now called for are those with direct impact on the world. And so it plays the game: skills, skills, skills (whether epistemic, occupation-specific or generic skills[3]). These are forms of instrumental knowing: they assume that knowledge can be wrought upon the world with calculable and predictable effects, effects that are measurable. Knowing is prized now that it can be measured: give us your knowledge and we'll give you our metric comes the call from the wider world; and the university succumbs to this calling. The vocational becomes a vocation.

And let there be light. The ocular metaphor is potent (Barnes, 1977). Present in Plato's allegory of the chained prisoners in the cave having to come into the light to leave mere illusion behind them, and for the shadows to be turned into figures, the metaphor has continued to the present day. The Enlightenment captured the metaphor and gave it a systematic treatment. The university sees itself in that way, as a site of pure reason, even despite its new drive to demonstrate its performative credentials. The university believes that, through whatever discipline, it offers a disinterested position from which to shed undistorted light on a situation. Even lecturers in business studies see themselves as in the business of the study of business as much as a study for business (Macfarlane, 1994).

Purity and enlightened reason on the one hand; performativity and economic reason on the other: the university sees itself in both camps at once. It embraces the new stance of performativity while refusing to disinvest itself of the older stance of disinterestedness. Does this self-identity hang together? Can the university be a site of disinterested reason while also giving to society the new forms of knowing that society calls for? The light may be going out; but perhaps new – and different coloured lights – are coming on.

Values, what values?

The light shed by disinterested reason was its own value. Knowledge as its own end: that was the central idea of Cardinal Newman (Newman, 1976). Buttressed by other ideas, such as the 'philosophical' view that an unencumbered relationship with knowledge would bring, knowledge being its own end needed no further justification. The illumination that pure reason would bring, shorn of the worldliness of professional knowledge, was clearly a good in itself. For Newman, a liberal education was precisely one that was free from, untainted by, worldly preoccupations. Such a stance towards knowing would bring that 'philosophical' outlook because it would offer a disinterested vantage point.

A consequence of this intellectual heritage of disinterestedness – of which Newman was a representative – is that the university has been ambivalent towards its value-base. Is it value-free or is it value-rich? The university wants to claim that its hard-won knowledge is value-free and yet not value-less. Its value lies precisely in its being value-free (Wolff, 1997 edn). The university wants it both ways; and perhaps it is right.

At its back, the university hears the murmurings of Auschwitz (Stryker, 1996). The value-free search for truth led, on some readings, to Auschwitz (Baumann, 1991). The disinclination to take on board the values that knowledge might be asked to serve or to question the ends to which it might be put: such value freedom led paradoxically to an instrumental view of knowledge such that it could be put to any end. The university, especially the German universities, was doubly implicated in all this. On the one hand, it was active in pursuing knowledge as its own end: the means became the ends. Ends were not up for independent scrutiny, for that would have required recourse to a set of values that was simply not available. The university had no defence, no way of falling back on a value-base of its own, since it had eschewed values: its knowledge was devoid of values. On the other hand, and as a matter of fact, the German universities had largely fallen in with the role cast for them in supporting the Nazi regime (Nash, 1945). This was consistent, after all, with value freedom: if values were off limits, it could hardly matter to what end the university put itself.

Value freedom, then, seems to be a cul-de-sac, robbing the university of any security and making it a prey to be used for any purpose. On the other hand, modernity appears to place in doubt the possibility of securing any set of values for the university to hold on to in the pursuit of its activities. To say that knowledge is its own end may seem to be a way forward but it turns out to be an empty slogan. Either we can fill out the end that knowledge serves (as its 'own end'), in which case we would have to resort to a set of values that would require separate justification; or we rest with the dogma of knowledge as its own end (Nisbet, 1971), which in turn renders the knowledge vulnerable to any kind of value takeover.

In the face of these considerations, the postmoderns have gone in two directions. On the one hand, they have declared that no universal values are available. In such a world, presumably, the university has no responsibility to uphold a larger universe of value: it just makes its own values in the world. This stance leads directly to the marketized university: the university's values are those that are sustained by the markets in which it can find a living. Postmodernism has been accused of being a conservative force but, here, things are worse than that. For postmodernism – taken up by the university – allows the university simply to become the dependent variable of the markets that assail it. Postmodernism is a value system supporting the big battalions.

On the other hand, other more conscience-striken postmoderns, being disinclined to countenance such an uncertain and vulnerable future, want to reinject a value basis to contemporary activities. The main strategy offered lies in tolerance (Squires, 1993). If postmodernism reminds us of difference, it also implicitly calls for tolerance. Quietness, openness and charity: this is a path opening up for postmoderns who want to hang on to a value basis (even as other postmoderns prize noise, glitz and self-expression). There are two problems with this idea of tolerance.

Firstly, if tolerance is to be serious rather than superficial, it has to lead to a situation in which mutually conflicting viewpoints can engage with each other. But thoroughgoing postmodernism removes the possibility of difference finding points of agreement which can form the basis of such engagement. That's the trouble into which Habermas ran with the postmoderns: his validity conditions of a rational discourse are, for them, just an attempt to smuggle in universal connecting tissues which postmodernism has outlawed.[4]

Secondly, tolerance as a strategy for the university is empty at best and liable to surrender it again to the forces of instrumental and economic reason circling around it. Without other values – repudiated by postmodernism – the tolerant university has no way of discriminating between the just and the unjust uses of its services.

The university in the contemporary era is unsure of its value basis; and that is to put the matter charitably. More accurately, the university declines to concern itself with its value basis, as it attempts pragmatically to assure a place for itself in the wider society. And yet, in reality, the inner sense that there are limits to what we may take a university to be stubbornly remains. Whether over the acceptance of a donation from an ethically dubious source, the silencing of academic views for fear of difficult publicity, or the difficulties faced by women lecturers in gaining senior posts, concerns arise over activities of the university.

Certainly, examples such as these raise the issue as to whether our value sensitivities are specific to the university *sui generis* or whether our value concerns are simply the importation of wider social and civic values into the university. Accepting donations from an ethically dubious source or placing a ceiling on opportunities for promotion for women, for example, would constitute moral failure in most domains. Such examples speak of civil and even human rights which have nothing to do with the university as such. So, perhaps the university is devoid of a value base of its own after all.

The third example – the silencing of academic views for fear of difficult publicity – suggests otherwise. Admittedly, there is an equivocation over the term 'academic' here: does it refer to views that are academic in character or that are simply expressed by academics? However, the point is that a university cannot, with dignity, retain the title of 'university' unless it upholds the collective virtues of tolerance and respect for persons. Indeed, such collective virtues in a university setting become extended into responsibilities of persistence and unflagging inquiry. Individual moral virtues of courage, diligence and carefulness also flow, in turn, from such collective virtues and responsibilities. A university is a site of collective and continuing inquiry or questioning: that recollection alone generates a horizon of values within which the university must remain and which the university must always keep in view.[5]

A university that did not abide by such values would forfeit any right to a public recognition of itself as a university; and, in practice, that would almost certainly happen. The widespread antipathy to granting even the honorific title of 'university' to certain private sector enterprises with instrumental agendas, which are liable to limit the scope of inquiry, is testimony to the tacit sense that there are value-laden boundaries to what we take a university to be. Furthermore, the difficulties that any 'new universities' face in establishing themselves as bona fide universities in the public consciousness also confirm that there are normative dimensions in carrying the title of 'university', even if what counts as a university continually slides and widens.

Burning one's boats

But perhaps that horizon of values is just a legacy of a past age. Whether under the banners of consumerism, of markets, of economic regeneration or of postmodernism itself, perhaps we should eschew such values. Perhaps that horizon of values is fading, in any case. And perhaps, too, those values are being replaced by new values, in which visible performance, immediate impact and competence in all its forms – including managerial competence – are given high marks. Away with the old values; in with the new – and not before time.

The university is at a value-fork. Faced with two sets of values – rooted respectively in dialogic life and in performativity – it is stuck fast. It is ambivalent towards the new values: part of it feels distrustful, even hostile, but it recognizes that in them lies some kind of security, position and social acceptability. Money, influence and visible action await. In the knowledge society, a new and central role opens up for the university. The university can see not just financial security but also a recognized pivotal position in the new world order. On the other hand, it dare not yet abandon its traditional values. It cannot yet bring itself to burn its existing value boats.

The university fears a position in which it becomes simply a dependent variable, yielding up to the economy and to the consumer those gifts that they demand. Those values that spoke to a position of some independence retain their allure, if only negatively: the university cannot be sure that performativity offers a position of any security in the long term. And, anyway, the notion of the university as an independent variable, and the values that sprang from such a calling, paradoxically until very recently rendered a position of high status. Poor but rich at the same time: economically poor but rich in esteem. It was not a bad position in which to be.

And so the modern – or, rather, the post-modern – university is stuck fast. Glitz or virtue: these are the callings that appear to lie before it. And often glitz is chosen before virtue. Research 'findings' are announced, even to the world's news in much-heralded press conferences, but prematurely as it turns out. Or a university's Senate agrees to take a donation from a corporation, subsequently only to find that the sources of the donation are suspect in certain ways. Yet virtue has a habit of having the last word. The research 'findings' cannot be replicated and the researchers in question lose something of their standing; the donation is declined. The university holds on to its traditional value-base, even while it accedes to the new glitz that beckons it.

The university, then, is one institution that has not been detraditionalized (Giddens, 1995). The old self-understandings and sets of values live within the new; and necessarily uneasily. Old values; or new values; or both sets at once? (The other alternative, that of no values at all, is no position at all, as we have seen: it opens the way for all kinds of instrumental takeover.) The old values appear to be passé, not acknowledging the 'real world' in which the university has to make its way. The new values may appear to be value-less: that's their value. But the values of performativity and consumerism *are* values, even if their outcomes are unpredictable.

And so, not wishing to burn its value-laden boats, the university tries to have it both ways at once: collegiality and performativity; inner-worldly and outer-worldly. The university dare not abandon completely its modern calling of disciplinary authority for a postmodern calling of performative impact. The university contents itself that these are not conflicting values but are complementary. Performativity, it tells itself, only gains authority by being anchored on the bed of disciplines and their communicative networks. Even the external world tells the university that this is so. Transferable skills have to be 'embedded' in conventional curricula: that is the message from on high (in the successive reports on the university).[6] Performativity *and* collegiality: the boats do not have to be burnt after all.

Having one's cake?

But is that right? Does it make sense? Are the values of performativity and collegiality not conflicting sets of values? If that is so, how do we understand this determination of the university *and* the wider world to see the university hang on to the old values? Is this a sign of poor collective logic or is there a larger story to be told? The latter is the case.

There is here, as it might be put, the issue of compatibility, an issue that crystallizes around a crucial distinction. The sets of values to which the university is attracted may be:

1. conflicting but compatible; *or*
2. conflicting and incompatible.

Is the unease that the university feels the unease simply that of handling complexity, of an information overload that springs from coping with multiple agendas; in other words, a conflict, yes, but which is ultimately resolvable? *Or* is it the unease of the guilty conscience, of wanting to have one's cake, of sensing deep down that the value sets are incompatible and that one set is superior to the other and is now being devalued? This is a crucial issue – in some ways, *the* issue – before us.

It could, of course, be a bit of both. The university may have won its public esteem through its attachment to and upholding of independence, integrity and openness. These are values that have received high marks and have helped to sustain a sense of a 'higher' learning being on offer, the 'higher' in this case being that of a higher order of thought, if not action, which these values have generated. Now, the university is beguiled by the glitz of money and influence, of immediacy and impact. Performative goods such as these are attractive and – speak softly – somewhat shoddy at the same time. They are shoddy in the sense of being less valued as ultimate ends. The university struts its stuff, showing off its latest acquisitions, its new buildings, its lecture theatres with their information technology facilities, its named chairs and even its research facilities; but, deep down, it senses that it is not, ultimately, for such showiness that it is valued in the wider community.

Perhaps, then, the values by which the modern university lives are neither straightforwardly incompatible nor conflicting. The discomfort felt by the university is that of a fall from grace: no longer does the university occupy a position of disinterestedness. Purity has given way to highly visible taintedness. Not just in the world, but of the world. That is the university's *necessary* position in the contemporary era; and yet, the university feels discomforted by it.

At worst, then, it appears that the university's discomfiture arises from its trying to uphold values that are only mismatching. One set of values speaks to disinterestedness and one set speaks to action-in-the-world. The one receives high marks on the university's conscience; the other receives high marks from the university's accountant and press officer. The discomfiture is only that: just an unease in acting two parts at once. There is no fundamental conflict here, much less an incompatibility. The university's conscience is easily assuaged. But, in the end, the university remains troubled, and for good reason. The different values that pull the university pull it in different directions. Disinterestedness is set against interestedness; critical commentary is set against action-in-the-world; understanding is set against performance; and impartiality is set against partiality. There is at least tension here, if not downright incompatibility.

So our earlier question repeats itself. This ambiguous positioning of the university – its determinedness to be seen to be delivering, to be getting things done, to be adding value in measurable terms on the one hand alongside its refusal to disavow those callings of higher virtue – calls for an explanation. Is it a matter of poor collective logic or is there a larger story to be told? The idea that all concerned, both within and without the academy, have been bewitched by a set of logical fallacies does not make any sense. This is not a matter of logic, even if the position in which the modern university finds itself is illogical. Such discursive positioning, such apparent superfluity of values through which the university constructs its identity in the modern world, needs a larger explanation than either faulty logic or evaluative greed.

A new enlightenment

The discursive universe is expanding. The stories by which we understand the world, ourselves and our relationships to each other are proliferating, and the university is implicated in all this for it is a key point of energy in this discursive expansion. There is no stable state (Schön, 1971). All is unstable, an instability that is partly of the university's own making.

In this discursive maelstrom the university faces, it is sometimes suggested, a crisis of legitimacy (Delanty, 1998a). Buffeted hither and thither by conflicting discourses, the university comes to see itself both as an engine for economic regeneration on the one hand, and as a repository of traditional academic virtues of scrupulousness and scholarliness on the other hand. Consequently, the university's value base at best becomes more diffuse if it does not dissolve altogether. The university concentrates on its own survival and public projection, securing its financial and its moral base from any quarter that will provide it. The university is a nice example of the end of ideology, a doctrine that it has promulgated itself. If the university survives, if it can secure customers for its services, then it generates its own legitimacy; or so it hopes.

The university is willing to live with these tensions; that much is clear. But, as we remarked a moment ago, other voices reinforce the discursive ambiguity facing the university. Even as the calls for a more performative university are heard, other calls now urge the university not to abandon some of the older callings through which it has constructed itself, callings that appear to summon up deposits of past traditions. Breadth, depth, critical conscience and even independence: these are just some of the callings now urged upon the university and which are resonant of certain of its traditional self-understandings (NCIHE, 1997). Just as the university felt that it was being called upon to shake off its past practices and become modern in character (not postmodern) in order to perform effectively in the world, so it finds that it is being encouraged to retain much, if not all, of that earlier framework. After all, it appears that the wider society sees something, at least, in those earlier callings which is of value in the contemporary era.

The stories of enlightenment are turning out, it seems, still to have attractions in them and not just among those within the academy who yearn for a quieter, simpler age. The wider society now calls on the university to live up to its own rhetoric: the world, the global age, now needs a university sector in much of the self-image that it has constructed for itself.

So the university has friends in the wider society and even in high places. The dominant interests and discourses of society provide a space for the university, a space in which the conventional university can find itself still prized. A University of Industry may be joined by a virtual university of the Internet, and corporations may term themselves 'universities', but old-style universities will not yet be homeless. They will engage in cosmetic changes – taking on more part-time students, continuing to set up research partnerships with industry and displaying themselves according to instrumental performance indicators – but, essentially, they will remain faithful to the more traditional callings of generating knowledge and new understandings around structured discourses *and they will be expected to do so.* Disciplines may themselves broaden to embrace fields of action, multidisciplinary frames of engagement and policy studies, but the idea that a university is structured around conversations that are largely academic in character is not seriously in question.

The discursive conflicts that the university finds itself having to handle are partly of its own making: the university is prized in the modern era precisely for its capacity to generate new frames of understanding. But those conflicts are also partly the result of the conflicting callings to which the university now finds itself accountable. The plea for 'diversity' in a system of mass higher education (NCIHE, 1997) is simply a recognition that individual universities will find their own point of equilibrium between these conflicting callings; it does not mean that institutions that go under the name of 'university' can abandon any significant portion of the framework of criteria by which the title of university might be justified.

We have not, then, reached nor are we in any prospect of reaching a situation of 'anything goes' so far as the fulfilment of 'university' is concerned. Even the fraught debate about the presence of research as a necessary condition of what it is to be a university is testimony to the wide acknowledgement that there should remain boundaries to the scope of the institutions that take the title.

A suitable metaphor to capture the discursive positioning of the university system in the wider society might be that of a number of constellations among the larger galaxy. *Each* university constitutes, as it were, a constellation of discourses within the expanding galaxy. Every now and then, shooting stars are seen as new connections are made between the constellations and the larger galaxy (between a university and the wider society). The university retains its enlightenment function towards the wider society but in a new form. Now devoid of the ideological baggage that came with that

function (of spreading the light of reason), the university fulfils that enlightenment function simply by adding to the discursive universe. The university
sheds light by generating new forms of understanding of the world; and the
wider society urges it on in this function.

Ideological paradox

The university can no longer pat itself on the back for promoting universal
– or even societal – Reason (with, as it were, a capital R). The university can
no longer persuade itself that it is either the arbiter of reason or that reason
constitutes a neat unity to which the university has privileged access. But a
more challenging role is opening up. The university has both to engage
with the wider society and to contribute to its intellectual capital in ever
wider forms.

Enlightenment lives. Yet the suspicion remains, even within the university,
that the university has sold its soul. Yes, it can add to the forms of knowing
and understanding in the world, it can widen our sense of the world we are
in, and it can make the world a more perplexing place to be in. It can and
it does do all of these things. Resonances, then, of the Enlightenment
project are still felt. Even emancipation can be claimed as a story for the
contemporary university (CVCP, 1996). But something is missing or, at
least, is no longer a major part of the story.

For the university, enlightenment is in danger of becoming an operational
project. Enlightenment had been connected with a sense of improvement,
less in man's material conditions and more in human being as such. Through
reason, through theory, we were improved as human beings (Habermas,
1978 edn). The transformations that reason offered were not transformations in our capacity to extract surplus value from our environment or,
indeed, from each other; quite to the contrary, they were transformations
that enabled us to inject value into our environment and our transactions
with each other more fully. We saw what we did not see before. The world
was represented as a richer, more complex and more subtle world. Our
relationships with the world and with each other were transformed through
the new insights alone. Whereas that Enlightenment was contemplative in
character, the new Enlightenment is operational in character. It promises
added value, not in insight as such, but in the additional value to be yielded
from our additional knowledge of the world and of each other.[7]

The university is heavily implicated in all this. From transformation-as-
emancipation to transformation-as-sheer-performance: this is the key shift
that threatens in the Enlightenment project as the ideological basis of the
university. The university is apparently listening just to some – and the more
obvious – voices around it and is missing the more subtle external voices
that call for a wider interpretation of its role in a global age.[8]

We have not reached then, as some would say, the end of ideology.[9] That
it appears to be so is testimony to the power of the new ideology in so

cloaking our perception of the world and of our educational practices that, at first glance, we are in danger of losing that older contemplative view. The critical voices are there and they are still allowed to be heard; but only in limited measure and, then, only so long as there is a sense that this and that critical voice may assist the operational agenda. Critical reason may have a performative role in showing up the operational limits of our current practices. It *can* add to surplus value and economic positioning. So the presence of critical reason should not be taken as a sign that the contemplative view of Enlightenment is still with us. Read carefully, it may be precisely a sign that the performative view of Enlightenment has overtaken the university.

But, as we have just seen, we should not lightly assume that we are seeing a wholesale ideological repositioning of the university. Contemplative university becomes performative university: this may be a tempting reading but it cannot be an adequate reading of the situation before us. The university is a carrier of multiple discourses: the contemplative view of the universe is still to be found – and wanted – even as it is overlaid by agendas of modernism and performance. The university offers an ideological admixture of old and new forms of enlightenment at the same time.

There is a paradox at work here. Enlightenment for understanding and enlightenment for improved performance: the university is not only representative of both ideologies but it is also *called upon* to sustain both ideologies. It is not going to be permitted to relinquish the contemplative Enlightenment project even as it acquires a new project of performative Enlightenment. Accounting for and understanding this paradox will occupy much of our attention in these explorations.

In playing its part in the production of performative reason, is performative reason colonizing the university such that other values, even if present, are so residual as to offer no real counterbalance?[10] In that case, the university – even though it might house many discourses – would come to be dominated by the values of performative reason: if it works, if it secures the survival of the university and if it offers instrumental added-value, then it is justified. It is not clear that the university has any value anchorage which will act to resist such operational wilfulness. It is not clear that a separate horizon of values has any significant place in the life of the university. The separate values are there but, now, they are apparently marginal to the main project. The large multifaculty universities, with their recurrent budgets of several hundred million pounds, their several thousand staff and their large student populations, just have to get by, securing customers for their various services at viable prices. If they can do that, they appear to be prized. The successful universities are those that are demonstrably adding value. This performative reason supplies its own values.

Conclusion

Enlightenment lives; but of what kind? Has the wattage been turned down, the university consigned to its enlightenment role in the interstices of its

new and larger performative role? Or are there new forms of enlightenment being urged upon the university? Is the university in such danger of
being seduced by the glitz and glamour of the new performativities opening
up for it that it fails to notice the quieter murmurings that seem still to
require that it hold to its earlier callings? Voices in the wider society speak
of knowledge, breadth, critical reason, freedom and even critical conscience,
but voices speak more loudly of skills, impact, standards, accountability and
efficiency (NCIHE, 1997). It is the louder and more strident voices that are
noticed by the university. Even while the wider society is hesitantly intimat-
ing that it has need of universities that live up to their own rhetoric as
guardians of reason, so the university seems intent on construing itself in
ever-narrower frames of self-understanding. A trick is being missed.

The failure is understandable. The role of performative reason heralds
an immediate and visible place for the university in the centre of late
modern society. Its capacity to generate forms of knowledge (through its
research activities) and forms of knowing and understanding (through its
teaching function) which have demonstrable use value is what will sustain it
in the new order. The university has that on good authority. The knowledge
society needs universities but on condition that they offer the performative
reason now in demand. Criticized on both fronts (research and teaching)
for not responding to this new agenda, the universities are anxious to demonstrate that they fully understand and are prepared to meet the role now
extended to them. Research will have demonstrable 'impact' and will secure
funding from industry; teaching will 'embed' key skills. The new role becomes
an ideology: the university understands itself in this way and is keen to
project its increasing performative credentials.

In this process, the self-understanding of the university as a vehicle of
enlightenment changes. We do not have to say that contemplative Enlightenment is being replaced wholesale by a performative Enlightenment. All that
needs to be claimed is that performative Enlightenment is now a rival ideology even though contemplative Enlightenment – for better understanding
– remains in the university's interstices. If that more viable argument can be
plausibly made, then we are facing the prospect of the end of the Western
university and the emergence of a new kind of university; one that embraces
the role and values of performative reason.

Whether this matters will depend on the losses and the potential disbenefits
on the one hand, and the new opportunities that may be opening up on
the other hand; and these, as we have intimated, may be largely overlooked
and yet turn out to be significant. The examination of the balance sheet lies
before us.

3

The Ends of Knowledge

And of knowledges there shall be no end

The problem with knowledge for the modern university is *not* that knowledge has come to an end. Rather, it is that there are now many knowledges vying for a place within the university. It is not that the clerks have lost their monopoly over the production of high status knowledge (Hague, 1991); it is that they have lost their monopoly over the definitions as to what is to count as knowledge.

As a result, the university is swamped with rival claimants for worthwhile knowing. Is a course to be constructed around contemplative knowledge, that so-and-so is the case; or around knowing-in-action; or around understanding-through-communication; or around critical action; or around action learning? Are the 'skills' to be domain-specific or are they to be generic, transferable – so it is hoped – across situations and knowledge frameworks? Is the knowing in question to be acquired through a deep embedding in a tradition or is it to offer an overarching 'metaknowing', such that one has the capacity to approach a domain with energizing and fruitful knowing strategies? Is knowing a matter of understanding large conceptual schemes or is it a matter of determining strategies that will carry one forward effectively in large-scale endeavours (through 'policy studies')? Is knowing essentially epistemological or ontological in character: is it cognitive or has it much more to do with one's state of being-in-the-world?

That a curriculum is such a site of epistemic contest is a cameo of the way that multiple knowledges nowadays knock on the door of the university, asking to be let in. The ways in which we engage meaningfully with the world, and so frame what counts as knowledge, proliferate. It is accepted that knowledge about the world has to be complemented by forms of knowing in the world; but it is also understood – in many professional areas, at least – that having an understanding of oneself and of ways of communicating seriously with one another are themselves important forms of knowing.

So, for example, consultancy comes to rival research; or, to be more accurate, there comes to be no sharp distinction between the two activities. Knowing-in-the-world (consultancy) not only comes to be accepted as a valid form of knowledge but the distinction between it and knowledge-of-the-world ('research') is often impossible to determine. Making the distinction between research and consultancy in universities becomes a pragmatic and even a micro-political matter, dependent on the resources that flow from the different categorizations. However, what appears to be a purely bureaucratic matter is also, and more fundamentally, an epistemological matter deriving from the definition of worthwhile knowing in the university.

In the modern world, there is no end to this proliferation of definitions of knowledge. The knowledge society (Stehr, 1994) values, celebrates and upholds knowledge. But that very development, of society giving high marks to knowledge, brings in its wake challenges to the definitions of knowledge held by the university. Why should the wider society accept the definitions of knowledge that have grown under conditions of knowledge production in which the clerks were largely in control (Gellner, 1991)? Of course, it does not. But that lets the epistemological cats out of the bag. They scamper about, delighting in their freedom and in the fuss made of them. The wider society calls for an ever-widening variety of forms of human being. Far from our witnessing the end of knowledge, of knowledges there is no end.

A practical interest

Some believe that we are witnessing the end of disciplines (Gibbons, 1998). The reasoning is straightforward. Disciplines were formed as the outcome of a mode of knowledge production in which the academics were supreme; indeed, in which the academics became an academic class (Gouldner, 1979). Now, academic domination over knowledge production is not exactly threatened – except in teacher education – but it is dented. So-called 'producer capture' is ended by a combination of forces: the state, the economy and the market all become independent variables reducing the degree of control by academics over the production of knowledge.

The sociological story has not been fully worked out. Precisely how, in what ways and to what degree in different fields of inquiry the academics' control has been relaxed is not yet understood. What is apparent is that those movements are uneven both across disciplines and across institutions. That unevenness is considerable. In some fields indeed, especially as professional domains seek to advance their status by calling upon higher education to offer a definite entry route, academics become the new producers. The professions – such as nursing – yield, even if nervously, their control to share it with, if not to hand it over to, the academics.

However, while relevant, the sociological story is not our main concern. Of more moment is the accompanying philosophical story. In all this movement, as the interested parties call upon higher education to meet their interests, fields of inquiry themselves start slipping and sliding. Scott (1997) talks tellingly of an 'epistemological wobble'. But the situation is more fraught than a single wobble. It is more like a motorway pile-up: the vehicles are slipping and sliding in different directions all at once and, as I have just intimated, some may even be going 'backwards' as the academics gain control for the first time.

Epistemologically, then, the university has lost all sense of direction. To say that it is searching for new epistemologies would be too charitable. Buffeted on many sides, it becomes what it can be. The configuration that knowledge assumes – in business studies, chemistry, nursing studies, economics, leisure studies *and in all the other fields* – is the separate outcome of the play of forces both within and without the academy. Action learning, strategy, elaborate theory, communication, and the 'solving' of practical problems: these are just some of the elements that might be found in the constitution of a characteristic knowledge field. And each of these elements takes on a particular form in different fields of inquiry and/or action.

This elasticity of epistemological elements infects – we might say – even sub-fields of inquiry. Optoelectronics suddenly appears within electrical and electronic engineering, not just because a new portion of the natural universe has been discovered but because new technologies – such as lasers – themselves become a site of interest.[1] The interest is not purely intellectual but is also practical in orientation. Research monies become available because of the potential *practical* yield from the new site of epistemological interest.

This practical interest is increasingly present, at least as a background presence. Perhaps not every field is yet coloured by its presence and a single field will vary in this respect across its sites.

A research or a scholarly centre may have a greater or lesser practical interest. Partly, this will be due to the way in which the centre situates itself within the field: does it have an interest in the more technological, policy or professional elements? Partly, too, the degree to which a practical interest is present is dependent on the possibilities open to the field to secure allies for its projects and underwrite its future (either directly, for example through financial support from pharmaceutical companies; or indirectly, by the academics themselves setting up their own companies to market their knowledge products). No matter what its extent or its influences: the practical interest spreads. The academy's epistemologies were always social in character; now, they are becoming practical in character too.

Have we then, in this practical interest, a new organizing principle for knowing efforts within the academy? Perhaps the current messiness represents a transition period, essentially from knowledge as contemplation to knowledge as *praxis*.[2] In another fifty years or perhaps a hundred years (comparatively short periods in the history of the university), the practical interest will be transparent and near universal.

That may well happen. We could be at just such a turning point in the history of the Western university. But, for our purposes, we do not even have to be anticipating such an epistemological break for the present situation *already* to have taken on a character of fundamental significance.

It may be responded that there is nothing new in there being a practical interest within the university: the mediaeval university was explicitly a set of professional schools and, implicitly, its students were preparing themselves – through their studies of rhetoric and logic – for the life of the clerkly administrator. But the point mistakes the changes now underway. It is not that in the new incorporation of the practical interest in the university we are seeing a return to an earlier practical interest. No: this interest is entirely new.

What a performance

Lyotard (1984) offered us a story of this newness. For him, 'performativity' captured the epistemological changes we are witnessing in the academy. Knowledge is now judged not on its power to describe the world but through its use value. Knowledge has to perform, to show that it has an impact on the world. Enlightenment – not a term deployed by Lyotard in this context – becomes a function of the illumination afforded by knowledge through its power over the world: we see anew how the world may be brought under control or how it may fit with our wider purposes.

This 'performativity' thesis was coupled, in Lyotard's analysis, with a larger thesis about the arrival of postmodernism in the academy. In this larger thesis, knowledge splits apart epistemologically and morally (to use another non-Lyotardian term): under conditions of postmodernism, Knowledge becomes knowledges. As the large stories of knowledge creation and dissemination – for truth, for equality and for emancipation – fall away, each knowledge form ends up fending for itself. Any sense of common language, common traditions and common ideology recedes: all that is left is each knowledge becoming its own language game, intent on forging a life and a place for itself in the world and in its own way.

This wider story faced Lyotard's 'performativity' thesis with a dilemma. On the one hand, the postmodernism thesis offers a refinement of the performativity thesis: it tells us that what counts as performing, as having a use value and as having a legitimate impact, can take many if not an infinite variety of forms. Especially in a situation where knowledge is subject to the claims of the market, where many now press the right to exert their claims on knowledge acts, performance is bound to take many forms. 'Knowledge' comes to have no definite form, no conditions and no limits. Accordingly, 'forms of life' in the academy proliferate.

On the other hand, the performativity thesis speaks ultimately of power, and in two senses. Firstly, there is, explicitly, the power exerted by knowledge in its different domains. Secondly, and implicitly, there is the power over the definitions as to what counts as legitimate impact. Lyotard's 'forms of life' notion (taken from Wittgenstein) suggests that anything goes: there are no boundaries except those surrounding a form of life. But we do not live on a level playing field: our epistemological options are not open. The playing field is sloping. There may remain in the academy a 'life-world' demand: mature students may look forward to their weekly visits to their part-time classes for the 'therapeutic' revivification that they receive. But the dominant players in the academy are now those of the economy and technology. So performativity takes on definite hues, even if pretty well every colour can be detected in the total quilt.

Shades of performativity

'Performativity' looks as if it can offer a new universal story of the modern university. Whatever our value orientations to the idea, even if we feel uncomfortable about the attitudes that it seems to imply are now endemic in academe ('if it moves, measure it; if it cannot be measured, it is of no value'), it looks as if it is capturing something of general significance. So it is; but it also provides traps for the unwary.

Firstly, there can be no substantive general definition of performativity. What counts as performance or use has to be worked out in every field and sub-field; and even there, in each field, the domains of knowledge creation (research) and of knowledge acquisition (teaching) are different. To that extent, the postmodern story is right. There are literally infinite possibilities for thought and action in our developing efforts to understand the world; and the academy is party to this continual stretching.

Secondly, the boundaries between purity and application dissolve but, in the process, the elements multiply; they are rarely extinguished. Performativity rides on the back of contemplation. For example, in languages, global economies and global labour markets prompt a widening of the field to incorporate additional languages for mainstream study *and* offer opportunities for greater impact: 'discourse' is taken up as a practical as well as a theoretical concept.

Thirdly, performativity occludes the extent to which dominant players have the power to determine what is to count as a satisfactory performance. 'The market is always right' is a message that stands behind performativity. But the epistemological market – like all markets – is uneven; worse, it is sometimes rigged. Putting it formally, use value is coloured by exchange value. The big prizes of status and finance are to be secured only if one is seen to have impact; and major impact requires buyers for one's epistemological products (whether in the shape of Research Councils or corporate organizations). That much is apparent; no-one takes pains to hide *these* material aspects of performativity. But an illusion of equality is all too frequently portrayed in, for example, the published performance indicators which imply that all epistemological fields are equally placed to demonstrate their capacity to perform.

Performativity beckons as a new universalizing theme, seeming to make sense of the changes befalling the university. Beyond its epistemological fields, the idea of performativity seems also to do justice to the way in which the modern university has to be seen to be performing, whether in its local region or globally. The university's glossy brochures proudly exhibit these performances, whether in joint endeavours with industry or, indeed, with another university on the other side of the Earth. Yet, precisely because it has immediate attractions and obvious visibility – in new buildings, in new joint activities or in new forms of lecture – performativity masks the differences both between fields of inquiry and between the variable forces that bear upon them, producing the shape of their own performativities.

So the performativity thesis holds traps for the unwary. But we need to distinguish *two performativity theses*. One thesis underlines the overt features of epistemological performance: income, economic regeneration, making friends and influencing people, and securing one's public status and professional security. In themselves, these features of our knowing efforts are not malign. Nor do they conflict with the fundamental purposes of the university as the disinterested search for knowledge and the promotion of a disinterested understanding. But behind this showy form of performativity stands another which heralds the end of the Western university.

This other performativity is one in which the features just picked out become ends in themselves. From the point of view of the university, there is nothing wrong as such in making money or in winning friends and influencing people. For too long, there has been a temperament within the university which has poured scorn on such activities. That puritanical strain is now disappearing: academics can make their fortunes (earning more than their vice-chancellor) as they convert their ideas into technologies and, in turn, launch companies to market those knowledge products. Instrumental reason can be accommodated, even within the university. The difficulty in all this arises when such activities and pursuits become constructed as knowledge activities.

The point is not one about individual motivations, interesting as that may be. It is a more general point, at once social and epistemological in nature. *All* knowledges are, in effect, performativities of a kind. The value of Lyotard's analysis lay, therefore, not in his idea of performativity as such, but in its drawing to our attention that we are now witnessing a change of fundamental proportions in the kind of performativity now developing in our knowing efforts. Lyotard was not concerned with or, rather, overlooked the showy performativity all too often apparent today. Instead, Lyotard argued the more radical and more problematic thesis that our criteria of truth are changing so as to incorporate performativity itself. Use values are introjected into our knowing efforts. All too easily, we become servants to and carriers of this strident performative ideology.

We are all performativists now

If *this* performativity thesis is correct, it spells the end of the Western university. Such language may seem excessive: it is not. The significance of such a shift in our knowing efforts can hardly be overstated.

As we noted earlier, ever since its mediaeval foundation, the Western university has looked to the domain of work as a characteristic feature of its self-constitution. The 'ivory tower' university was simply a phase that the modern university went through while knowledge production was under the sway of the academics. It did not represent the true university. So there is nothing singular as such about the university standing in a close relationship with the wider society.

But that is not at issue in the emergence of the new performativity. What is at issue is the infusion of use values into the university's knowing efforts. Its epistemologies are sliding from being contemplative to being pragmatic in character. Its concepts, its theories and its ideas are infused with the world of action. Nor is this simply apparent in such fields as business studies, nursing studies, transport studies and education; and nor, additionally, is this feature only to be found in the technologies now ranging beyond engineering to include biotechnology. It is also to be found in the more contemplative fields.

For example, semiotics may appear to be a disinterested study of signs but it has come to take on a pragmatic character partly through the power of its own insights. Getting on and getting ahead is now seen to rely partly on the power of signs and – whether in advertising and marketing or in one's self-presentation – semiotics is now being given a use value that it could not have comprehended previously. In the process, the study of signs is altered with its knowing efforts being focused tacitly on its use values. Its concepts and ideas are now developed, even if unknowingly, partly with an eye to this newly found use value.

In other words, whereas the showy version of performativity wears its performativity on its sleeve, in the epistemological version performativity creeps in surreptitiously and nestles in the frameworks of understanding inhabited by the academics. It gains its power not by supplanting contemplation but by living happily with it. For example, to return to an earlier example, optoelectronics – a sub-field within electronic engineering – is a matter both of understanding optical technologies (such as lasers) *and* of extracting greater effects from them. Being part of the constitution of the emerging knowing frameworks *and* going hand-in-hand with contemplation, this epistemological performativity is pretty well hidden. This is a real embeddedness: contemplation and performance in bed together.

Performativity, then, comes in two versions: a practical or, indeed, exhibitionist variety and a more subtle epistemological version. The exhibitionist variety is there for all to see in explicit performances in which knowledge is put to use, or is displayed in showy configurations. The epistemological variety is more hidden, embedded in emerging concepts and ideas and in new sub-fields of inquiry and their associated operations.

Of course, both versions have their own variants. The practical form of performativity may be associated with the field itself and with driving up the price (literally) of the knowledge products in the wider market. The epistemological variety of performativity may be associated with more contemplative forms of inquiry within the field, through its manifold forms such as action research, policy studies, experiential learning and problem-solving. Of these two versions of performativity, it is the epistemological variety that is the more significant because it strikes deeply into and at what it is to know. Through the insertion into the academy of this performativity, what it is to know is being transformed from knowing as contemplation to knowing as performance. To repeat, this shift spells the end of the Western university. (This development is *not* totally a matter of regret.)

Admittedly, there are counter-charges to this position, that things are not black and white, that in no field do we see pure performativity in any event (there is always a mix of performativity and contemplation); that fields of study vary in their susceptibility to this performativity; and that, in a mass higher education system, some universities will be less vulnerable to such an infusion. (The more 'élite' universities are assured of a student market for their knowledge products; moves towards performativity can be resisted to some extent.)[3] All these qualifications are valid but neither singly nor collectively do they shake the main argument that, in epistemological performativity, we see the closing of the Western university.

The first counter-charge – that of cohabitation – I have dealt with: cohabitation strengthens performativity rather than diminishing it. The second and third charges – in essence, those of systems complexity – are valid but, again, can be overplayed to such an extent that they buttress performativity. For systems complexity, read the story of postmodernism: things are so complex that there is no one grand story. At this point, Lyotard went wrong. He undercut his performativity thesis with his postmodernism story. Performativity has undertones of modernity in supplying means to ends, it is fast becoming a new grand narrative and it is sponsored by the state. In each of these three respects, the postmodernism story implicitly denied the performativity thesis, proclaiming that the epistemological slate was being wiped clean. Nothing is further from the truth. In this performativity, a new unifying narrative is emerging, one that strikes at the core of the Western university as a site of disinterested reason.

Vive la différence, yes. Let us be epistemological egalitarians, but if only it were true. The truth is that we are all – or almost all – performativists now.

An unknowable world

The world is radically unknowable. That this is so is implicit in the thesis offered by Giddens (1994) on 'manufactured risk'. New knowledge spawns new understandings. Some new understandings may lead to changes in our wider environment, whether in our technologies, our social policies or our social institutions. Very often, those changes bring unforeseen problems calling for attention. As Giddens points out, we do not have to cite mega-problems such as the changes to the natural environment being wrought by the emission of hothouse gases. Our social institutions are also affected by our new self-understandings: there is an ecology at work in the social environment just as there is in the natural environment. As our sense of the fixity of social roles, gender identities and family relationships changes, so in turn new patterns of relationships evolve having repercussions for welfare, housing and educational policies and practices.

This is a brave new world; it is not for the faint-hearted. We never shall get on top of this world; it continually slips out of our grasp. Through our knowledges, problems – empirical and conceptual – open up for our attention. This is fine; the university will be in business for a long time to come after all.

But a couple of twists to this story are in order. Firstly, we can usefully put Giddens together with Lyotard. The situation of manufactured risk (which Giddens observes) has come about very much as a result of the performative lurch in our epistemologies (which Lyotard noted). Epistemological performativity breeds manufactured risk. That is the whole point of it. It is knowing that is intended to produce effects on the world; it is not an accident. Accordingly, manufactured risk is a *necessary* by-product of the new epistemological age. It is not happenstance. Our new knowledges are predisposed towards changing the world, whether natural or social, and so are continually ushering in new worlds. We cannot now retreat to a more contemplative relationship with the world around us.

The second twist to the prospect of unlimited knowledge problems is that the logic of our situation can be understood as one of expanding ignorance rather than expanding knowledge. This is the thesis of Lukasiewicz (1994) in his brilliantly entitled *The Ignorance Explosion*.

For a number of reasons, knowledge has got out of hand. It grows so rapidly that we cannot keep pace with it. In terms of our social systems, our technological systems and the wiring in our brains, the expanding knowledge universe exceeds our capacities to process it and to understand it. It could be said that there is nothing new here; that providing that it resides in a public forum available for interrogation, we are still in the presence of knowledge. Academic libraries fulfil just this storehouse role. It may further be observed that Popper's (1975 edn) description of objective knowledge as forming a World Three was precisely 'knowing without a human subject'. Knowledge does not have to be publicly proclaimed and fought over to count as knowledge.

All that is true but the objections miss the main point, namely that knowledge production is now completely out of kilter with knowledge comprehension. There is at work a weird economics of knowledge production. In the old days, even academics needed an audience for their attempts to disseminate their claims to knowledge. Now, that relationship has broken down. Academics no longer need an audience for their wares. The market, in the form of kudos for 'public' research and scholarship, works to favour textual production as such irrespective of whether there is an audience for the product. 'Get that paper published' becomes an academic mantra of our times, a situation which (in the UK) the Research Assessment Exercise has only exacerbated.

The result of this curious, producer-dominated, knowledge economy is that academic texts are proliferating at an exponential rate, and far faster than can be comprehended. In this situation, the library-as-storehouse metaphor may be beguiling but it is misleading. For the storehouse metaphor implies that all its contents could in principle be accessed, but that is not the situation in which we find ourselves. Our knowledge texts continue to expand at an ever faster rate so that the storehouse continues to expand and the proportion of its contents that will remain virtually imprisoned also continues to grow. Knowledge production and knowledge comprehension: the gap between them widens evermore.

A new illiteracy

A consequence is that academic texts become reduced to the status of data, indistinguishable from the many other forms of data now available, accessible through computerized media (Midgley, 1989). In turn is generated a need for *data-handling skills*, the competencies that apparently can bring the ever-proliferating data under some form of control. But each of those three terms – data, handling and skill – betrays the character of the human capabilities now sought. They are themselves technical operations that, in the process, supplant understanding, interpretation and the adjudication of meaning. The human mind, in this conception, is reduced to a data-processing brain, handling and manipulating data. The associated learning organization is simply a set of systems of information-handling capacities. Both at the personal and the organizational levels, understanding is surplus to requirements.

To return to Popper (1963), inert knowledge is not knowledge at all: it becomes knowledge when it is subjected to a public examination of conjecture and refutation. Without that process of public and critical dialogue, we are in the presence not of knowledge but of assertion. The new phenomenon of knowledge products out of control, therefore, presents a paradox. We are part of the knowledge society but it is also one now characterized by ignorance.

There is yet another form of expanding ignorance. This is the ignorance created by the proliferation of academic discourses as new fields evolve and sub-fields arise, both features of supercomplexity. Under such conditions, *academic illiteracy* grows. Efforts to advance academic literacy are seen worldwide in the 'academic literacy' programmes put on for students. Whether those courses are effective or not is beside the point. Their mere presence is a symptom of the burgeoning forms of 'academic' life associated with an increasing range of epistemic fields and practices. It may be true that multidisciplinarity and interdisciplinarity are recovering somewhat as fields of inquiry draw on each other for new resources. But the continuing formation of knowledge fields necessarily creates academic illiteracy for the new outsiders.

The knowledge explosion, then, produces an ignorance explosion. There are the insiders and the outsiders; and there are the problems of information overload. New forms of communication struggle to address the widening gap between expansion and comprehension. Journals give way to abstracts, abstracts give way to conferences and conferences give way to the Internet. Knowledge production and validation reflect successive forms of the compression of time and space. In the process, knowledge comprehension degenerates into a mere information-handling capacity. The result is that knowledge continues to expand beyond our powers to have command over it.

The world, which has become what we have made it, is now beyond our knowledge reach. We are ignorant of the world that we have created. It is an unknowable world.

It will be all right on the night

Is all this the voice of Jeremiah or of Cassandra? Is it an exaggerated story of doom and foreboding or is it an accurate story unlikely to be believed? Some would indict my account not just of undue pessimism but of a more serious felony, that of relativism. It could be alleged that behind all the talk of ignorance, performativity and epistemological pile-ups lies an alliance with relativism. It could be said that the real purpose of this depiction of epistemological waywardness is to endorse it. This story of the end of knowledge is actually a plea in favour of its end. The story of performativity is, in reality, an admission that this is the new verisimilitude: truth is what works. Epistemological nihilism is, in actual fact, here being defended, not attacked.

Fearful of such epistemological nihilism – with its lurking spectre of Nietzsche[4] – some shuffle uneasily. Surely, there must be some way out of this hole. So some brave souls are beginning publicly to declare themselves in favour of knowledge and truth (Norris, 1996); their kind of knowledge and truth, at any rate. But this is a move that is as unnecessary as it is wrongheaded.

None of the points made earlier about the epistemological sliding in front of us constitutes an attack on the possibility of gaining knowledge as such. The problem is not knowledge as such but that our legitimate knowledges expand and move. The modern university is not so much deprived of its epistemological foundations as it is suddenly presented with all kinds of epistemological foundations, with new ones – performative ones – claiming special privilege. So the spectre of relativism is falsely identified. As well as being unnecessary, it is wrongheaded because it is liable to lead us into unrealistic and totalitarian responses, insisting dogmatically on certain forms of knowledge and truth as the true ways to epistemological enlightenment.

Another response to the situation that we have charted is both more timid and more subtle. The timid will simply assure themselves, if not others, that things will fall out well in the end. There is no problem to which we cannot address ourselves seriously, if not solve outright. The very expansion of knowing frameworks and approaches yields more and more knowledge resources – involving action, interaction and communication – which are able to bring more and more problems under control. Let's not worry until we have to do so.

This is a philosophy of 'it will be all right on the night' and, deep down, we know that we hold it more in hope than in judgement. Our consciences are salved for the moment but, we sense, there will be a reckoning in the end. This response evades the issues presented here and which continue to gnaw away at any sense that knowledge can provide a universal project for the university.

Another, less charitable, description of this philosophy would be that it is one of muddling through. Just keep going; deal with such problems, be they substantive or epistemological, as they arise. We seem to have got by, so far. But this is amnesia and bad faith rolled into one. Remembrance of Auschwitz in the recent past and acknowledgement purely of the possibility of ecological chaos in the very near future (by the end of the twenty-first century on some current predictions) should pull us up short.

Conclusion

Our efforts to procure a secure relationship with the world through our knowing efforts are in trouble. We are not at the end of knowledge, but we are at the end of any legitimacy for our knowing efforts.

We ought to be well-off, epistemologically speaking. To the more contemplative forms of knowing have been added those intent on effecting changes in the world. Nothing so crude as the mere addition of knowing-how to knowing-that is the sum of what is before us. The significance of the new performativities lies in their seeping into concepts, frames of understanding and orientations to the world. Nor are we seeing a simple replacement of knowledge as contemplation by knowledge as performance. All kinds of knowledges and, therefore, performativities are to be found together, and are more or less accommodating to each other. The contemplativists and the activists rub shoulders in the same university department and teach on the same course. Normally, civil warfare does not break out for the parties share the same concepts.

It may be said that in the 'risk society' (Beck, 1992), unless our knowing efforts take on a more performative function, we shall all be dead, literally. But this performative role into which knowledge has been press-ganged is itself helping to generate the very problems that knowledge is being called upon to address. There is no escape from this vicious circle; only a chasing of one's own tail with increasing speed. Through the performative turn that knowledge has taken, we are liable to end in a merry-go-round devoid of humanity. Unless we can supply a new legitimacy for our knowing efforts, the university is doomed to become the handmaiden of a nihilism that is largely of its own making.

4

The Fading Constellations

Conceptual riches

Knowledge and truth, then, no longer supply a firm framework for the university. Impregnated with agendas of performance and achievement, they no longer offer any security in themselves as justifications of the university. Knowledge and truth begin to offer a firm foundation only when backed up by supplementary premisses (that they come in many guises; that claims to know are worthwhile if they provide us with greater control over the world; and that the university is properly an institution for solving the problems of society, if not of the world). Since any such supplementary premiss is debatable, knowledge and truth are now robbed of their power to supply an indisputable underpinning for the university.

However, not all is lost. A corollary of the difficulties that have befallen knowledge and truth is that all kinds of other conceptual possibilities are opening for shoring up the university and for giving it a sense of purpose. The difficulties that knowledge and truth face arise partly because universities have gained a *wider* legitimacy than attaining knowledge and truth for their own sakes or even for their power to enlighten. The universities have now come *into* society and, indeed, into the world. Many hopes are invested in them by multiple constituencies. Accordingly, public purposes for the university multiply. We seem to be embarrassed by conceptual riches.

Attractive constellations

We shall come to the main claimants in a moment. But it is worthwhile pausing to make a general observation. It is clear that there is no single story to be told which can in any way do justice to the university in the modern world. There can be no essence of the university in any simple sense. This is so for three reasons.

The first two are straightforward. Firstly, large multifaculty universities – and even relatively small institutions – are a conglomerate of knowledge factions, interests and activities. We cannot assume that the manifold activities of the 'multiversity' have anything in common (Kerr, 1972). It follows that the notion that there could be a single binding characteristic that all constituent parts of the university share, that there could be an essence, has to be suspect.

Secondly, any mass system of higher education can be examined for the differences *across* its universities. Do all universities conduct research to any significant degree? Do they all admit part-time students? Do they all see themselves as having an international reach? Do they all engage deliberately with the local community? Do they all use the Internet to deliver their courses? Systems will vary as to the extent to which there are significant differences between their universities: from some perspectives, universities may – in some countries – appear remarkably uniform. No matter: even if there are centripetal forces at work producing similarities, there are also at work even larger centrifugal forces producing differences (Scott, 1995).

Whether internal to each university, then, or across the system as a whole, no simple single story is going to capture the character of the university. However, there is a third reason which tells against any impulse towards essentialism but which yet opens up a more fruitful line of inquiry. This is that, in any event, even our dominant ideas are always hedged in by a penumbra of other ideas. Our ideas are refined, qualified and given shape and colour by connecting ideas. In other words, the notion of there being a pure essential idea which somehow captures our activities and concerns is itself misguided. What might be more promising is the notion, suggested by Richard Bernstein (1991), of a constellation of concepts. That is, an interconnecting set of concepts may begin to fill our sense of what we are about. For example, we have already seen how knowledge and truth are connected to further ideas of reason, enlightenment, disinterestedness, power and control. Some of these ideas pull against each other but that is the nature of a constellation: entities setting off pulls and pushes among themselves.

So the idea of a constellation of concepts tells against essentialism but opens up the prospect of a more informed and a surer insight into the character of the university. Knowledge and truth and their surrounding constellation of concepts turned out, in the post-modern age, not to hang together in any consistent way. That constellation therefore has had to be abandoned; but perhaps there are other more plausible candidates that help us to understand the post-modern university. We can identify five further constellations.

The constellation of production

Trying to insert itself as the dominant set of ideas by which the modern university should understand and conduct itself is the constellation of production.

In the constellation of production, we find as interconnected ideas those of work, the economy, the vocational, competence and skills. This constellation is not finding things particularly hardgoing. It has many supporters, not only outside but also within the academy; and there, it has its adherents among both staff and students. It is not, however, fully endorsed, either within or beyond the academy; and even among its adherents, there are strong endorsers and there are more cautious endorsers.

Nonetheless, the line-up of endorsers is impressive. The state and the world of work itself (by no means undifferentiated, with significant differences of nuance between the multinational corporations and the smaller firms and between the private and the public sectors) drive the associated agenda forward.[1] Economic regeneration, economic competitiveness and skill upgrading are the watchwords. This is an agenda and a constellation of ideas that have been widely assimilated into the academy. And not reluctantly either: the academics often have one foot planted firmly in the world of work, and may through their own business ventures be adding to the production process itself. At the same time, students – if they are not already working – may be taking up employment, even if unwillingly, in order to finance their studies; or are likely to have their minds partly on their career and are wanting to ensure that their studies assist in the shaping of that biography to come.

Work will always be with us and it is right that the university should have it more in its sights than in the past. However, despite the energy invested in it, the constellation of production cannot supply anything approaching a satisfactory story of the modern university, tempting though it may be.

Firstly, work itself is just part of life; it is not life itself (White, 1997). Increasingly, efforts are made to persuade us to the contrary: the dominant discourse of our age is that of work and the economy. All other aspects of life are marginalized or are made to appear as work. The end product, the outcomes, the value-added and the performance indicators: these are the criteria by which activities are now often to be judged. But this discourse is itself challenged in its sought-for hegemony.

Secondly, work is far too differentiated to offer a stable unitary dominant idea. Captivating as it might be, work is an umbrella concept under which go many kinds of disparate activity (Handy, 1990). Again, many would reduce work to that work which is susceptible of a means-end calculation (cf. Arendt, 1958). Such a reductionism can do no justice to the multifaceted character of work.

Thirdly, in many of its senses, work is diminishing. It appears that work of any continuity is being structured out of the reach of a significant portion of the population. Crudely, although the estimates vary, durable work may be denied to around one-third of the population, with another one-third holding on tenuously to some form of work, albeit of a relatively predictable kind. A secure hold on work, and it tends to be the more conceptually challenging forms of work, is 'enjoyed' by the remaining one-third. Mass higher education has become a universal education for that last third. To define higher education in terms of work is to demarcate it as an activity more or less permanently out of the reach of the remaining two-thirds of society (Reich, 1992; Hutton, 1995).

Lastly, and most significantly for our purposes, work itself is changing. That, it will be said, has always been the case. But the changes taking place are so far-reaching that what counts as work is slipping beyond any definition. The portfolio worker (Handy, 1990) is on the move in more ways than one. She does not just add discrete work commitments but finds herself engaging in different milieux with different kinds of discourse and with radically different forms of engagement and communication. Work is now experientially challenging because it yields no definite boundaries: this worker has to make it up as she goes along.

Paradoxically then, just as it seems that, in work, a universal and defining purpose for the university has arrived, it dissolves in the same moment. Work cannot provide the university with a new legitimacy.

The constellation of democracy

A third constellation of concepts through which the modern university has come to understand itself – beyond knowledge and work – is that of democracy, justice, citizenship and community (cf. Carr and Hartnett, 1996). Who could not be in favour of democracy and social justice? But they won't do, either, as an underpinning for the university.

The university *is* a player in the discourses of society: it helps to shape them, produce them and disseminate them. It is right that access to those discourses should be as open as possible and that they should be disseminated as widely as possible. 'Access' and 'participation' have justifiably become key watchwords of the modern university: for too long, the university has limited both access and dissemination and is having, even now, to be reminded of its responsibilities in this regard (Bourdieu and Passeron, 1979; NCIHE, 1997).[2]

The concepts of democracy, justice, citizenship and community *are* important concepts: they speak a language of inclusion rather than of exclusion. They have to be part of the realization of the modern university. But they are about means, not ends. They are like markers on the roadside, giving us an indication of where not to go but no indication as to where to go. Admittedly, there are objections to this view. Three, in particular, deserve attention.

Firstly, it may be said that the idea of democracy can indeed impart ends as well as means (Gutman, 1987). The pursuit of a more equal society; the extension of life chances, especially to those who enjoy few of them; and the enhancement of a more democratic society: these ideals could impart purposes and policies to the university. Ensuring equality in its employment procedures; within its admissions policies, discounting advantages accrued through an applicant's social environment; and offering support to students, not just financially but so as to enhance their confidence to undertake their learning challenges: policies such as these would constitute a start in the desired direction. These policies amount to a neutral stance: we shall endeavour not to add to your disadvantages through the way in which we relate to you.

In addition, a much more positive stance might be opened up by the university. It could engage vigorously with the local community at all levels, and with all kinds of agencies and organizations, seeking to widen access to its programmes through working with local employers, by making available its programmes through modes of properly supported independent study, and by providing a crèche and other facilities. On this reading of the constellation of democracy, each university should be a people's university.

Undoubtedly, a busy programme of reform, action and engagement opens up from such a reading. But it should not be mistaken for a reformulation of the ends of the university. Even when understood as the promotion of democracy through the widening of life chances; even when followed through into the academics' own discourses so that, for example, they are encouraged to be inclusive rather than exclusive of gender and race: even then, despite much possible busyness, fervour and public declaration of its equal opportunities policies, we are still in the realm of means, not ends. It is true that these means are sometimes taken up as ends, but such a stance is wrong in principle and wrong in practice.

It is wrong in principle for the democratic motivation to furnish ends for the university because it takes the collective eye off the ball. It changes universities from knowledge institutions into social institutions. It places as primary the university's social responsibilities as against its responsibilities towards knowledge. It is possible to run the two missions together, as did Davie (1961, 1986) in his *The Democratic Intellect* but, even within his way of looking at the matter, Davie understood that the democratic leaning was a qualification to the claims of the intellect.[3] To claim democracy and justice as one's major emblems would put an end to any prospect of the university having a distinctive contribution to make to the production and dissemination of knowledge. Such a move would lead the university to renege on its primary responsibilities.

But it is also wrong in practice for, in privileging justice over knowledge, it surrenders to the dominant forces the definitions of knowledge. This is what the university has, in some way, to contend against. The playing field is unbalanced. Accordingly, the social justice agenda could end up by having the opposite effect to that intended: the university will have cast for itself the role of securing access to the dominant discourses, so shoring up the inequalities of discourse and of being in the world. The democratic intent is in danger of undermining itself.

That despatches the contention that democratic ideals can furnish us with ends for the university. We turn, then, to the other two objections to my repudiation of the constellation of democracy.

The second objection is that the learning society requires universities to be democratic in their character. If society is to become a learning society, then it has to become a learning society *in toto*. A half or a third of a learning society is no learning society. Accordingly, universities must play their part in generating the learning society by becoming democratic institutions. The reasoning is well-motivated but it is flawed. Even if we add in the missing premiss that the learning society is necessarily a democratic society, it does not follow that the university has itself to be a democratic institution.

We might distinguish between the substantive and the procedural senses of the democratic university, that is, as a democratic institution in itself and as one intended to bring about a more democratic society; and we might add that it is the second of these meanings that is at stake here. That is, in promoting the learning society, the university is also promoting a more democratic society. But we are no further forward. We are only being given a tautology; or, at most, being informed about a legitimate reading of the learning society (Coffield, 1997; Ransom, 1994). The really substantive issue about the kind of learning to be promoted still lies before us. Accordingly, the learning society story – interesting as it might be on another occasion – is here a blind alley.

Lastly, it might be countered that the democratic constellation supplies *the* story for the modern university. Precisely because what counts as knowledge is up for grabs – or so it might seem – at least we can fall back on the idea of democratic dialogue as the basis of the communicative structure of the university. Indeed, if universities are not to fall prey to any passing totalitarianism, we *have* to fall back on such an account. There is much in this, essentially the Habermassian riposte to postmodernism. But here, to mix up this important point about the structure of rational dialogue with the larger story about democracy, social justice, citizenship and community is to commit a category mistake. The two matters should not be conflated.

We can, then, dismiss the constellation of democracy as forming a foundation for the modern university. Its concerns are real, but they are sideshows. They are not the main event.

The constellation of self

A fourth constellation of ideas which can be summoned up as a conceptual foundation for the university is that in which autonomy, personal development, personal fulfilment and personal realization figure strongly. This constellation – the constellation of self, as we might term it – assumes prominence as a combination of the arrival of a mass system of higher education and the parallel emergence of a market. The character of that market – more quasi-market than market – can be sidestepped. What is significant is that these two features – mass higher education plus market – reduce the power of the academics as providers and raise the power of students. As a result, the academy is obliged to give consideration to the personal aspects of its students. Give them what they want has become an unspoken but lurking consideration in the academy.

However, there is more to it than that. Higher education, especially in England, has been seen as a form of character training, particularly in the arts and humanities. The tutorial system in the ancient universities had – whatever its financial and even its educational flaws – the merit of putting students on the spot, of requiring them to give of themselves and more fully to become themselves. Something of that thinking remains in the interstices even of the mass higher education system so as to retain a little of its perhaps unique 'intimacy' (to draw upon Scott's (1995) evocative term). In parallel, the German concept of *Bildung* speaks to a form of personal development accruing as a result of an individual's active search for truth.[4] A truth-oriented discourse compels the formation of personal qualities. Truth and moral virtues go hand-in-hand. There is, therefore, deep in the Western university, a longstanding receptivity in favour of the student developing as an individual independently of any market.

But more generally in higher education, as a feature of the Western university, lies the idea of autonomy.[5] In particular, it is understood that truth-telling is ultimately a matter of autonomy. It is not just that in giving an account, one is expected to come forward with one's *own* account and be ready to back it up with one's own reasons. It is that, in the idea of truth, there is a strong sense of commitment at work. In stating such and such, I am saying not just that it is true and that I am justified in saying such and such but that I believe it to be true (Ayer, 1956).[6] In other words, I am making a personal commitment to that truth claim.[7] This is partly why many find higher education to be a demanding affair: they are required to give of themselves, to produce their own autonomy. Truth-telling is not just a matter of intellect but also invokes each of us as autonomous persons. Higher education has to be a highly personal matter; the university is necessarily an institution that takes people seriously as persons.

This view of truth-telling does not exhaust the personal component of higher education. Especially in a mass higher education system, individuals will place on the university large hopes of personal development and even personal fulfilment. Whether they are those who are mid-career but without a degree, those who have a degree but who are now struggling to find their true métier, or those who are nearing retirement but who 'missed out' on a degree when younger: all these and many more turn to the university to enable them to become something other than they are or have been. Nor do they look to the university solely or even mainly in instrumental terms. They look to the university to help them to realize personal hopes and ambitions connected with their sense of themselves as persons.

For an institution that has built itself on matters of utility, the economy and the intellect, these are extraordinary hopes to come its way. Many students, however, are surely destined to be disappointed because the degree of the personal that they wish to invest in their learning is unlikely to be recognized and reciprocated by their universities. In a mass higher education system, the personal is an increasingly unmet set of hopes.

Partly, this failure is the result of reduced student contact; but, all too often, that is an excuse for the failure to comprehend and to resonate with this set of claims on the part of the students. There is a mismatch at work: the academics look – rightly – for personal fulfilment in their research and their scholarship, but they fail to create the pedagogical conditions under which their students can live out their own parallel hopes and so make *their* learning a fully personal experience.

The personal dimension is in trouble, then, in a mass higher education system precisely at the point at which it claims and deserves new attention. But there is a yet deeper reason for its difficulties.

The problem posed by the set of concepts marked out by the constellation of self – autonomy, personal fulfilment, personal realization and personal development – is quite simple. This constellation is built upon the belief that there is a personal identity and that the task of higher education lies in developing it. But in this postmodern age, personal identity is itself a problematic concept (Usher and Edwards, 1994). The self is dissolving, if it hasn't yet dissolved.[8]

The constellation of self, it should be clear, represents an important set of ideas and is worth hanging on to; indeed, it is to be fought for. Educational transactions are about the self, especially in higher education where notions of 'finding oneself' still have resonance and where one's students may, with approval, describe teaching sessions as 'therapeutic'. We might say that a genuine higher education calls for the injection of self into its epistemologies. Through their utterances, through taking up measured stances in the world, students have not just to give of themselves but also to become themselves, to constitute themselves.

But a story of higher education written up purely or significantly through this constellation of concepts – which puts the personal in the shop window – remains problematic if only because the self is problematic in this postmodern age.

The constellation of critique

A further, and arguably the defining, constellation of ideas which might provide a foundation for the modern university is – as we might term it – the constellation of critique. Here, we find such associated ideas as critical thought, higher education as opposition, critical self-reflection, dissent and even revolution. In this constellation, we find the hope that higher education can offer a countervailing force in society, distinct from and, if necessary, in opposition to the dominant voices of the day. It follows that, if this hope is to be realized, the university should enjoy a definite autonomy in its own right. Putting it more formally, we might say that the university should constitute its own discursive space in society.

There is, of course, a sociology which brings up short this set of hopes of the university. Even in its weaker form – that the university does not have to engage in revolutionary acts but should stand ready always to offer a countervailing viewpoint – the university has to admit that it no longer enjoys academic autonomy, even if it ever possessed it.[9] If it is honest, too, it would admit that the constellation of critique has long been well down the list of its self-understandings. The limits of its academic autonomy have not been so much imposed upon as self-imposed. The university has allowed itself, discursively, to become incorporated into the mainstream of the discourses of society; indeed, in this global economy, into the discourses of the world.

We might even be charitable and observe that the university has formed a contract with society[10] to pursue its own activities precisely because they appear to be useful to 'the knowledge society' and are generally, therefore, going to endorse the state's projects. In any event, the university is mindful of the power of the state to contest its own power: the shooting dead of the four students in Kent State University (Davies *et al.*, 1974) may now have faded from the collective memory but the university feels that it will get along better if it negotiates a deal with the state. This is not a university that will frighten any horses.

Quite apart from the ways in which the sociology tells against the constellation of critique, more fundamental – philosophical – considerations loom into view. Herbert Marcuse (1968; 1969) tried to sketch out a theoretical standpoint justifying the university as a revolutionary force. The argument turned on the way in which, for Marcuse (1968), the university was simply the inheritor of a 2000-year long faulty logic of reason: a logic that had led to the domination of a technological reason, a reasoning that had cast its net over mankind itself, so producing *One-Dimensional Man.*

Alasdair MacIntyre (1970) pointed out the self-contradiction contained in Marcuse's charge: the totalizing logic couldn't be as totalizing as all that if Marcuse had managed to shake himself free of it. But, not to be undone by such a charge, Marcuse pursued his argument, claiming that there could, in fact, be an alternative science which did not base itself on technological reason. In turn, Jurgen Habermas (1972) gently reminded Marcuse that there was an alternative way of making room for other forms of human reason and that was by rescuing those alternative forms that were actually embedded in reason itself. In particular, reason held within it both interpersonal ('communicative') and critical elements, since reason required both of these elements in order to work as reason.[11]

The constellation of critique, then, gets itself into unnecessary difficulties. Pragmatically, it is liable to overlook the power of the state to impose its will, if felt necessary. Philosophically, it pretends to inhabit an alternative realm of human reasoning and human being which is simply not available. It overplays its hand, believing that it alone has access to pure reason; and it cuts the ground away from itself, overlooking the possibilities for immediate impact that lie *within* reason.

The idea of critique turns on there being available an alternative framework from which the critique can be mounted, whether we are concerned with propositions, social institutions or personal actions. But the trouble, in the postmodern era, is that we can never get to that secure ground from which critique can be mounted with any confidence. We can never fully guard our rears, as it were: we are always vulnerable to being outflanked. No framework is impregnable. Popper (1975 edn) would have admitted as much, and still held to the idea of objective knowledge. But the postmodern insight presses the point to its ultimate and discomforting conclusion. No utterance can be made with any security. The whole idea of critique, as a result, turns out to be built on shifting sands. There are no secure foundations to be gained here.

The constellation of emancipation

The final constellation claiming our attention is that of the constellation of emancipation. In part, we have met it already amid the constellations so far encountered, especially those of democracy, critique and the self. But it is a constellation in its own right, even if it intersects with others.

In this constellation, we find the ideas of emancipation itself, liberation and freedom. Held jointly with the constellation of self is the idea of autonomy and with the constellation of critique is the idea of critical self-reflection. Again, this is an important set of ideals.[12] But it, too, is in some difficulty in the modern era.

Firstly, it is in danger of becoming froth without substance. Emancipation sounds like the sort of thing we can sign up to with a clear conscience: who wants to be enslaved after all? But under what conditions is emancipation to be achieved? Is emancipation an outcome or a process: is it an achievement or a task? Who decides when the state of emancipation has been achieved? Is it the emancipated or some disinterested party? And how is it to be achieved? Critical theory tells us that it is by the individual being emancipated: the patient must administer to himself.[13] Even if there is something in this, how does it apply to higher education? Does it mean that we can do without teachers?

It is not that well-founded answers to these questions cannot be forthcoming. It is that, in relation to the idea of emancipation as a theory of and for the university, the questions just keep on coming. For example, is it achieved by the individual or collectively? Is it to be gained theoretically or practically? Is some kind of personal transformation necessarily involved? And so on, and so on.

Why is this? Why should the idea of emancipation generate so many questions? At one level, the answer is simple. It is that emancipation is not just a story but a large story, a grand narrative, under which so many other hopes, ideas, theories and viewpoints have their place.

Emancipation reminds us of ideals with which the Western university can be legitimately associated.[14] It connects too, as we have seen, with other large ideas of critique, of self and even of democracy. This interweaving of grand narratives, in the centre of which sits that of emancipation, gives this constellation a particular strength. But it is in danger of being just a glitzy story, jostling with others for attention and – in the end – of having little or no substance.

We should be suspicious of emancipation. In it lurks the danger (we can use the term) of ideology, of having others' interests read into the student's interests. All too easily, as a pedagogical aim, it can become a cover for imposition rather than emancipation: being emancipated in a pedagogic situation can be a case of we know best. Even to say that the task of emancipation rests with the student takes us no further forward, for the definition of the criteria for emancipation will still remain – if we are not careful – with the powerful. If we say to the contrary, that it rests with the powerless, that can mean very little in higher education in an advanced economy where, as we have seen, definitions of knowledge abound but will repose ultimately among the powerful.

In short, the constellation of emancipation turns out to be froth without substance. As a backing in itself for the modern university, it is just not up to the job.

Conclusion: a necessary incoherence

So let us be shot of all of these six sets of ideas as a way of understanding the modern university. Knowledge, production, democracy, self, critique and emancipation: none offers a firm foundation for rebuilding the university. It may be said that we have to work with all of them. This may be the case, but the difficulties in doing so have to be recognized.

Firstly, one by one, the constellations tell no specific story. At the extremities of each are ideas that pull in different directions. Emancipation, as we saw, can be read as a collective or as an individual story. Democracy can be read as a matter of input or output, of access or of the university contributing to an equalizing of discourses. Self can be understood as the configuring of self through the academics' discourses or through the student's wider social being. Even the utility inherent in production can be understood in specific or more general terms: skills for the here and now or metaskills to cope with the unexpected. Accordingly, quite different educational strategies may be legitimately read off from any one constellation.

Secondly, the grand narratives conflict. The fundamental clash in the modern university is that between instrumental reason and reason guided by a collaborative search for the better argument; in the terms of our constellations, between the university itself being seen as a set of production processes and as a site of undistorted critical dialogue in which the ideas of truth, democracy, critique, self and emancipation all have a place.

Put like that, it seems that the forces of production must be swept away by the combination of all the other five constellations. That, in the real world, we know that they are not is testimony to the strength of the constellation of production.

This antagonism shows itself in the university in the tension between managerialism and collegiality (cf. Trow, 1994). Being guided by technical reason, by a determination to get things done so as to turn the university into an efficient site of production, on the one hand; and being guided by a willingness to hear things out, to go on examining the issues and allowing all parties equally to have their continuing say, on the other hand: both sets of motivations cannot easily be followed simultaneously without some sense of unease. That is the condition of the modern university: that technical reason and dialogic reason continue to slide against each other with an inevitable sense of upheaval.

The modern university is a site of tectonic plate movement. *Both* technical reason and the ideal speech situation have a place, even if neither is to be found in its true form. They have a place because *both* are embedded in the university. These different stories of the modern university cannot easily be held together, but they are both now social facts of the constitution of the university. Consequently, the university is without any coherent purpose beyond the jostlings of rival aspirations. It is utterly incoherent.

The third reason why none of the six stories will do as a legitimation of the modern university is hinted at by postmodernism. Postmodernism asserts that there are no universals in the contemporary era. Postmodernism has in mind claims to knowledge, ideologies, views of the world, conceptual frameworks, the self and values; in short, our hold on the world. To this assertion, we can note that, in an era of postmodernity, society is undergoing massive forms of change. Globalization and detraditionalization are the features of this era. Massive movements of capital, twenty-four hours a day, across the world, aided by the information technology revolution, are the motors of this incessant change and associated conceptual challenge.

The six sets of ideas that we have just looked at are inadequate because they rely on some sureness, some sense of stability and some sense of the enduring. No such stability or durability is available to us in the modern world. Whether in terms of ideas, of values, of what is to count as knowledge, or of our own sense of ourselves as having secure personal identities, we have to accept that we are in an age of change and uncertainty. 'Age' here has to be interpreted generously: there is no end to this condition that can be envisaged, only more of the same in ever-quickening form.

For these three reasons then – the internal tensions within the grand stories, the conflicts of the grand stories and the loss of security on which they depend – the modern university is condemned to live with incoherence. There is no way round this situation. We have to address it, head on.

Part 2

Supercomplexity and the University

5

The Constellation of Fragility

New or old underpinnings?

All the available stories of the university are suspect. Both singly and in combination, they present problems. Where, then, can we turn? What cluster of concepts or ideas is going to furnish us both with a realistic sense of the position of the modern university and with a notion of how it might constitute itself productively and effectively in the world in which it finds itself? To put the problem more formally: the university has been delegitimized. From where, then, does it gain a new legitimacy?

The problem is complicated for a reason that has not yet been brought out but which has been implicit in our discussion. One of the dilemmas facing the modern university is not just that it is being built on conflicting stories, nor just that some are old and some are new (there are strata of stories within it *and* they are all jumbled up). It is not even that its major story – that of knowledge – is undermined by the situation of radical uncertainty with which the university is faced such that knowledge itself becomes problematic (the emperor's new clothes syndrome). The fundamental dilemma is one of values. We touched on this matter in Chapter 2. There, we noted that the university seems unable to shake off its value inheritance and become fully modern: much as it embraces the outstretched arms of instrumental reason, production, utility, measurement and performance, so the university also hangs on determinedly to old-fashioned stories of collegiality, pure communication, independence and critique. We also noted that the wider society, even as it is urging the university to become *moderne* in character, is also encouraging the university to retain and even to articulate its more traditional value background.

Is this, to repeat a question we posed earlier, a matter of faulty logic at work? Or, irrespective of whether these value systems are compatible, is it a case of the university wanting to be all things to all people? *Or* is there a larger story to be told: that, despite the apparent and even the actual incompatibilities involved, the university is *irredeemably* wedded to those older values while finding it necessary to come to some kind of accommodation with, if not actually embrace, the newer values? The question has, of course, to be nuanced: before 'university' stands, in the shadows, the qualifier 'Western'. The idea that the university is irredeemably wedded to certain values makes sense only if we understand the university in a particular context and tradition of dialogue and debate connected with a sense of human virtue, a context and tradition that goes back to the Greeks.[1]

Or is there a yet further story to be told, one in which the modern world is cast not as a vengeful slayer of the university but, rather, as *in need* of the traditional university, as least in some senses? In that case, the challenge before us is to understand the sense in which the traditional value background can be recast such that it does duty for the new demands being placed upon the university.

We are faced, then, with a conundrum. The university is clearly disinclined to shake off its historic value base: it shrinks from being 'detraditionalized'. Traditions live on; they can be a long time a-dying. But, in re-establishing foundations for the university, do we attempt to build on those traditional foundations, do we find room for them such that they support a wing of the building but are not the underpinning for the main structure, or do we see them as supporting the building as a whole? A glitzy new building is going up; we are all pretty well agreed on that. Everyone is scrambling to engage the best architects, literally and metaphorically. But there is much less agreement on the nature of the foundations. The conundrum is this: does the new building require new foundations or should we shore it up on the old? Or, is it even yet a matter of putting in new foundations alongside the old?

Resorting, in response, to the term 'the Western university' will have different resonances. To align oneself with the notion of the Western university is already to commit oneself to certain values and traditions. To go on to say that certain conceptual foundations are necessary for any university that sees itself in that tradition is hardly more than a tautology; at best, the point simply reminds us of those values and traditions. The real issue, of course, is why should one wish to make such an alignment? If we are to enter the brave new world that beckons, if we are to build a set of foundations that will serve the university for the next millennium, shouldn't we now shake off the old entirely? Doesn't real modernity, let alone postmodernity, require nothing less of us?

At this juncture, I wish simply to put this issue on the table. It is crucial that we are alert to it as we continue our inquiry. We have now reached the stage where we need to start on the conceptual reshaping of the university. But the task has to be tackled in such a way that we give ourselves the best opportunity of pulling it off. Like quantity surveyors, we have to ensure that we arm ourselves with the proper and complete resources for undertaking the task successfully. That means being alert to its full dimensions and challenges. And they, in turn, include facing up to the issue of the value base of the university: is it something that we can make up as we go along or is it, to some degree, determined for us? If we are going to shape a building that we can, with any legitimacy, call a university, perhaps our value options are not entirely open after all.

So here is the conundrum of putting the university on a firm foundation for the next thousand years. The sheer unpredictability and uncertainty of the future require that we do not, in advance, box ourselves in by declaring ourselves in favour of any particular value base but, yet, the very idea of the university in such an age may require that we hold fast to certain values – even amid its already conflicting value base. To endorse an earlier implied point, we may need to find a way of having our conceptual cake and eating it.

A state of ignorance

Let us identify the conceptual resources that we need in the task of reshaping the university. I have suggested that the world is radically unknowable. Every framework for knowing and every sense of the world, of ourselves and of our relationship to the world is contestable. Very well: let us define the nature of the modern university around this realization.

Instead of assuming that knowledge is available to us, and that through knowledge lies power, let us be somewhat more modest. Instead of knowledge, let us turn to ignorance. Let the modern university be built upon the realization that we shall always be behind the game, that the world will always be beyond our full grasp, that all our frameworks for being, understanding and acting will always be challengeable and that we will always live in a state of perpetual conceptual mortgage. Let the modern university not be dismayed by this realization and not see in it an affront to its dignity; let it instead revel in the uncertainty that surrounds us and to which the university contributes in substantial measure. What cluster of concepts, in that case, opens up?

The constellation of concepts I want to invoke consists, in its inner circle, of four concepts:

• uncertainty;
• unpredictability;
• challengeability;
• contestability.

To these four concepts I would add others such as ignorance itself, contingency, instability, risk, turbulence, volatility, disturbance and even chaos. These concepts constitute the outer circle of the constellation. Together, all these concepts speak to the world we are in, a world in which all our frameworks are contestable and are contested. It is a fragile world, a disturbed world. Following the styling of the six constellations that we encountered earlier – and dismissed as not being in any way adequate to the modern university – we can term our new constellation the constellation of fragility.

The notion of fragility is liable to create unease in the heart and mind of many a university's chief administrative officer. The new buildings to be seen out of the window and those being erected alongside seem substantial enough. Despite the pleas of pretty well every system of higher education for more money, the university seems a robust enough institution. The name of a wealthy donor adorning the new building is testimony to the capacity of the university still to win and retain friends in the right places to secure the necessary continuation of its funds. Fragility neither is appropriate to this state of affairs nor is it the kind of idea with which we wish to be associated. We are made of sterner stuff and we want the world to see it.

But the fragility in question here is not about buildings. It is not even a matter of the university's annual accounts, although they are often nowadays in a state of continuing fragility.[2] Rather, *this* fragility is about the conceptual base of the university: can a clear set of reasons be given as to why those buildings are being put up? Do the reasons that are forthcoming have anything to do with a sense of the purposes of the university? And, while those purposes are today's purposes, can they be said to have any durability to them or are they purposes summoned up to deal with the here-and-now exigencies pressing on the university?

The point is not that there is some stable set of purposes available which is being overlooked through pragmatic manoeuvring. It is, indeed, that the position of the university is one of fragility and that, therefore, any new shaping of its conceptual foundations has to take this fragility on board.

That the chief administrative officer is likely to exhibit some nervousness in the face of alleged fragility is understandable. Fragility is not a stance that comes comfortably in presenting the university to the university's Funding Council. It carries overtones of weakness, both managerial and moral. (The chief administrative officer knows that, of course; his tough demeanour is one of bravado, knowing that much is gained in this fragile world through bluff.)

All too easily, therefore, a value component is read into the notion of fragility: it is seen as a charge to which one has to respond. And a charge often brings forth defensiveness. But the notion of fragility should not be misunderstood. In this context, no value component is included in it. This use of the term is entirely descriptive. It is a reminder of the world that the modern university is in, wherever it is and in whatever system of higher education it finds itself. It is a world in which our descriptions and our frameworks for coming into a relationship with the world are always incomplete. Knowledge escapes us; we have to accept that we are in a perpetual state of ignorance.

That we are in a perpetual state of ignorance and that all our efforts to deploy our knowledge are in a state of fragility need give us no cause for concern. What it does mean is that we have to take this state of affairs on board in reshaping the university's conceptual foundations. This situation is akin to erecting a tall building in an earthquake zone: we have to allow for the likelihood of earthquakes and ensure that the framework going up has a degree – but not too much – of flexibility in it. Fragility requires a structure both robust and flexible at the same time: it has to contain a degree of tolerance. What, then, might our conceptual structure look like?

The constellation of fragility

I said earlier that there are four concepts that are key to understanding the post-modern university: uncertainty, unpredictability, challengeability and contestability. They have distinguishable features but they also have inter-linking features. While a number of other concepts are associated with them in the constellation of fragility, it is these four that stand at its centre.

Uncertainty is that state of being in the world in which one is aware that one's state of mind is itself open-ended. Uncertainty is that state of being in which one cannot be certain. Uncertainty is partly cognitive, but it is prim-arily experiential: it is an expression of one's mode of being in the world.

Unpredictability is that state of knowing in which one cannot predict with any security what is likely to happen at some future moment in time. It is a much more bounded concept than uncertainty. It has point in situations where one would wish to form expectations about the world. A state of unpre-dictability exists where one cannot tell what is going to happen. Science and technology, in their broadest senses, are sites where we seek predict-ability; but so, too, are our ordinary experiences as actors in the world.

Challengeability is that state of affairs in which our assumptions about the world are subject to counter-intuitive experiences. It is that state of affairs wherever we can be caught out. Suddenly, something takes our breath away; we have the stuffing knocked out of us. The assumptions on which we depended, but of which we were hardly aware, are – in the same moment – both revealed and found to be inadequate.

Contestability is that state of affairs in which a proposition or framework might be subjected to the counter-punch of a rival proposition or frame-work. It indicates a situation in which competing voices might wish to be heard and can be heard.

While their emphases vary, these four ideas all exhibit five features. Firstly, they contain both cognitive *and* experiential aspects. Secondly, they indi-cate the possibility of an undermining from the material world, from the world of human agency or from the world of ideas. Thirdly, they speak to an openness in our capacity to act in the world as well as to understand it. Fourthly, they could come into play in the presence of either collective understandings or those of individuals. And, lastly, they have point in rela-tion to understandings which could be highly systematized or which could be tacit assumptions, of which we are hardly aware.

We can depict the four concepts in the following table:

	World	Self
Cognitive	Unpredictability	Contestability
Experiential	Uncertainty	Challengeability

It will be clear that this tabulation is crude since, as we have just seen, all four concepts have resonances with all four moments at the ends of the two polarities (world/self; cognitive/experiential). But each, I suggest, has its centre of conceptual gravity at the points denoted. The table is also crude in implying that there are sharp boundaries between the four concepts. Again, it has just become apparent that they inhabit very much the same territory as each other; they are not just interconnecting but are overlapping concepts.

These four are the bright stars, as it were, in the constellation of fragility. But, as we noted, there are other concepts orbiting around them, including those of disturbance, ignorance, contingency, instability, risk, turbulence and volatility. It is this conceptual constellation which enables us both to understand the position of the modern university and to indicate the possibilities for its reshaping such that it is in fair shape to face whatever the future may bring at it.

Never a dull moment

The four concepts – of uncertainty, unpredictability, challengeability and contestability – are sociology and philosophy combined. Sociologically, they point up the conditions of the world in which the university finds itself today. It is an age of uncertainty and unpredictability because it has become an age of challengeability and contestability. Partly due to the earlier success of the university and to the spread of an educated population, we live in an age in which there are no ultimate authorities. Every educated person feels that she or he can challenge and contest the definitions of the world with which she or he is confronted. Medicine, science, high culture, politics, religion, economic arrangements and, of course, education itself: the accounts on offer in all of or concerning these domains and others are contested and challenged. As a result, more and more accounts of the world arise and more and more interventions in the world occur such that the world becomes uncertain and unpredictable. In turn, new definitions of the world arise, bringing in their wake new accounts and new interventions. And so the cycle of challenge and unpredictability continues in ever more rapid revolutions.

It will be said that much of the unpredictability of modern life arises outside the university in every sense; that much of it – economic and technological – is quite independent of the university. But that suggestion has to be qualified. For many, if not most, of the economic and technological changes have their sources in the university, either in its knowledge products or in its knowledge capacities residing in the minds of those who have passed through, whether as students, researchers or members of faculty. The recurring claim that knowledge production is now distributed far beyond the university is misleading, therefore, if it is taken to mean that the new production of knowledge would and does occur without the presence of universities. Very often, the symbiotic relationship – between the university and the wider world – is visibly affirmed through science parks and the clusters of new technologies that grow up around universities. But such visibility is not a necessary symbol of this interdependence. The proliferation of sites of knowledge production is a demonstration of the success of the university. But now, the university has to generate a new sense of itself amid the very unpredictability that it has brought into the world.

That the university should face up to these facts of life, therefore, is only right if somewhat ironic. For the university is, thereby, only looking at itself, the university having contributed in large measure to this cycle of unpredictability. It has done so through the proliferating accounts of the world it generates in its research and scholarship;[3] through its direct interventions in the world; *and* through the reflexive and critical capacities it engenders in the population by means of its teaching activities (with learning being undertaken as a form of pre-experience and post-experience). In having its gaze directed, therefore, to the cycle of unpredictability, the university is merely looking at itself and at the repercussions of its own activities.

These, then, are the sociological facts of life to which the modern university has to become accustomed; and they are captured in our four key concepts. But those four concepts – of uncertainty, unpredictability, challengeability and contestability – tell also, as it might be termed, a philosophical story. As well as depicting the world we are in and have to confront, they open up to us a view of the world to which we might aspire. As well as an 'is', there lies an 'ought' in these four concepts. Implicitly, to hold up these four concepts as key to the understanding of the idea of the modern university is to say that the life held out by these concepts – of utter uncertainty – is preferable to a life of certainty; that unpredictability is preferable to a world in which tomorrow is as today; that challengeability is preferable to a situation of dogma; and that contestability is preferable to a situation in which authorities rule by decree.

To speak of fragility, it is apparent, is not to invoke a life or a world that is meagre, frugal and weak but is, when backed up by the four concepts to which I have pointed, to open ourselves – and here the university – to a life that is challenging, certainly, and even daunting. A world in which *nothing* is unambiguous or free from being contested is unsettled, if not unsettling. But it is also a life that is, for those with fortitude and imagination, one that is stimulating, innervating and simply interesting *per se*. It may be regrettable that, just for one day here and there, one cannot get up in the morning with any surety as to what the day will bring; but at least, for those with the energy to face it, there will never be a dull moment.

Reflexive reconstitution

The problem for the university is not its psychology; there will always be those within it who are either embracers of the unknown or mistrustful of it. The problem lies, again, in both its inner sociology and its philosophy.

As a social institution, it has built itself on the known. It pretends to the world that it can secure knowledge (at least, that is what it tells the research councils and other sponsors of its research); it demarcates academic life into separate territories in which academic identities are formed, feeling assured that the boundaries of those territories have logic to them; it sorts its students into definite grades within a tight classification, as if there was a further assurance in the precision of those sortings; and in its newly emerging operations in the world (its 'consultancy' activities and its technologies), it implicitly says 'trust us, for we see things as they really are'.

It is time that these self-assurances and self-understandings were abandoned. Instead, the university should be embracing and be projecting a more modest but more realistic version of the situation. It is that its offerings are tentative responses, possible readings and suggested ideas for action and intervention. This is a much more modest role than that of producing and disseminating authoritative pronouncements; but it is a more honest role, given the situation of utter contestability and uncertainty in which the university finds itself.

If, sociologically, the university is going to find the abandonment of its faith in knowledge difficult to undertake, philosophically the task is going to be even more difficult. Sociologically, it will fear – wrongly – the loss of status and influence that will ensue. Philosophically, however, it will shrink from the whole idea that knowledge is not available to it. It has built its whole sense of itself on the idea of knowledge; as Nisbet (1971) put it, more tellingly than perhaps he knew, the belief in knowledge has become *the* academic dogma. If not knowledge, then what? What conceptual framework could possibly replace it? Uncertainty, unpredictability, challengeability and contestability: this constellation of fragility will hardly seem an attractive prospect as a *Weltanschauung* for the university. The university has too much invested in the constellation of knowledge to give it up unless some compelling reasons can be found.

The university will not be persuaded by logic. It never has been, despite its declarations in favour of reason. The important distinction made by Michael Argyris and Donald Schön (1974) between espoused theory and theory-in-action could have pointedly been turned inward to the university itself. Logic never was the university's strong point. Since it has had within it for nearly one thousand years philosophers who have cautioned against the idea of knowledge and has failed to pay heed to their observations, it is hardly likely to start doing so now.

Another tack is therefore required. The university will be afraid of being found out, of losing its capacity to influence those around it. It will doubt that industry, let alone the taxpayer, will continue to support it if it proclaims the end of knowledge and, instead, raises a flag on which flies the emblem of the constellation of fragility. But it shrinks from such a prospect unnecessarily. Indeed, a new opportunity beckons for the university.

If the world is one that is characterized by uncertainty, unpredictability, challengeability and contestability, then the university has an unparalleled and an unrivalled opportunity to become the key institution in the world. It will become such a pivotal institution precisely through its insight into the character of that world and through the human capacities it will sponsor to confront that world. Knowledge in any simple sense is not available. Instead, what it can offer is what it has been doing for eight hundred years: perpetual critical scrutiny of what it encounters alongside its creative offerings. These two capacities – creativity accompanied by critique – are the capacities that a world of uncertainty and contestability requires.

Sociologically, such a role and a self-presentation on the part of the university injects into society helpful monitoring capacities that, at the same time, extend the range of the possible.[4] Philosophically, it retains for the university a connection with the ideals of the Enlightenment but now abandons the metaphysical baggage of 'knowledge' that accompanied it. The modern world is such that we can never get on top of it in any absolute way. It will continue to slip from our grasp. Accordingly, while entrenching its capacity to add to the complexities of our world, the university can open out to us the prospect of increasing enlightenment. For just as the complexity of the world expands – partly through the university's own endeavours – so too our capacity to understand, to interpret and to act in enlightened ways expands.

Far from reducing the role of the university, the replacement of the constellation of knowledge by the constellation of fragility opens out to the university a new and more important role. Knowledge and control are not, thankfully, available. (That belief partly led to Auschwitz.) What is both necessary and possible – just – is an enlightened societal self-monitoring. The university can become a pivotal institution in this process of collective self-enlightenment. The constellation of fragility opens up the prospect of a reflexive reconstitution of society.

The uncertainty principle

What emerges from our discussion is the uncertainty principle. The uncertainty principle has three elements to it. It is that the university is an institution that (i) contributes to our uncertainty in the world (through its research and consultancy); (ii) helps us to monitor and evaluate that uncertainty (through its work as a centre of critique); and (iii) enables us to live with that uncertainty, through both the operational capacities and the existential capacities it promotes (in its pedagogical activities).

There are three things to note about this uncertainty principle. Firstly, knowledge figures *not at all* in this triple-fold principle. Although it is not practically possible to surrender the ideas of knowledge and truth, the postmodern university can go a long way without resorting to such metaphysical notions.

Secondly, research and teaching are retained as independent elements in the principle but are reformulated in terms of the notion of uncertainty.

They will and should continue to have a place in the future university, but only if they are cut free from the notion of knowledge and recast in terms of uncertainty and, thereby, brought within the ambit of the constellation of fragility.

Thirdly, introduced into the principle, alongside the expansion of uncertainty (research) and the inculcation of the capacity to understand and to cope effectively with uncertainty (teaching), is a third element, that of the monitoring and evaluation of uncertainty (critique). It is a crucial part of the principle, but how might we understand it?

In this third element of the uncertainty principle is held out to the university a role in critiquing the discourses of the wider society (to which the university has itself contributed). Precisely because the post-modern university understands that there are no certainties, that there are no ideas that cannot be qualified, that the world is one of infinite etceteration, the task of monitoring those accounts that are available in the world becomes more important. We have no direct access to the world: we have access to the world only through our accounts in it. Our activities, our technologies and our institutions, as well as the world itself, are 'known' to us through the descriptions we have produced.[5] The university has a responsibility, certainly, to add to those accounts, to compound the complexity of the world. But it also has a role to shed light on the manifold accounts that exist. This role has tended to be known as scholarship, an activity that becomes crucial in offering us new interpretations of the already existing accounts.

This role, long established in the university, takes on a new resonance in the world and makes new sense of the incorporation of the university into the wider society. The world itself is an uncertain place; our accounts are contestable. The university reinvigorates its role as a critical voice in society by holding up those accounts and subjecting them to searching examination. The ideologies that bombard us (the apparently authoritative statements from the government and various state agencies through which we are expected to understand our world and the stories sanctioned by the professions about themselves and their views of the world) and the cultural images and sensations that surround us: the university has a responsibility to put them under its forensic microscope. Absolute knowledge will not be forthcoming, but different and even more insightful accounts of the world might emerge. At least, we shall not be left to the mercy of the accounts that come to us from the big battalions.

Scholarship, then, can and should take on a worldy role. It should turn away from its role of being an introverted conversation among the academics (in which, for those who want to know, we are given a new insight into what x said of y who had commented on z). The never-ending character of that cycle of communication had become self-indulgent and unnecessarily so. Now, a more extrovert role beckons of commenting on the discourses, stories and accounts more widely available. In taking on this wider role, scholarship assists the formation of a more rational society.

The post-modern university, then, lives out the uncertainty principle. It plays its part in adding to the uncertainty of the world and reinterprets higher learning as the formation of the human capacities to live without fear in such an uncertain world. But also, in its monitoring role, the post-modern university plays a steadying role in enabling all of us in society – and, therefore, the world – to distinguish sense from nonsense, well-informed accounts from uninformed accounts, and enlightenment from ideology. The post-modern university is a necessary part of the 'reflexive modernization' of the wider society (Beck, Giddens and Lash, 1995).

Conclusions: a world without knowledge

There are no assurances in this world. There are always qualifications, nuances and refinements, if not downright full-frontal challenges, rebuttals and exocets. This fragility extends to our frameworks for interpreting the world. It is not so much a runaway world (Leach, 1968) as an ultimately fathomless world, not because we are devoid of resources – conceptual, human and technological – for handling it but because we are replete with resources. Our conceptual cup overfloweth.

In this situation, a new constellation beckons for the university. Its brightest stars are the ideas of uncertainty, unpredictability, challengeability and contestability. It has associated with it a number of lesser stars, including those of ignorance, risk, turbulence, complexity, instability and even chaos. Here, if anywhere, in this constellation of fragility, is a set of ideas around which the university can be reconstructed and can regain its legitimacy.

The university cannot duck out of this challenge. It might pretend to do so, comforting itself that it knows what it is about. But, deep down, it knows that things cannot go on as they are: muddling through is not good enough. The wider society, indeed the world, wants, needs and deserves something better from its universities.

The wider world is looking for three things from its universities: a continuing flow of new stories to add to those that we already have in the world (and it will help if the new stories are cashable in some way); a critical interrogation, and even rebuttal, of existing ideas; and the development of the human capacities to live both at ease and purposively amid such uncertainty. All this the university can provide; but, first, it needs to rid itself of its pretentiousness, of its claims to know things, of its inner sureness about being an authority on matters and of its tendency to conduct inner conversations of the elect. We live in a perplexing world, a perplexity that is partly of the university's making. The university had better help us to live in that world.

6

Supercomplexity: the New Universal

The new universal

The notion of the university gains its point in two ways. Firstly, the term 'university' speaks to the idea of *universitas*, that is, a guild or corporation. The mediaeval universities were, in their origin, just that: groups of scholars who formed themselves into self-governing guilds. Their establishment as formal foundations, with designated powers to award degrees – that is, the setting up in each case of a *studium generale* – came later, as did the colleges. The idea of a *universitas*, then, denoted a mutual recognition of the members of the association and a common language (that of Latin): each could understand the others and all understood each other as sharing in a common cause (Cameron, 1978). In the beginning was unity-through-dialogue.

The second sense of the university, as being in principle a site of universal knowledge, is more modern. By 'universal knowledge' is meant not that the university should necessarily embrace all fields of knowledge – although in it should be represented a wide range of knowledge fields – but that it should exhibit an openness towards knowledge. It should understand that the boundaries of knowledge are nowhere fixed and that the source or character of legitimate ideas, qualifications and commentaries cannot be specified *a priori* (Popper, 1966). This sense of the university offers a unity-through-metatheory.

Both of those ideas of the university are now buried in its deep strata, but on them has been built organically a more modern sense of the universal character of the university which is also germane to our purposes. It is that human reason can be developed and can be institutionalized. Human reason has a number of characteristics, including a determination to get at truth (which is independent of opinions or values), an openness to criticism, a willingness to treat as equal all those who wish to join the conversation and a capacity to liberate (from superstition, ideology and delusion). These features of human reason are part of the heritage and the supporting conceptual framework of the Western university and are held to be universal in character.

However, the postmoderns like to declare that there are no universals. They enjoy making this observation of the world that surrounds us. They *delight* in doing so. In other words, they are not just recording neutrally, as it were, how things are. For the postmoderns, the fact – if, indeed, it is a fact – that there are no universals is a state of affairs to be applauded. It is a welcome state of affairs. It is even – speak softly, softly – a new universal.

If the postmodernists were right, the university would be in difficulty. Ideas of universal reason, communication, truth, knowledge and openness: all would have to be jettisoned. They would have to be repudiated as the detritus of the modern age and, far from offering a means of enlightenment, would serve only to shackle us. Get rid of them. For the postmoderns, such a clearing out would, indeed, amount to a clearing out of the stables. We should tackle the task enthusiastically, and not delay ourselves with pious thoughts about humanity or what we might be losing. A brave new world awaits.

Why the postmoderns think this way is not, fortunately, our concern here. The point is that there is a value element written into the postmodernist story. We are being told not just that this is how things are but also that we should warm to this situation: it is a situation greatly to be admired. The wish, too, is party to its fulfilment: in endorsing postmodernism, its adherents hope to bring that world into being even more fully.

We can reflect that if, on any occasion, values and wishes are mixed in with observations and judgements, we may justifiably be sceptical of the veracity of the story being opened out to us. So, too, it is here. This is not to rubbish the postmodernist story as such, but it is to urge caution: we may be being given a lopsided story. And that is the case; the postmodernists overplay their hand.

Universal leverage

That there are no universals is itself a universal. The aphorism carries three sentiments. Firstly, the statement captures our modern condition; nothing less than that. Specifically, it does two things. In declaring the impossibility of establishing universals in the modern world, it underlines the radical challengeability of every attempt we make to understand the world and to gain a meaningful hold on the world. It endorses the constellation of fragility as the expression of the world in which we find ourselves.

Secondly, however, it declares that this state of affairs *is* itself a universal. This is a truly global state of affairs and it is against the horizon of such a global state of affairs that we have to understand the university. So, paradoxical as it may seem, the very fact that we find ourselves saddled with unpredictability is itself now predictable. This is a sure ground – of a sort – on which we can move, can establish our institutions and our frameworks of thought and action. That nothing is certain is itself a certainty. We are justified in taking this point seriously, as a firm base on which we can move forward.

Thirdly, the proposition (that there are no universals is itself a universal) gives us grounds for hope, after all. It recognizes that there may be validity in the postmodern story: we just may live on shifting sands. There may be no secure footholds. But, precisely in making this observation, it offers hope. For the act of making the observation amounts to forming *an understanding*. Even amidst chaos, in other words, the exercise of our own understanding provides a leverage through which we can insert a distance between ourselves and our murky surroundings. We do not have to be sucked into the quicksands.

All this amounts, it will be observed, to a disinclination to buy the postmodernist story hook, line and sinker: there is, yet, space for human reason to work. But it also amounts to a qualification of the Habermassian project. Habermas (1990) wants to hold out the prospect of there being universal reason and has taken on the postmodernists on their own ground. Just as they demur about the idea of universal reason, so Habermas attempts to identify the presence and the basic elements of universal reason. But, if the Habermassian project is to be realized, the tactics have to be altered.

It is possible to allow the postmoderns to have their say and to endorse what they have to say, short of the point where they are liable to run themselves into a self-contradiction. We can go with them in their pointing up the ultimate challengeability of every framework for action and understanding. That, of course, includes the character of the framework in which they make such 'observations'. We do not have to assume, à la Habermas, that there must be universal conditions of human communication obeyed tacitly even by the postmoderns themselves. We cannot even assume that a tacit appeal to human reason is present in their discourse. What we can do, however, is to observe that the postmoderns' story is itself a contribution to the very complexities that they themselves are pointing to, complexities that are *apparent to human reason*.

Much as the postmoderns attempt to do so, therefore, they cannot get entirely behind human reason. Their utterances may bear witness to there being no universal features of human reason and communication (and that is why, to be charitable, so many are incomprehensible): there may be no universal validity conditions upheld *within* their offerings. To that extent, the Habermassian project gets off on the wrong foot in its assumption that there must be binding conditions of human communication. But where it does score is in its pointing out that the postmoderns can never get behind themselves. Purely in making utterances that are more than mere grunts, in offering additional points of meaning to the world, they are adding to its complexities. Inadvertently, they affirm the very conditions of complexity to which they are pointing; they do not stand outside them.

To say, therefore, 'that there are no universals is itself a universal' is to say much. It is to say to the postmoderns that there are limits to postmodernity. It is to say that there are features of the world that we can assuredly agree on, namely its challengeability, contestability and, thereby, its ultimate negotiability. And it is to say that the recognition of *this* universal of ultimate complexity can give us – even if somewhat surprisingly – some sure ground on which to move forward, even if we have always to be checking that peculiar sureness. The cracking ice holds.

Supercomplexity

The world is such that not just our propositions, our theories, our actions and our social institutions are contestable; rather, the world is such that the very frameworks by which we might try to come into some kind of determinable relationship with the world are themselves contested. It is this contestability of our frameworks that characterizes the postmodern condition. Lyotard was partly right and partly wrong. Yes, the postmodern shows itself in 'an incredulity towards metanarratives' (Lyotard, 1984: xxiv) but this isn't because metanarratives are on the way out. To the contrary, we are bombarded with them and increasingly so.

Our especial postmodern difficulty is in choosing *between* metanarratives, or large stories of the world. Do we embrace science or mistrust it? Do we hang on to the welfare state or, instead, look to individuals to take responsibility for themselves? Do we abandon religion or seek to welcome new religions? Is it important, in managing our public institutions – such as universities – to ensure that decisions are made and that things get done or to find ways of encouraging the members of those institutions genuinely to engage with and to come to new understandings of each other? How do we apportion relative priorities between freedom, justice, responsibility and equality? Does social change spell social progress? Is science a force for increased rationality and control or is it an ideology serving particular interests? (Feyerabend, 1978). And so on and so on.

In this situation, we are assaulted by large ideas through which to interpret ourselves and our hopes. There is no incredulity towards large stories as such; to the contrary, we are obliged to give credence to so many stories, all competing for our attention and our allegiance. Our discomfort arises in realizing that putting all the stories into an orderly picture is impossible for, if they do not conflict in a logical sense, they do at least speak to different kinds of human aspiration which would lead us in different directions.

We are entitled to name this situation as one of *supercomplexity*. We are in a situation of supercomplexity when our very frameworks for making the world intelligible are in dispute. The resulting fragility that confronts us is not that our frameworks are dissolving as such; rather, it is that for any one framework that appears to be promising, there are any number of rival frameworks which could contend against it and which could legitimately gain our allegiance. We do not know and *we cannot know* with any assuredness who we are. We approach, it seems, a situation of collective anomie. There are no secure holds on the world.

It is not just that we have to grapple with different theories or ideas; for example, that doctors or lawyers will often come to quite different judgements

about the same situation. Rather, the very frameworks with which we understand the world, ourselves, our practices and our environment are themselves
contestable. What it is *to be* a doctor or a lawyer in the modern world is
disputed. The frameworks through which we interrogate the world and find
our way in it are multiplying.

Supercomplexity is, therefore, not just hyper-complexity (Delanty, 1998b:
109); it is not just an extended or an expanded form of complexity. It is a
higher order form of complexity. It is that form of complexity in which our
frameworks for understanding the world are themselves problematic. It is
that form of challenge in which our strategies for handling complexity itself
are in question. It is a higher order complexity in which we have to find
ways of living and even prospering, if we can, in a world in which our very
frameworks are continually tested and challenged. This supercomplexity is
the world in which we all live.

The university is triply implicated in this world of supercomplexity. Firstly,
it is one of the institutions principally responsible for producing this state
of affairs. Certainly, the mass media, the global economy with its increasing
momentum of change, and the widely dispersed sites for knowledge production are all playing a part. But the university has to bear a particular
responsibility for generating this state of affairs in that, precisely, this is
what it is paid to do. We require of our universities that they come forth
with radically new ways of understanding the world. To the extent that they
fail to do this, they fall short of their responsibilities.

Secondly, a high proportion of the frameworks for understanding the
world has received some kind of critical scrutiny within the university. The
motor-car has furnished one framework for being and self-identity in
the modern world. Clearly, the university does not manufacture motor-cars,
but it can – and does – study the manufacture of motor-cars. In so doing,
it produces contesting frameworks for understanding the motor-car. Is the
car to be understood as the largest element in manufacturing industry
and, therefore, to be protected? Is it an undue consumer of the Earth's
resources? Is it the most dangerous polluter of the Earth's ecology? Is it, yet,
a means of personal projection, the most obvious way in which we can
attempt to present ourselves publicly in this postmodern world of image?
(Baudrillard, 1987). These are not just multiple frameworks, they are contesting frameworks. And this contestation is characteristic of the contestation of frameworks with which we have to grapple several times a day in
making our choices, our statements of who we are and our interventions in
this world.

Thirdly, the doubts and difficulties that many experience as part of living
amid supercomplexity are expressions of psychological structures of tolerance, openness and reflexivity towards new ideas that the university has
itself developed.

In this triple association of the university in supercomplexity, we see
again but at a meta-level the triple responsibilities of the post-modern university: (i) to help to generate supercomplexity, to interrogate it and to

inform us about it; (ii) to help us to weave a way through it, and to develop defensible stories about the world, including ourselves; and (iii) to develop the ego structures such that we can live at peace with ourselves and with each other, even amid supercomplexity, *and* such that we can make purposeful but reflexive interventions in the world. The university nurtures supercomplexity, keeps it under review and helps us to live with it and through it.

Brave new world

The world is radically unknowable. *Every* framework for knowing and every sense of our world, of ourselves and of our relationships to the world and to each other is contestable. We cannot know who we are or what the world is like. Not just every proposition and theory, not just every stance, principle or action, but every set of assumptions, tacit understandings and inner beliefs from which those thoughts and actions spring: all are challengeable. There is no security. The philosophers have long told us that. Nietzsche was only following Heraclitus: all is flux; any semblance of stability is just a self-imposed delusion, a mere comforter.[1]

The sociologists have caught up with the philosophers at last. The sociologists of the early nineteenth century sought, through their espousal of a society built on reason and positive knowledge, to offer a framework for conceptual and social progress. But that project is now called in question by a new world order. Just as it seemed as if we were getting on top of things in our social arrangements such that we could begin to contemplate the end of history (Fukuyama, 1993), the sociologists – not to mention the environmentalists – point out that we are in a runaway world. In this new order, postmodern-*ism* can be seen as the cry of angst emitted by those who cotton on to the unpredictability now sharply posed by postmodern-*ity* (Aviram, 1992). Amidst the global economy and detraditionalization, there is no social stability and, in turn, no secure conceptual hold on the world for which we might reach out. Those holds that appear to have some firmness crumble in our grasp.

The university is in some difficulty in all this, to put it mildly. Firstly, it sees itself as having something to do with knowledge. Secondly, it likes to believe that it is in the vanguard of progress. Clearly, in this new world order, both of these self-beliefs are problematic. Thirdly, and even more problematically for the university, the disturbance to our frameworks in the modern world is not just intellectual in character but also challenges our sense of ourselves and our sense of right action. When all our frameworks for understanding the world become questionable, then so does our sense of who we are *and* how we might reasonably act in the world and in relation to each other. There is a double existential quality, therefore, about the unsettling position in which we find ourselves: the domains *both* of self-understanding and of action are implicated.

'Brave new world' admirably sums up this situation. To pick up the Shake-spearean sense of the term,[2] we are faced with a world full of show: it contains many things that are new to our senses, disturbing and captivating at the same time. In our responses, delight is matched by awe, wonder is matched by anxiety, attraction is matched by fear. But there lurks as well the Huxleyian sense that *this* brave new world is largely manufactured by us and contains within it oppressive capacities. In turn, that understanding prompts the realization that it is only brave souls who are going to be adequate to the challenge of this ever-perplexing world. A university worthy of the name, therefore, will certainly go on adding to the complexities of this brave new world (it is not a 'university' if it is simply echoing existing descriptions of the world); but, through the higher learning that it offers, it will also provide the wherewithal, the human qualities of courage and resili-ence, which will enable individuals to cope with *and* to live in this world.

A universal responsibility

The world is a disturbing place to be in. But this disturbance, to which the university is contributing in no small measure, is not just an intellectual disturbance. It is a disturbance within individuals as persons. Ryle (1949) got it askew. For him, what you saw was what you got: man was a one-dimensional being whose mind was indissoluble. But living in the modern world calls for a multitude of aspects of being to come into play and to do so simultaneously. Acting, monitoring oneself, knowing-in-action, feeling, giving of oneself, being willing, and taking the plunge: all these can go on at once and *all are separable*. It is hardly any wonder that there is an inner disturbance, even if it is hushed up. Any one of the multitude of human capacities that come into play is a site of potential disturbance.

This fragility, to repeat, has been caused in large measure by the univer-sity. It has generated, directly or indirectly, many of the contesting concep-tual schemes, experiences, technologies and systems that gnaw away at these components of human being. Adult students understandably exemplify much of the ensuing angst. Their subjectivities – to use a voguish term – have been disturbed; and given that the university is party to that disturbance, there is a nice irony and fitting justice in their approaching the university to assist them in working through that angst.

So higher learning becomes a form of therapy, then? Or, for the younger students, provides the meta-capacities to cope with later disturbance, so that they can apply the therapeutic techniques to themselves? The questions imply a criticism and suggest that higher learning is ill-conceived as a form of therapy; and that, instead, the university should find its role in the life of reason, albeit in a life of reason under new management. The questions hanker after a sense of the university as a site of pure intellect, as one devoid of emotions. But that is to look to a lost world, a world that was sure of itself and in which frames of understanding were relatively stable. That world is gone.

The argument, then, emerges clearly enough:

1. The university has, in part, brought about supercomplexity.
2. Supercomplexity involves a disturbance of the whole person.
3. The university, then, has a responsibility to enable individuals to prosper amid supercomplexity.

The university has helped to bring about a brave new world; indeed, to cause both its internal and the external conditions. It has rendered our frameworks for grappling with the world problematic; and, in so doing, it brings unceasing turmoil to individuals as persons. Objective and subjective conditions of supercomplexity are the product of the university's work. In this post-modern world, the university has to shoulder its share of the responsibility for coping with supercomplexity. The university generates supercomplexity: that is the task of its research and scholarship. But it can also help us to live with supercomplexity: that is its educational role.[3]

Under this dual conception of the university amid supercomplexity, research and scholarship are reframed. Research can now be understood as the means of production of supercomplexity. Teaching, by contrast, becomes the management of the human relations of supercomplexity.

However, in this latter reframing of the university's educational task of enabling us to cope with supercomplexity, the university is given a new responsibility. We might say that there is nothing new here because many universities, at least in the Western world, have prided themselves on educating 'the whole person'. But the educational responsibility that arises from taking supercomplexity seriously *is* new in that it now becomes precisely a universal responsibility resting on all universities that would place themselves in the Western tradition: it is a new universal as such for the university. It is also new in that the conditions that it addresses are new. And it is new in the still further sense that it arises organically from the university's other activities of research and scholarship in their generating supercomplexity itself.

Derrida (1992) considered that it makes sense for us still to talk of the university and 'responsibility' in the same breadth. He did not, however, furnish us with any clear idea as to the nature of that responsibility. I believe that, in this educational task of enabling us to live with supercomplexity, we have found it: this is the new responsibility of the university.

It is a brave new world: the university is active in generating its richness, its complexity, and its rate of conceptual *and* technological change. But it is also a brave new world in that it produces phenomenological disturbance calling for lifelong meta-qualities of fortitude, resilience and courage. The responsibility for developing these qualities must fall upon the university.

The virtues of the university

The university is a meta-institution. Through its internal discursive spaces, it contains the inherent capacity to go on inquiring about itself, to generate an ever-evolving sense of itself and continually to replenish itself. The university is an institution that speaks unto itself. The university, to employ a contemporary idiom, is a learning institution. It is never still; it places itself on the table for discussion. It is a restless institution; it will not take itself as fixed in any way. It is an institution that critiques its own character as an institution. It is, to repeat, a meta-institution.

This both is all to the good and contains a double irony. It is all to the good because, if they are to survive, universities will have to contain such self-learning and self-generative qualities (Weil, 1998). This holds for any organization in the modern world. The reflection holds the double irony in that, firstly, as we have seen, the university has itself helped to generate supercomplexity which, in turn, renders organizational self-reflexivity a necessary condition of survival. In this sense, the university is only meeting the bill that it has landed us all with.

Secondly, despite being castigated for not being in the real world and for not taking on the proper managerial disciplines of that world, the university can demonstrate what it is to be a successful and adaptive organization. The university is ahead of the game; and nor should this be surprising since it has had eight hundred years' practice.

We can say, therefore, that the university is – or should be – adept at handling metacomplexity. It contains within itself the capacities for responding with vigour to supercomplexity. How is this possible? What is it about the university that creates such a happy situation?

The essence of the answer has already been given. The university is a site of competing discourses. One of its tasks, through research and scholarship, is to expand those discourses. A hallmark of the university in the Western tradition is that its discourses are open-ended (cf. Horton, 1971). Admittedly, this is as much a piece of rhetoric as reality. Becher (1989) has shown us that: the university's 'disciplines' are a matter of boundary maintenance. Foucault (1977) went further and showed how the disciplines, being bounded discursive systems, could serve as instruments of power and domination. But, for all that, disciplines still contain space for criticism and rebuttal (even if you have to be a fully paid up member of the fraternity to gain a hearing).

Disciplines, then, despite their empirical selves, contain discursive potential, even if that potential is not always realized. Institutionalized as sites of debate, academic life offers discursive space. Leavis' (1969: 6) credo, his encapsulation of the conduct of literary criticism, was only an extraction from the general conditions of academic life: every statement, every utterance and every academic act contains an implicit invocation, 'this is so, isn't it?'. To put it more grandly, *something* of the tacit validity claims that Habermas (1989; 1991) claimed to have identified are embedded in academic discourse. Academic practices invite rejoinders. They have a stubborn openness about them.

It is this openness that supplies the capacities of academic life to confront and to handle supercomplexity. Through this openness, disciplines generate their own self-reflexiveness and, in turn, they gain the suppleness that enables them to respond tellingly to supercomplexity; indeed, to contribute to supercomplexity itself. It is early days: not all disciplines are responding as yet. History courses may offer units in which history is itself examined; in contrast, such 'autocritique' may be absent from the more scientific disciplines.[4]

So then, openness, suppleness and self-reflexiveness: these characteristics of the university enable it both to contribute to supercomplexity and to make its way amid supercomplexity. These are organizational virtues, certainly. They give the university what it – and any other knowledge-based organization – requires in a context of supercomplexity. But organizational virtues gain their strength by becoming personal virtues as well. Openness, flexibility and self-reflexiveness: these are just some of the personal qualities – or, as we can say without awkwardness, virtues – that the academic life calls for (even if it does not always have its request fully met).[5]

This argument, that there exists the prospect of a symmetry between the organizational and personal qualities of academic life, should not be misunderstood. It is not an empirical claim about the university. It is a reading of its character as a social institution and of its prospects. The discursive structures of the university produce a certain openness, even despite inner and outer attempts to close off that openness. This reading is a form of critical theory in action: it is a reminder of what the university is at its best moments and contains within itself a potential for the future. The university can claim to be, in this sense, a virtuous organization. Virtue has a timeliness about it. So it is with the university. If it can get its act right, the university – in an age of supercomplexity – is an institution whose time has come.

The limits of supercomplexity

Virtues are not necessarily virtuous. Openness can be too open: one can be open to, and unduly swayed by, ideology. One can be so flexible that one holds only to the voice that was last encountered. One can be so self-reflexive that one ends up doubting any view that one might form and so[6] be paralysed into inaction. Accordingly, virtues only gain the status of virtues when held in due measure alongside a panoply of other relevant virtues and which, taken together, supply a form of life that is reasonably coherent and that can be justified in its totality.

Two other virtues can be pushed to extremes within the rational life. One is that of a love of truth; the other is that of courage. Together, they can produce Dr Strangelove. A love of truth can lead to a narrowness of vision, to a pursuit of minutiae and to an obliviousness to the effects that the truth-seeking process itself might have. To that end, for example, ethics committees have been widely established in Western universities so as to provide assurances that the wider environment – whether human, animal or natural – is respected. Courage, on the other hand, can turn into a will to power, a non-reflexive determination to dominate: my view is greater than your view; my insight is more penetrating than your insight; and my truth will yield more value to mankind than your truth.

These reflections have implications for our larger story about supercomplexity. The Western university has evolved through a value background, which itself has expanded. That value background includes the idea that certain things matter, such as a willingness to search for truth, respect for others in a truth-oriented conversation, tolerance of rival views, a willingness to be self-critical and a prizing of courage to proffer new ideas. Supercomplexity puts question-marks against all and any such values. In an age of supercomplexity, all large stories – or frameworks, as I have called them – are on the table for examination, if they have not been consigned to the waste-paper bin.

Supercomplexity places our values in question. In an age of supercomplexity, no value or set of values can be given an easy ride. But the downside of being overly gripped by supercomplexity is a sense that, ultimately, nothing matters. In such a climate, knowledge can be torn apart from its ethical anchoring and become a will to power.

Accordingly, in an age of supercomplexity, the value base of the university is on a cusp. Supercomplexity calls for a determination not to be overwhelmed by a sense of ineradicable uncertainty: openness to new ideas has to be matched by a courage to withstand the battering of newness and to be prepared to drive through one's own point of view, or to act in one's own way. But that very set of virtues – of determination, of a willingness to reach out to new positions and new stances – can lead to a will to power. Nietzsche (1988 edn) is the supreme exponent of this awkwardness. On the one hand, he shoots through the pretentiousness of claims to know and in so doing compounds our complexities, removing all our earlier anchors; on the other hand, he opens the way to a will to power.[7]

Supercomplexity, then, has its limits. It may seem as if it describes our contemporary situation *tout court*. If we put a boundary around it, it may seem impossible to imagine that the space beyond it has any content. But we have to go into that apparent void. Supercomplexity is a universal but it is not the universe. It has to be contained. We have to find the conceptual resources to get beyond it, to limit it, and to guide our efforts to situate ourselves in its midst.

The university has helped to beget supercomplexity. Very well. But the university cannot wash its hands of the matter. Otherwise, the university would have brought into the world a child about to turn into an adult without values. Accordingly, a further responsibility opens up for the university amid supercomplexity. It is that of maintaining the value background – its own value basis – which helped to produce supercomplexity. Of course, this is a paradoxical situation. Just at the moment that the large stories by which the university has projected itself into the world come up for radical scrutiny, the university has to go on holding on to those values. The university has produced supercomplexity but now it must stand outside supercomplexity and, in effect, dare it to do its worst. The university's values are larger than those of supercomplexity. After all, supercomplexity is bereft of values.

Conclusion

The university has to live through supercomplexity; it cannot afford just to live *with* supercomplexity. The prospect opening up before us is that the university will content itself with the latter definition of its role. It will go on expanding our understandings of the world and our self-understandings. It will extend our possibilities for action, for having demonstrable effects in and on the world, and for securing more (income, profit, resource) from the world. It will continue to add to the complexities of our world, secure in the understanding that the more frameworks we have, the better. The more possibilities, in turn, unfold for securing our ends in life, in society and in the economy.

Seen against that definition of the university's role, higher learning becomes a process of implanting in students coping mechanisms at least and creative capacities at best. All that matters is getting by and, preferably, 'adding value' to the world. As graduates, individuals perform; they thrive; and they are 'successful'. They can live with supercomplexity. The university secures anew its legitimacy in the post-modern world.

All this is a huge agenda for the university. But it is to do insufficient justice to the potential of the university. And it is to fall short of the ultimate demands of our planet. Amid supercomplexity, more can and should be required of our universities.

What is required is the capacity to tame supercomplexity, to inject a value structure into it even as all value structures are put in the dock. The university has to hold on to the value systems that helped to generate supercomplexity – of openness, courage, tolerance and so on – even as supercomplexity puts those same values under the microscope. Supercomplexity has its limits: it cannot help us to form a sense of what is right, how we should collaborate, and how we might relate to the world around us. Supercomplexity deprives us of a value anchorage for answering such challenges. The value background that spawned supercomplexity, on the other hand, can help us to do just that. The values implicit in rational critical dialogue helped to generate supercomplexity and they can help to keep supercomplexity in its place.

Adding to supercomplexity and helping us to live with supercomplexity are, then, insufficient specifications of the role of the university. To those two responsibilities, large as they are, we now have to add a third, that of doing justice to the value structure that helped to produce supercomplexity. The ladder of the university's value background has to be kept in place, not kicked away.

7
The Conflict of the Faculties

Introduction

The idea of supercomplexity drives a stake through the heart of the university. The university – the Western university – has built itself on a self-understanding that it was a force for reason. Yes, its contemporary form has embraced technology in the broadest sense. Science is on the way to being transformed as the handmaiden of technology. But still, despite these changes, despite the forceful entry of the university into the world – as an actor in the world rather than a mere commentator on it – the university could content itself that all its activities were embodiments of reason. They could be grounded in reasons. Evidence could be brought forward, evidence that had stood the test of robust scrutiny. But, as we have seen, supercomplexity puts in doubt this whole enterprise: reason itself is up before the courts.[1]

Reason is embattled. The postmoderns say that all frameworks are suspect. But that is an ideological position, which tells us more about the postmoderns than about frameworks: the postmoderns have an angst about frameworks. So we can bracket off that concern, to some extent. The idea of supercomplexity, on the other hand, is of a different order. For that idea implies not that frameworks are suspect but that they are all criticizable. There is no framework that we can hang on to with any security: all are fragile.

Popper (1963; 1977) said, too, that all frameworks were criticizable and then, in his theory of critical reason, tried to put the framework of critical reason beyond criticism. He failed to heed his own observation. Supercomplexity reminds us that we cannot get behind our frameworks to secure a safe redoubt. Reason cannot be made secure.

So the idea of supercomplexity drives a stake through the heart of the university, the Western university. It denies the security of the university's self-belief that, deep down, its activities are reasonable for we can no longer be assured that *its* reason offers us firm foundations. The university's buildings continue to go up, but they are built on flimsy conceptual foundations.

It may just be that the topping-out ceremony will have to be conducted without any conceptual foundations being put in place.

Kantian murmurings

In the old days, a writer proclaiming 'the idea of the university' could point to a favoured discipline as the embodiment of reason. For Kant – surprise, surprise – that discipline was philosophy. Philosophy could claim this role because it was pure reason. It was not so much that the other disciplines were aimed at bringing about effects in the world, that they were 'vocational'. Rather, they dealt with the world of mere appearances. Philosophy, in contrast, was concerned precisely to get behind appearances to uncover the structure of the world as such. It was an exercise in pure reason, uncontaminated by appearances. Kant's category of the synthetic *a priori* embodied this idea perfectly: human beings had knowledge of the world through their reason alone, independently of the evidence of the senses.

Inevitably, this view of philosophy explicitly set off philosophy against the other disciplines. For Kant, *The Conflict of the Faculties* (1992) consisted of philosophy on one side and all other disciplines on the other. The conflict arose out of the different roles that the disciplines were playing, a division of labour that had its basis in the epistemological status of the disciplines. The practical disciplines dealt with appearances and helped us to gain ascendancy in that world; philosophy dealt with the reality behind appearances and enabled us to gain a pure understanding of the noumenal world.

Kant termed the practical disciplines 'higher'; he termed philosophy the lower faculty. 'Higher' has here to be understood as derivative: the practical faculties were higher in so far as they rested on philosophy as the lower faculty. The conceptual and the practical weight of the university rested on philosophy. This was a conflict of some stubbornness since it reflected a metaphysical view of the way things were and the separate roles of the different faculties within that world view. There was a kind of resolution precisely in that the faculties *together* reflected the ultimate structure of the world. Unity through disunity. On the Kantian conception, the university could hang on to its sense of itself as reflecting the universe: all knowledge reposed in this university. The real and the apparent: all were united.

Only disconnect

In the Kantian conception of the university, philosophy played the key role: through philosophy, the university could fulfil its mission of uncovering knowledge of the real as opposed to the apparent universe. But this was a view that would not and could not survive the test of time.

There was bound to be something suspicious about philosophers giving the primary role to philosophy: the university's conscience, if not its soul, was safe with the philosophers. Yes, the unity of the university was dissolving as faculties gained their separate identities. But, properly understood, unity could be preserved, even amid the developing conflict. The faculties just had to remember their distinct roles: each had its place. The only difficulty – if, indeed, it was a difficulty – was that it turned out that philosophy was more equal than the others. Accordingly, whatever other faculties a university might have, it had to possess a faculty of philosophy. Without it, a university could not claim to offer insight into the real constituents of the world; it could only play with its appearances.

But how could the philosophers be rumbled? For the story they offered was *their* story. This idea of the university was, in essence, a philosophical story. It could just be that the philosophers were not speaking only in their own interests. Perhaps the story of the university *was* philosophical. After all, the university could not be understood without giving some attention to knowledge. And it was the professional job of philosophy to give us some insight into the nature of knowledge. So perhaps the philosophers are in a special, and almost divine, state in relation to the university: their views on the nature of the university just might have merit after all.

But there remains something suspicious about the argument. The philosophers are positioned such as to offer us a particularly penetrating set of insights about the university *and*, by sheer chance, it turns out that philosophy takes the golden palm. No university is complete without philosophy because it is philosophy that alone has the prospect of gaining access to the world in itself; all the other disciplines deal simply with aspects of its appearance.

There are two problems here. Firstly, is it possible to offer a disinterested story of the university? If the philosophers cannot be trusted, who can? At least, the philosophers are the professionals when it comes to knowledge. They are epistemologists: they are supposed to know about knowing. But if their story is saturated with interests, to whom can we turn with confidence? Later, a different story was told: we heard from Leavis (1969) that English literature in the form of literary criticism was to hold centre stage in the reshaping of the modern university. But Leavis was a literary critic. Is it, then, in principle not possible to escape a particular set of interests in working out general accounts of the university?

Secondly, if general stories are to be mistrusted as being imbued with debatable interests, is the university not then doomed to a new conflict of the faculties? The modern university, now lacking any discernible centre or animating idea, becomes simply a collection of epistemic tribes (Becher, 1989), attempting to define the boundaries of their epistemological territories (even while reshaping them). This, surely, is a key feature of the modern university, that it is becoming a set of separate groupings jostling for space, for epistemic and professional security. The groupings overlap and interconnect, and are always on the move; there is no stability.

And so the university disconnects within itself. But disconnection does not entail excommunication. The disciplines will not seek to drive each other out. The powerful seek only to marginalize the weak. In this current conflict of the faculties, extinction is not necessary: marginality alone will bring silence.

There is no altruism; no sense of doing justice to the academic cause; and no fear of ensuing guilt. On the contrary, in an uncertain world, you never know where you might wish to make an alliance. The external world presents more opportunities than it presents threats; and so the universities develop by epistemic growth and through a reshaping of their epistemic forces. The humanities may feel, in episodic bursts, that there is a 'crisis in the humanities',[2] but they still retain their presence in the university. They even expand, relatively and absolutely. Their presence is required, however beleagured they may feel. Their voice may not be heard as it once was, but it is not silenced. The university would sooner add to its voices than expunge any of them.

The contemporary conflict of the faculties, therefore, is subtle, nuanced and *sotto voce*. It is not that everybody knows his or her place. Rather, there is an expanding universe of epistemological space. Space is provided for multiple identities as well as for fragile identities. In such an expanding space, new configurations are taking shape: new stars and galaxies emerge and older ones fade, temporarily at least. Whether we are seeing the formation of an alternative universe is a moot point: just as the astronomers talk of parallel universes, so it might be that a new kind of epistemological universe is emerging out of the old. There is no single story that can explain how and why the configurations are taking the shape they are. This is a haphazard universe.

Timeliness

The epistemic space of the university is a four-dimensional space. In looking at some clusters of fields of knowledge, we look into the past; in others, we look to the future. For Helga Nowotny (1996), the arrival of 'the extended present' is a symptom of postmodernity: as we live in the present, so we now cannot help but also attempt to anticipate the future. This feature, this sense of the present being in-time, was and is characteristic of modernity. The postmodern spin is that, under conditions of postmodernity, we attempt – crazily – to bring the future into the present. In doing so, of course, we only speed up the present, as it were; the future always awaits, ever more uncertain partly because of the quickening that we have brought about in attemping to get ahead of the future. But academic thought, in some of its strains at least, has long attempted to read the future. Ecology, astronomy, sociology and, more recently, design: they have a timeliness about them in a particular sense. They are embedded in-time: they read the past partly to understand the future. The present can never be captured. For disciplines such as these, the present is not a serious category of thought.

Today's map of academic life is not easily drawn. Criss-crossings and over-lappings there undoubtedly are, but so are there distances and repulsions. Some drawing together occurs but uneasily; elsewhere, fission occurs and new stars are formed.

In itself, all this movement with its inner tensions, with different orders of magnitude across the galaxies and their stars, would amount just to a condition of extreme complexity. Supercomplexity arises when the separate elements come to operate under their own rules and motivations, and so become disconnected from each other. And that is exactly the situation into which the post-modern university has drifted. There are – it would seem – no general rules that hold the university together; nor is there any single set of ideas that supplies any unifying ideology; and nor, as a final resort, is there any discipline that can seriously lay claim to holding some kind of signal position[3] and that, thereby, can act as a kind of epistemic supernova under whose light all others are drawn.

The post-modern university has become disconnected within itself. The conditions of supercomplexity without the university have inevitably found their way into the university. There are no binding allegiances, no common rules of the game, and no sets of ideas – educational or otherwise – which thread through all its knowledge fields. The very difficulty of basic terminology is testimony to the presence of supercomplexity: do we talk of disciplines, subjects, fields, domains or some other entity in order to capture the basic building blocks of academic life? The terminological difficulty arises not just because there is no agreement about the form and purpose of academic inquiry, significant as that lack of agreement is. It arises because we no longer possess any agreement as to what a university is for.

In short, the inner disconnection of the university is a sign that the university as such has succumbed – as it was bound to do – to supercomplexity. Admittedly, the post-modern conflict of the faculties is rarely overt. For the most part, the distance between the parties allows for uneasy cohabitation. Mutual incomprehension is the condition of this fragile peace.

Making it work

Supercomplexity arises when we are faced with conflicting frameworks with which to understand a situation. That is to say, we have on our hands not just different theories or ideas, for they can be offered within a single framework to comprehend the situation in question. Rather, we have on our hands two or even more ways of coming at the situation such that the different theories or sets of evidence can get no purchase on each other. The parties to the dispute talk past each other because they are seeing the world quite differently.[4] It is not even that they are speaking different languages, as it were, for languages can be translated: there are points of contact that allow a translation to be formed (and for translators to gain a living). Under conditions of supercomplexity, it is not at all clear that there is any point of contact between the disputants; there is no obvious form of mediation available.

This is the condition of the internal state of the post-modern university. That disputes do not continually break out between distant faculties is due to the fact that hostilities are seldom commenced. There is seldom any apparent need for them. Academics like the easy life. They have enough on their hands dealing with those in their own camp. The really serious disputes within academic life are among those working apparently within the same discipline. On examination, those disputes characteristically take one of two forms. Most usually, they are rival views on the fundamental theories or paradigms within the discipline. The biologists dispute the validity of the Darwinian story but they still recognize each other as biologists. Sometimes, however, a dispute harbours fundamental disagreement about the nature of the discipline itself. Under these conditions, the likelihood arises of fission, a splitting to form new epistemic units.

Epistemic fission takes essentially two forms. Firstly, it arises from the emergence of different views of the disciplinary framework within the academic community. Secondly, fission can take place as a result of the importation of ideas and sentiments from outside the academic world. It is here that the conditions of supercomplexity in the university reveal themselves most starkly.

In one sense, the 'outside' is drawn narrowly: it is the domain of work. Learning matters, we are told insistently, but it is learning in relation to the domain of work. Accordingly, lifelong learning is renamed 'lifetime learning', since worthwhile lifelong learning is not lifelong at all but is learning through one's working – and therefore, on this reckoning, productive – life.

But the domain of work can also be drawn widely. While taking its cue from the rising stars in the world of work (currently, the biotechnical and the information technology fields), the onus is placed on the university to define work. 'Work' is more verb than noun: inquiry, research, knowledge and study are worthwhile provided that they *work*. What is to count as work is left unspecified. Some crude performance indicators are called up to fill out the character of allowable work, such as the proportions of graduates passing into specific occupations in the labour market and the proportion of the gross national product spent on science and technology, but it is recognized that these are crude. More important is that the various disciplines should recognize themselves in a vocabulary of enterprise, skill, knowledge, vocational and the productive; within, as we put it earlier, the cluster of production (Chapter 4).

Many will say that there is nothing new here. The university is simply being reminded of its mediaeval calling, to ally knowing about the world with acting in the world. Indeed, in the non-specificity of 'work', all kinds of creative opportunity are being opened up to the university to demonstrate its worth. The productive can take many, if not an infinite variety of, forms. Productivity shows itself, to use another term, in some kind of pay-off. The pay-off need not be straightforwardly economic: it might be political or

social (political science, sociology and international relations all demonstrate their capacity to provide a pay-off by assisting in the resolution of
political and social 'problems', and even on an international scale). The
humanities and the arts self-consciously demonstrate their capacity for 'value-
added' by contributing to the cultural infrastructure of society. The point is
that the added value cannot be assumed: it has to be demonstrated and in
terms other than those drawn up solely inside the academy.

The apparent breadth and freedom to fill in what counts as work, productivity and value-added betrays, therefore, a further narrowness. What
count are effects in the world. The effects are not specifiable but there are
general expectations asking to be fulfilled. A significant term is that of skill.
Situations demand skills for their successful handling. One judgement to be
made of research and knowledge, accordingly, is whether they lend themselves to the formation of skills. Again, skills are not simple: on this reckoning, they are societal, organizational and personal.[5] But, for all their manifold
forms, they are coming to shape our evaluations of acts of knowing.

The fork of instrumentalism

Far from being a reincarnation of the traditional relationship between theory
and practice, this new order presents us with an inversion of that relationship. Previously, effective action drew its justification from being infused by
validated knowledge. The action was enlightened by knowledge; knowledge
put to work produced action. The action did not exist in advance of the
knowledge brought to bear in a situation. Now, the requisite and identified
skills specify in advance the knowledge and even the research that is necessary. This is a nonsense, but it is the situation in which we find ourselves. It
is a nonsense because this inversion simply and literally will not – in the
long run – work.

This is the fork of instrumentalism. On the one hand, it dares not allow
complete freedom to research and scholarship, not so much through a fear
of being subverted but through a sense of the valuelessness that will result.[6]
'Value-for-money' is the cry of this calling. In repudiating this freedom,
instrumentalism denies to itself ideas that it might find useful, even in its
own terms.

On the other hand, in attempting to specify in advance the knowledge
and research necessary for effective action, it limits the action to the known
boundaries. Instrumentalism not only limits research but also limits the
very action that it would promote. Correctly, this *Weltanschauung* rechristens
action with the term 'skill', for the reduction of open-ended and enlightened
action to predetermined skill within definite boundaries is the inevitable
result. That such a double closure could be on the cards at the time of global
uncertainty is bizarre, but it remains the case.

It may be said that both prongs of this fork are misdrawn. On the skills
side, for example, it may be said that narrowly focused skills are passé;

instead, what are now required are transferable skills, core skills, key skills or some otherwise named form of generic skills. On the side of research, knowledge and scholarship, it may be said that 'pure' inquiry is still valued and that, indeed, across the world the funds of the state are devoted to it. Neither work nor inquiry is being boxed in.

Both arguments fail, however, and they fail together. Even if widened to encompass 'transferable skills', we are still in the presence of a skills-oriented conception of work. And even though discrete pools of 'pure' inquiry might be tolerated, they are so in the hope if not the expectation that they may, in the long term, have something to contribute to the productivity of the commonweal. The reckoning is held in reserve but, sooner or later, it will come into play.

Philosophy, we can note, is a dying species within academia; but now, it is promoted in virtue of the general transferable skills that it supposedly develops. Its capacity for enhancing our understanding of ourselves and our world is not on the agenda, since the particular forms of enhancement in evidence here, from the perspective of utility, even offer – say it quietly – a negative value. It is not just that utility may be questioned but that its delivery may be held up through the process of questioning.

The work ethic, then, is a constituent of the conditions of supercomplexity facing the university. Disciplines will be more or less inclined to reshape themselves in the image of work (understood, to repeat, in the most general way). The degree of responsiveness varies across universities, depending on the extent to which they command resources independent of those of the state and of the world of work itself. Academics, too, are adept at giving the appearance of positioning themselves anew even though their self-conception remains unchanged. There is sometimes a difference between discipline-as-presented and discipline-as-practised. Academics, with their eye on personal and collective security, will happily present themselves as falling in with this work ethic, claiming that their discipline really does offer the general skills that are required; a happy coincidence, indeed.

If all disciplines were simply to succumb to this work ethic, we would not be witnessing an instance of supercomplexity. It is because the arrival of this work ethic is party to the expansion of the possibilities for self-understanding that supercomplexity is a legitimate term here. This work ethic presents new *and additional* forms of self-understanding to the university, to which the university has to respond. It is given no option but to address the new calling even while it attempts to hold to earlier forms of self-identity.

The new work ethic is both challenging and insistent, being backed by the forces of the state and by the world of work itself. Supercomplexity thus enters the university, but with an insistency that will not be evaded. Supercomplexity represents, as we have seen, the loss of any unifying large idea that would carry the university forward (except, perhaps, an idea that builds upon supercomplexity itself).

The welcome address uttered by the new vice-chancellor rings hollow, because it is hollow. It is devoid of content. At least, it might be thought, the university is free to determine its own 'mission', to 'position itself' as it wishes and to secure its own place in a diverse mass system of higher education. Supercomplexity surely leaves open an infinite number of readings and responses. But that would be a naïve reading of the situation. Some options are more insistent than others. The new work ethic, in reversing the relationship between work and knowledge, will not lightly let go. It is a calling that cannot be shirked.

Conversation – what conversation?

The Western university is based on conversation. No conversation, no university. It is as simple as that. The more tough-minded of the vice-chancellors, those who take seriously the appellation of 'Chief Executive' on their business card, would like to deny this point. For them, conversation is downtime. It is time without product. This is not, of course, to deny the desirability of certain kinds of academic utterances. Conferences that generate revenue and advance the university's position, the book launch, the inaugural lecture given with panache: these are permissible utterances. They are more than utterances: they are *events*.[7] Their product is the university itself. Conversation, on the other hand, is without point for it has no end: in a genuine conversation, each utterance may have its rejoinder in a further utterance. Real conversation is infinite in its internal character and, seen superficially from the outside, has no product.

But are the academics interested in conversation these days? Are they interested in engaging with others? Clearly, they are. Conversation remains central to the academic enterprise and not just conversation among the members of the inner group conducted in the pages of a small number of academic journals. A casual perusal of any internal newsletter or of the corridor noticeboard will show a plethora of open seminars and lectures, with and without external speakers. Indeed, the new technologies of email and the Internet have served to increase the number of communications. Despite the Chief Executives, conversation has not been quashed.

And yet . . . in the post-modern university, struggling with supercomplexity beyond and within itself, facing the demands of instrumental reason to balance the diminishing budget, conversation is bound to come under some pressure. Choices have to be made: do I write this paper, go to that seminar, or even attend the reception that the Vice-Chancellor has organized for those overseas visitors (and to which I have had an invitation)? Do I even make myself available to my students, doubled in number over the past few years? The space for conversation, accordingly, narrows. To the latest email, a one-word response, if indeed there is one at all, has to serve.

The possibility of conversation diminishes for yet other reasons. Under conditions of supercomplexity, the myriad of conversational communities will make their separate responses to the challenges facing them, as they perceive those challenges. Under such conditions, to the distinctive rules of communication and engagement characteristic of each sub-community is added a particular positioning, the formation of a discrete set of values, aspirations, regrets and even anxieties. The faculties diverge even more; they drift apart.

We may summarize matters by saying that large differentials in economic and cultural capital will deter conversation across the faculties. The poor know their place and the rich just don't notice them. But things are more complicated than that. The increasing gulf between the faculties is also political in character. The biochemist acting as an adviser to a multinational pharmaceutical company has more economic capital than the specialist in French history, but she also has more political capital. Her networks are likely to be more extensive and more linked with the powerful. She will know the senior officials in the relevant government departments as well as in the key cross-industry circles. Academic identity and satisfaction derive from such networks, but they are not simply intangibles. Networks, properly exploited, can call forth resources.

Conversation, then, under these circumstances, is likely to dwindle. The faculties have come to live profoundly different 'forms of life'. Not just their languages and rules of communication differ; their values differ, their holds on life differ and their worlds differ. Under conditions of super-complexity, such divergences are inevitable. The centre cannot hold for there is no centre. Natural selection will do its work. Academic life comes to take on such different forms that there will be and there can be no communication between them. Conversation does not die, but it retreats, to be contained in proliferating forms of local languages.

Is anyone there?

The university has already become a kind of virtual university. It is disappearing before our eyes. Its disciplines have different resources and different values with which to respond to the conditions of supercomplexity that face them. The separate universities, too, constitute an independent variable and each brings its own resources and values to bear in influencing the responses of the disciplines in its midst. In turn, the invisible college – the international community of scholars in a discipline – may or may not be a strong reference group for any university department. Increasingly, strong reference groups are to be found in industry, in the business world and within the professions.

The pragmatic responses of the various groupings within each university lead to quite different positionings in the world. Some, quite unselfconsciously, situate themselves in the world. They see themselves as solving the problems of the world. Others, largely without friends in the external world, hold fast to their scholarly values for that is all they have; and, in the process, they content themselves that they are the true holders of the academic faith. All kinds of intermediate positions are taken up by yet others.

This is not a university that falls apart in any straightforward sense. As we have seen, the conflict of the faculties in this post-modern age is remarkably restrained. The university simply dissolves. It has no unifying centre, no lingua franca and no unifying set of ideas. That universities are enjoined to set out their 'mission' and that so many of them fall in with this injunction is testimony to the fact that they have no obvious point or element that holds matters together. The existence of a mission statement is tantamount to an admission by the university that it is *missionless*: as a general idea, the university is without mission. This is inevitably the case as forms of inquiry come into being with quite different epistemological, social and political elements.

Sometimes, there may be epistemological collisions as different forms of inquiry bear in on the 'same' topic or issue. But, having quite different characters, for the most part they pull apart, going their own way. The study of texts, the identification of 'competent' performance, the determination of appropriate policies, the modelling of natural structures for technological deployment, the communicative reflection on action, the understanding of professional practice, the handling of complex problems in client-based situations, the framing of systems, the creation of technologies and the creation of human texts: all these and many more forms of inquiry and knowledge creation have their place in the university.

The university expands epistemologically; it is epistemologically generous. But its generosity betrays its emptiness: the process of admitting forms of inquiry into the university is without formal criteria. As an institution with rules of its own that governed what it is to know, the university is no more. There being no unifying sense as to what is to count as legitimate inquiry, new forms will increasingly appear and the gaps between them will accentuate over time.

Under these conditions, 'Is anyone there?' becomes a fair question. If the university, as a unified institution, is dissolving, its members have no common means of communication. Their values, their orientation to the world, and their sense as to their purposes, agendas and discourses: all are so diffuse that real communication becomes impossible. The university dissolves into its local constituencies. But, then, only they know each other who recognize each other. Short of becoming anthropologists of their own institution, its members can no longer know each other. Other than as shadows in the corridor, they cannot know who is there in any serious sense.

Someone is there, but who? How can we know them? If they do not share our values, our orientation to the world, our sense of the university (and they do not), what point of contact can there be between us? We may even attempt to communicate with each other in the dining room or in the committee room: the worst moment is that before the meeting starts when, in unstructured formless encounters, the parties attempt to gain a semblance of making contact. Deep down, it is understood by all parties that no such mutual understanding has been or could be reached. It is a silence of the deaf. The deafness is wilful, however: there is no real attempt to leap the chasm. It is seen as too wide. Incomprehension and, therefore, invisibility are the inevitable result.

Conclusion: conflict – what conflict?

Under conditions of supercomplexity, what it is to know the world is no longer given in any sense. In these circumstances, categories of academic, knowledge, disciplines and, of course, university itself become unstable. One uses such categories only with a certain shamefacedness. They have no uncontested unity on the one hand; on the other, they carry with them pretentious value-laden baggage – of enlightenment, truth, secure boundaries, and identities.

The university opens up to many kinds of inquiry. While it may not be true to say that anything goes, it is impossible *a priori* to identify any boundaries to the permissible forms of knowledge or rules that they should follow.[8] The professor of biotechnology looking to market, and even to patent, gene applications; the professor in management studies acting as a consultant to major corporations, advising on business strategy; and the mediaeval historian interpreting manuscripts: they live profoundly different lives because they inhabit different worlds.[9] There are no connections between them. New forms of knowledge handling connect neither with each other nor even with their predecessors.

Kant's notion of conflict is inapposite in this situation. Under conditions of supercomplexity, there are no common allegiances, but conflict does not break out. It does not need to do so. Under conditions of supercomplexity, there is room for all; well, virtually all. Also, conflict requires engagement. But, in the post-modern university, nothing remains that connects its parts or its inhabitants. All are nomadic, unsettled and confused. There is nothing to hold its inhabitants together. The university has dissolved. It requires no decentring from the postmodernists. It has decentred itself.

Unfortunately, the university has read only half the story of supercomplexity. If the university is to be adequate to the challenge, change and unceasing contestation in every dimension that is the world of supercomplexity, that uncertainty has to be mirrored in the university itself. But the decentred post-modern university, as we have seen, will do its best to avoid conflict, shun confrontation and sidestep unpredictability. Much as uncertainty presses upon it, the post-modern university would prefer to be a place of quiet and safety. These are tendencies that have to be combated.

Part 3

Reframing the University

8

Conditions of the University

Conditions of uncertainty

Two forms of uncertainty press upon the post-modern university: epistemological uncertainty and ontological uncertainty. The university has lost any sense of what it is to know as a universal activity and so it becomes a site of epistemological mayhem. Epistemologically, anything goes provided it can find backers. Within the same institution, if not on the same corridor, we find the cloner of sheep (if not of humans) and the producer of software programs *and* the interpreter of villagers in a rainforest. In this situation, categories of knowledge, truth and research lose their modern force. Even the idea of epistemology as a fundamental category of the university becomes problematic: it no longer offers any rules or conditions that knowing activities might have to fall in with. This is a situation of epistemological uncertainty.

But to this epistemological uncertainty is added an ontological uncertainty. The university no longer knows what it is to *be* a university. What are appropriate processes of decision-making? What are proper forms of inter-personal interactions on campus? How might we construe the pedagogical relationship where, for example, the students are not just adults but are very often older than the lecturers? We do not have answers to these questions. As a result, each university is developing its internal processes and forms of self-presentation in its own way. There is no common sense as to what it is to *be* a university.

We name a number of institutions 'University' but in their fundamental aspects – of knowing and being – it is doubtful that they have much in common. Instead, universities are sites of entrepreneurialism (Clark, 1998). What it is to know and to be in the late-modern university is a matter of the creative exploitation and imagining of opportunities: the only guideline is that the new initiatives should *work*. 'Quality' and 'excellence' are invoked as boundary conditions of the new initiatives but these are empty concepts, deriving their infilling from competing ideological agendas imported into the activities in question (Readings, 1996).

The university, then, is without foundations: it has no epistemological or ontological anchoring. It just makes things up – on both fronts – as it goes along. The working papers, the consultative documents and the statements of policy on higher education which flow from governments shrink, understandably, from tackling these issues, confining themselves to operational matters (of finance, structures and systems). The significant matters of what it is to be a university and what it is to know in a university are passed over largely in silence. The overt reason is that these are internal matters of the academic community; but, in reality, it is understood that these matters are now intractable. Better then to focus on matters that appear to yield a determinate *solution*. The idea of the modern university is left unaddressed. As a result, 'university' becomes simply a term. It is no longer a concept, standing for anything of substance.

Conditions of practice

In personal life, confidence is gained through the confirmation by others of the self that one is projecting; it is undermined when one's self-conception is denied by others. Similarly in institutional life. The self-understanding of a university is bolstered through confirmation by others; or, at least, by finding other 'universities' with which it can secure mutual recognition. 'Are you one of us?' is the tacit question underlying university life in a mass higher education system.

Assent to one's institutional self-image can be found in many quarters, both within and without the academic world. 'World' can be understood literally. Some institutions will so construe themselves as world players that they feel that they can neglect the views of others nearer at home: for them, their peers are a handful – perhaps just four or five – of other institutions around the world. Institutions exert their epistemological and economic pull (or not) within the worldwide academic market. Others will situate themselves closer to home and seek confirmation of their self-identity in the local community. For one, endorsement is sought from Harvard, Tokyo and Milan; for the other, endorsement is sought from the local councillors.

Endorsement can come in many forms. It may consist in being permitted to join a conversation: a university's likeness to other institutions is demonstrated in the networks to which the university is allowed access. (In the UK, a number of conversational circles have grown up among 'like' universities, the membership of which speaks of inclusion and exclusion.) It may be evident in the labour market, especially for lecturing staff: are they drawn largely from the region, or from the 'élite' universities, or even from across the world? And it may be evident in the business corporations that literally endorse a university, permitting their logos to be associated with those of the university. (At one time, the *lack* of such showy endorsement was a sign of one's élite status; now, the would-be élite universities compete for the endorsements of the greatest transnational corporations.)

Against this background, the practical conditions of what it is to be a university ease. You need have no angst that you are failing to consider what it is to know and to be within a university. You simply are what your friends and competitors allow you to be. That's it. If there are sufficient instances of confirmation of a university's self-image, it can 'be itself'. It becomes itself so far as it is allowed to do so by the powerful voices around it. In significant part, the university's internal processes and achievements will be the fall-out of this – now constructed from without – self-image. The university is constructed from without. Even its transactions behind closed doors – whether in the Vice-Chancellor's office, the teaching session or the committee room – can be read in this way: the general motivations, the institutional drive and values, and the tacit criteria for judgement (of activities and individuals) are all derived from the university's self-understanding as it is constructed by friends and foes around it.

Admittedly, this story can be overdrawn. Firstly, despite in many countries the state taking a closer interest in *its* universities, universities retain space of their own. It is in the state's interests to permit its universities space in which to contribute to the expansion of the society's intellectual capital. And, as testimony to the point, many states are now divesting themselves of detailed control of universities in favour of 'self-regulation' (Kells, 1992). Secondly, academics are adroit at representing themselves in the image of the other while retaining in essence their continuing values and practices: they are masters of the professional hoodwink. Thirdly, while there are tacit understandings within a mass higher education system as to the groups of universities that share likenesses, the boundaries of these families of institutions tend to be fuzzy. There is room for positioning, nationally and internationally. There is not all to play for but there is much to play for.

Yet, as we saw, the university is beset with its own epistemological and ontological uncertainties. It has to construct itself so as to yield positive effects amidst an unknown world: unknown externally and internally, and unknown epistemologically and ontologically. Even if the room for manoeuvre is limited, any university has to act and feel as if it were not. To think otherwise is the way to institutional atrophy.

Situational readings

Talk of institutional positioning, realization and construction implies the formation of strategies. But how, amid conditions of supercomplexity, are strategies to gain a purchase? If we cannot trust that tomorrow will be like today, strategies are liable to run into the sands. The dependence that some Western universities have come to place on the Pacific Rim as a student market has turned out to be misplaced as local stockmarkets have collapsed.

This is but a nice instance of the general point: under conditions of super-complexity, *all* dependencies – operational and conceptual – are suspect. What it is to know, what it is to be: all is fragile.

The second issue more particularly concerns universities as such: simply, what is it to *be* a university under conditions of supercomplexity? Are there any rules that the university should follow? Are there any principles that the university should attempt to maintain? Are there any processes of inter-personal engagement that are desirable, even under conditions of super-complexity? To invoke rules, principles and desirable processes may deny the 'university' just the freedom to manoeuvre that any institution requires for survival amid supercomplexity. But to surrender any sense of boundaries and conditions limiting what it is to be a university would result in robbing the notion of 'university' of any content.

It will be said that what it is to be a university in the late-modern world is necessarily fluid: institutions bearing the title 'university' have to be free to make their own movements, shaping their identity and their future as best as they can. In the process, the meaning of 'university' slips and slides. Universities are engaged in processes of tectonic plate movement, over-lapping each other, incessantly on the move and never quiet. Under these conditions, there can be no rules that govern what it is to be a university. Survival, accommodation, negotiation, achievement and performance: this has to be the vocabulary of the successful university.

Pragmatic accommodation: that could be said to be the watchword of the post-modern university. But the possibility exists that there is more to our understanding of the contemporary university than that. There are two kinds of argument that should exercise us.

The first is the *argument of coincidence*. The argument is that it just so happens that this very supercomplex world requires universities to hold on to – or indeed, in some instances, to acquire – the scaffolding of the idea of the Western university. Since, under conditions of supercomplexity, we cannot know or be with any security, the only organizational posture has to be one of critical dialogue and collective self-scrutiny. Recalling the univer-sity's dialogical heritage is no act of self-indulgence. On the contrary, if universities are to add positively to the intellectual and cultural capital of their host society, they have to maximize their critical, creative and dialogical capacities. The Western university can arise, phoenix-like, from its own ashes – and still retain the title of 'university' – because the university as a site of creative dialogue is now required by the very society that has been giving it a hard time of late and threatening its demise.

The second argument is the *argument of rationality*. It is radically opposed to the previous argument. It repudiates the idea that the late-modern world is calling for creative dialogism and, instead, declares that the university – precisely through its constituting, perhaps uniquely in late-modern society, a site of critical dialogue – can serve as a vital element in the maintenance and the furthering of the rational society. At the very moment when the discursive universe is closing, with the McDonaldization of the world (Ritzer,

1998), the university is now needed more than ever in order to maintain a site of discursive openness.

Could both arguments be valid? The first appears to be an argument of incorporation; the second an argument of resistance. Their mutual tension is itself an instance of supercomplexity: they are examples of the kinds of conflict to which the Western university is heir. But even so, the question remains: are the two arguments compatible or not?

Let us retrace our steps. We are examining three issues. The first issue is that of what, *in principle*, it is to be a university amid conditions of supercomplexity: under conditions of epistemological and ontological uncertainty, can we give any substance to the general character of 'the university'? The second issue is that of *in practice* being a university: how might a university construct itself amid supercomplexity? Thirdly, there is the issue of *purpose*: if realizing the university is to be more than pragmatic manoeuvring, a general justification is called for. *Prima facie*, the university as a site of dialogical reasoning seems a possible narrative, even amid supercomplexity. But there turn out to be competing justifications to this self-understanding and so the prospect of foundations disappears once again.

Against this background, talk of realizing the university has to seem to be, at best, muddled and, at worst, utopian. Either it is a matter of faulty logic or a matter of not living in the real world. But a third possibility exists. This is that realizing the university is difficult. The university may never be realized in any definite sense. The conceptual, practical and ideological challenges are real; they are not to be shrugged off. But why give up without a fight? Why abandon the project? That the university can never be realized in any determinate sense still leaves open to us the stance of *trying* to realize it. We might never pull it off; but we can tackle the task as if we might at least make progress. We can travel hopefully, even if we never finally arrive.

Conditions of the university

If the university cannot be realized in any determinate sense, its 'conditions' take on an elliptical character. The conditions that we might identify for the university as a project – in all its educational, societal and epistemological aspects – cannot be conditions that, even if instituted, will realize the university. No such conditions are available. At best, they are conditions that will give an institution a fair chance of approaching what it might be to be a university. There will always be a gap between the conditions of the university and their realization.

There is, therefore, a conditionality to the conditions. They are bound to fall short of their task. They *never could* bring about the university, fully and substantially. But there is also a conditionality to the conditions in that they have to become a set of metaconditions. If the university cannot be realized, if its conditions can only be expected to bring about the most efficacious positioning of the university amidst its epistemological and ontological uncertainties, its conditions must take account – as far as practicable – of those very uncertainties. Those uncertainties cannot be overcome; they exist, as we have seen, as the character of the university; as sets of epistemological and ontological conditions, indeed.[1]

Setting up pragmatic conditions of the university in an age of super-complexity cannot be a matter of first-order prescription. Rather, it is a matter of boxing cleverly and establishing the framework under which insti-tutions might bear the title 'university'. Activities, strategies and forms of engagement would then have to be worked out within those metaconditions. Amid supercomplexity, the conditions of the university have to be general and even abstract in nature. The modern vice-chancellor does not need to have his or her head in the clouds; but he or she does need – if the title of 'university' is to be honoured – to be able to form a vantage point above 'mission' and strategy so as to frame the conditions under which a 'university' might survive.

There are six conditions of realizing the university in an age of supercomplexity:

1. *Critical interdisciplinarity.* If the university is not merely to respond to uncertainty but is to engage with it and, thereby, to compound uncer-tainty, it has to be so constructed that such fresh perspectives are likely to be forthcoming.

   It may be said that, in this respect, the academics can be left to their own devices. The university is already a site of multiple discourses. Even so, a number of questions remain: is each university so structured as to engender the largest possible discursive creativity? Are the university's discourses, proliferating as they are, appropriate to an age of supercom-plexity? Is the discursive structure suitably nuanced to offering creative responses to the dominant discourses of society and, indeed, the global-ized economy? Are there opportunities for spontaneous and fruitful cross-linkages across the discourses represented by the university?

   Against the context of questions of this kind, the notion of 'critical interdisciplinarity' can only be a shorthand for the requisite form of discursive responsiveness and interplay.[2] It is an interplay that acknow-ledges that, in an age of supercomplexity, there are no disciplinary givens, that there are only – at most – forms of inquiry in which are inter-mingled many and varying forms of interest and purpose and that, therefore, one task of the university is to keep all forms of inquiry on their mettle. It is, accordingly, an 'interdisciplinarity' in that every spe-cies of inquiry may find itself interrogated by any other inquiry, if only cooperatively to put together a new research proposal. A discipline's space cannot be held pure to itself; it is subject to potential invasion from any quarter.

   But this interdisciplinarity is also 'critical' in that the increasing porousness of inquiry injects an extramural understanding of inquiry itself. A nervousness may develop in each form of inquiry; even a self-reflexivity may become apparent as it realizes that its discursive neighbours will not take it on trust. It has continually to be prepared to give an account of itself. If that willingness to be reflexive and to seek to offer a grounded account of the discipline's contribution emerges on its own account (and it is happening, especially in the humanities), that is all to the good;[3] where it does not (as in the natural sciences), the summons in favour of reflexivity will surely become more insistent. Claims to knowledge can no longer secure their own legitimacy. New domains open up, testing the old; practice is mixed with theory; and prescription is mixed with analysis. Implicitly, the new is critical of the old (too 'academic'); but, equally, the old is critical of the new (too 'practical').

The university can go with the flow; it can accept that the forms of inquiry to which it gives house room will inevitably rub up against each other. But, if it wishes to realize itself fully as a university, it will seek to find ways in which its discursive capital is capitalized fully and made to work for its living. No form of inquiry will be left to have an easy time, to find a secure redoubt for itself. Each will be brought into the open and made transparent. Debate, dialogue and communication will be actively fostered. Every form of inquiry will be valued, but the price of being valued will be transparency. Disciplinary collisions will not just be welcome; they will have to be deliberately brought about. Manufactured epistemological turmoil will be a sign of a university realizing itself.

In this way, through the resulting critical interdisciplinarity, the university can do new justice to the notion of the university as holding together the total universe of knowledge. The university becomes more than an aircraft carrier of multiple discourses; it becomes engaged in assisting novel juxtapositions of its discourses and, in the process, in creating new forms of knowing. In this university, there can be no hiding place.

2. *Collective self-scrutiny*. Supercomplexity calls forth reflexivity. When nothing is certain, fundamental concepts and frameworks are liable to come under scrutiny of some kind. The reflexive society is an inevitable outcome of supercomplexity.

However, amid supercomplexity, the university has a *responsibility* to make possible systematic self-scrutiny within itself. Such collective scrutiny should not be construed as a tactical move to head off 'the evaluative state'.[4] On the contrary, it is a necessary condition of the university creatively generating new perspectives for its activities.

The university likes to see itself in precisely this image: a self-critical academic community.[5] However, there are three shortcomings in this self-understanding. Firstly, it has for too long been more part of the rhetoric of the university's self-understanding than of its reality. Splintered by rival discourses and factions, the university, far from being a site of rational collective self-scrutiny, has long been a site of warring parties not exactly squaring up to each other but trying to avoid each other.

Secondly, with their professional identities framed within their local forms of inquiry, academics have come to exhibit a collective blindness about the university as such. This is hardly surprising: there is, after all, no collective *organic* language that the academics inhabit and through which they are members of the university itself. (The only collective language readily available to them is an imposed language of excellence (Readings, 1996), which offers no serious resources for collective self-scrutiny and is understandably eschewed in its being imposed.)

Lastly and most importantly, in an age of supercomplexity, collective self-scrutiny has continually to be reforged, reunderstood and recreated; and this, too, at three levels.

Firstly, that of membership: if the idea of a self-critical community is seriously to be instituted, its potential members can only become full members within an informed understanding of the kinds of complexity that make for the university's supercomplexity. There is, accordingly, an onus on today's university leader to impart that understanding. Secondly, that of critical scope: in addition to its being a site of cognitive knowledge, we have to understand the post-modern university as a site of action and identity. Accordingly, collective self-critique has to expand to embrace praxis and identity: it should take into account both the forms of engagement that characterize the university and the academic and student identities that it sponsors. Thirdly, that of the university as a transglobal organization: 'community' has to be understood not as given, in any sense, but as a set of challenges continually to be worked through and remade in every new encounter.

Collective self-scrutiny, then, is a condition of realizing the university. But, collective self-scrutiny has itself to be realized. Amid supercomplexity, it is a highly problematic notion; we can never assume that we understand its character. Collective self-scrutiny is not a natural condition of the academic community but then neither is 'community'. Community and collective self-scrutiny have to be made and remade, continuously.

3. *Purposive renewal.* It is tempting to say that – amid supercomplexity – the university has continually to replenish itself as a university. It does, but the point has traps for the unwary. If the university is now a problematic category, the institution cannot be reconstituted in any straightforward way. Renewal, replenishment and reconstitution: such terms, therefore, can be deployed only in a sense of their being in quotation marks. And yet, unless it wishes to become a shuttlecock buffeted by global capitalism, the university has to keep its purposes under review and continually to restate them.

Mission statements, accordingly, have to be reunderstood. They can be bland, offering no indication of distinctive purpose; they can be highly specific, and become checklists for ruling offside any development that might fall outside their scope; or they are felt to mark a debate that the university once held and, having been held, can be assumed to have put to rest all the major difficulties facing the university. But in an age of uncertainty, there can be no statement about the strategic purposes of a university that carries with it any durability. There can be no assurance about a university's 'core business'. Even that has to be continually revisited and reinterpreted.

Purposive renewal, therefore, has to be subtle in character. There can be no definitive staking out of purposes, of boundaries of activity, and even of aspiration. Instead, there *can* be a concerted dialogue over the positioning of the university amid its local, national and global competitors. There can be a conversation about the key challenges facing the university and a collective attempt to identify the new opportunities that may be opening. There can be a debate about the values that the university might be seen publicly to uphold and to identify the stances that might be taken up in the presentation of the university towards the relevant national and international agencies shaping higher education policy.

There can never be an end to conversations of this kind. This has to be a debate without end. Opportunities for debate have to be not only seized but also created; and that requires energy, effort and a style of institutional leadership that is seriously willing to engage with others.[6] Such engagement calls for unflagging energy that both takes account of others' viewpoints and attempts to move practices and perceptions forward, so that the University is better positioned amid supercomplexity.

4. *Moving borders.* In a university, in an age of supercomplexity, there can be no fixed borders. Borders, boundaries and demarcations: these necessary elements of institutional and social life have perpetually to be on the move in the post-modern university. They are and have been on the move anyway. Despite the accusatory jibes as to its inertia, the university has – for the most part – continually accommodated its organizational forms to the emerging challenges it has detected. The trick now is to bring that incessant movement into the lifestream of the university.

Academic life is brilliant at erecting enclosures and less adept at finding ways of dismantling them. Borders play an important part in securing identity of purpose, but the university has to find ways of making its borders transitory and of transcending those that are in place. University life has to become nomadic, where identities and purposes are lived out in border country.[7]

Borders are of two forms in the university, which is to say that there are two forms of structure at work.[8] Firstly, there is that of the map of inquiry represented by the university. At the personal level, the key question is: how do individual academics situate themselves in terms of inquiry? What is the field of inquiry, or indeed fields of inquiry, that commands their allegiance? It is these self-understandings that constitute and, in turn, are composed by the general map of inquiry.

Secondly, there is the bureaucratic structure of the university, with its departments, centres, units and even, perhaps, its modular degree schemes, and its semesters. Willingly or unwillingly, academics are having to find their place in this organizational structure and play their roles within it. Increasingly, the two structures are interdependent. Indeed, a feature of the university-as-organization is that the bureaucratic domain is invading the scholarly domain. Roles and responsibilities do not just conflate the two structures – as evidenced in the emergence of various kinds of curriculum and research managers – but are coming to give priority to managerial considerations.

Consequently, academic identities have to be formed across both epistemic and bureaucratic borders. But – and in both domains – identities are also formed vertically, within local units and at faculty, university and national levels. No level can claim privilege over the others.

The two kinds of map – epistemic and bureaucratic – are always changing, although unevenly. Within élite institutions, there remains considerable stability in both domains. Nevertheless, the maps are always having to be brought up to date. Even if the inhabitants are not restless and are not seeking change, the boundaries are not just changing but are giving way to different kinds of terrain.

In this situation, what marks out the supercomplex university is not continuous change – for that will happen anyway – but a readiness to comprehend and to address such instability. Borders cannot be settled; and passports cannot be issued, but only because there are no authorities to do the issuing. Instead, the boundaries have to be continually remade, with the inevitable resettlements and migrations. The post-modern academic is always in danger of becoming homeless, even if a temporary home has been found. The post-modern university is one that lives purposively with its uneasinesss.

Under conditions of supercomplexity, the borders have to be continually patrolled, not to keep them rigidly in place or to stop unauthorized émigrés but to keep under permanent review their appropriateness. Under conditions of postmodernity, the academics could be left to sort things out entirely by themselves. Nowadays, a role is extended to the university leader to assist in the continual redrawing of the 'map of knowledge' within the institution.[9] That vice-chancellors are taking up this challenge from a bureaucratic perspective is undeniable; what is less in evidence is a readiness to engage in reconstruction from a sense of the university's epistemological possibilities.

5. *Engagement.* In an age of supercomplexity, the university has to engage with multiple communities; and for two reasons. Firstly, there are many other producers or definers of knowledge in the wider society. The university, if it is to survive, will have to engage on that territory, with the newly emerging rules of knowledge production (Hague, 1991; Gibbons *et al.*, 1994). It will find itself forming alliances with industry, with professional bodies and with consultants in order to maintain its market share

of knowledge creation. In a world of supercomplexity, there can be no ivory towers.

The second reason in support of a policy of engagement is that, in the knowledge society, there are increasing numbers of clients for the services of the university. Indeed, the question arises as to whether a university needs students at all. Perhaps some 'universities' of the twenty-first century will offer their wares on the market and will decide that the teaching of students is insufficiently profitable – in several senses – to warrant its retention as a core activity.[10]

The recent report in the UK of the National Committee of Inquiry into Higher Education speaks approvingly of the universities as 'the conscience of society' (NCIHE, 1997: 79). A less value-laden way of making the point is that, in an age of supercomplexity, universities become sites of the production of multiple and *contending* perspectives. In the process, perspectives of the wider world are subject to counter perspectives produced within the university. But if the university expects to be heard in presenting those multiple stories to the world, it has to listen and to offer its stories partly in the language of the recipients in the wider society. In an age of supercomplexity, the university has to be prepared to listen as well as to speak.

6. *Communicative tolerance.* The university in an age of supercomplexity has to maximize opportunities for different voices to have a hearing. Communicative tolerance cannot be passive. It cannot just mean that I shall not prevent you from having a hearing. It is not just a matter of ensuring that no sanctions will fall unjustly on the maverick. Given the different levels of resources that different voices command, it is also a matter of different voices in the university being encouraged to express themselves.[11]

There may be a raised eyebrow at this suggestion: surely, academics need no encouragement to express themselves? But the university is saturated with organizational and epistemic power: many staff feel diffident about expressing themselves. Indeed, the 'modern' university regards silence as a sign both of high morale and that the university is operating 'efficiently'. The supercomplex university, on the other hand, will go out of its way to offer space to all to express themselves without feeling unduly vulnerable.

'Give us your ideas' has to be the underlying ethos in an age of supercomplexity. The large corporations in the private sector understand this nostrum. Such an ethos will make the university a noisier, a more unsettling, place to be in (Senge, 1990). But, in the university, quietness cannot be an indication of high morale.

Of course, the strategy carries risks. It will encourage the whistle-blowers.[12] But the university in an age of supercomplexity is necessarily living with risk. Whistle-blowers might not be popular; but they must be accepted as the price of maximizing views, ideas and fresh perspectives. And anyway, whistle blowers must take their chances: their views will be exposed to the critical gaze of even wider audiences.

Conclusion

If the university is to respond positively to an age of supercomplexity, if it is to be not just responsive to but to make its full creative contribution to the environment in which it finds itself, it has to fulfil certain conditions. They are necessary but not sufficient conditions. Their fulfilment cannot ensure that the university will remake itself effectively in the new world order. But they give it a chance of doing so. That is all we can reasonably expect.

Against these considerations, a threefold challenge for institutional leaders emerges. Firstly, there is the challenge of enabling staff to understand the manifold and conflicting nature of the challenges bearing in on them as academic actors; and to understand that the challenges will go on multiplying. There is no stable state and the instability will accelerate. Secondly, there is the challenge on institutional leaders to find ways of encouraging staff to go on addressing these challenges, to prosper amid the incessant turbulence of academic life (in both its material and its ideological aspects) and to develop the motivations to go on amid such unending challenge.

But thirdly, amid supercomplexity, institutional leaders have to find a form of institutional leadership that is neither managerial direction nor postmodern disengagement. It is a 'third way' of epistemological and onto-logical engagement, in which different intellectual groupings are brought together to understand each other and to engage with each other. Such engagement becomes a matter of identity reconstruction. The university has continually to remake itself; but it needs help. Amid the epistemological and ontological uncertainties of supercomplexity, a vice-chancellor intent on positioning the university to maximum effect has to become both a practising epistemologist and a practising ontologist. This is not a role for the faint-hearted.

9

A Suitable Ethos

Introduction

The managers shrink from the notion of ethos. Against them, it can hardly get a foot in the door. Its admission would present difficulties; it would cause them *to think*. Besides, what need has the managerial impulse of 'ethos'? For the managers, there are simply problems and challenges requiring decisions. If there is anything in the idea of supercomplexity, all that it requires in response is *super*management. If we are smart enough, we can manage our way out of trouble. Any residual difficulties are simply an indication that our management strategies have not been sufficiently clever or supple. Somewhere, given enough ingenuity, we can find a strategy to enable us to prosper. To any problem of the university, there is a managerial solution.

It will be clear that this attitude has to be rejected. Firstly, supercomplexity represents intractable problems to would-be managers: supercomplexity refuses to be managed. Of course, to admit as much is tantamount to an admission of defeat, from the managerialist outlook. In an age of supercomplexity, managerialism digs its own grave. But secondly, the managers cannot avoid *ethos*; managerialism produces an ethos in itself.

What, then, is to be the fundamental ethos of the university in an age of supercomplexity? What is to be the value structure of the post-modern university where nothing is certain and where it is faced with conflicting agendas?

The dispassionate umpire

One response is to assert, even with some vehemence, that the university should become a site of value freedom. Post-modern society is awash with multiple values, even multiple value systems. Indeed, the presence of overt value systems on campus can drive out the conditions for rational debate. 'Political correctness', for example, can lead to *The Imperilled Academy* (Dickman, 1993). Very well; let the university become a moral haven, an antiseptic for moral fever. Moral ardour has to be dampened if the university is to thrive. The ethos of the university, accordingly, should be that of the dispassionate umpire, not taking sides but ensuring that the conditions of open, balanced debate are upheld.

Under this conception of the ethos of the university, its watchwords might be thought to be neutrality and impartiality (Montefiore, 1975). This stance could turn into a kind of Pontius Pilate philosophy, a washing of the hands to the effect that it does not matter what is done or said, just so long as all have their dialogical chances. It is the discursive egalitarianism of the marketplace in which fortune will favour those with the most power or money. If that is not to be an unintended outcome, then the communicative rules that the academy upholds will have to be substantive as well as regulative; they will have to rule out certain forms of utterance. But which utterances are to be prohibited? Is a platform to be extended – or not – to certain religious or political groupings? Are the values of the greens and their concerns for ecology and the environment explicitly to be embraced (notwithstanding their sometimes violent tactics)? In either case, the answer is not transparently obvious: the principles of open debate could legitimately point in different ways.

In short, the concepts of neutrality and impartiality yield no straightforward strategies for campus conduct. It is unclear, therefore, however beguiling such concepts may seem, that they can offer the basis for establishing an ethos for the university.

This is inevitably the case amid supercomplexity. For, under conditions of supercomplexity, the very rules of debate are themselves in dispute and the very frameworks by which we understand ourselves and conduct ourselves are contested. That there is disagreement over whether certain groups and even certain views should be allowed a hearing is testimony to a lack of certainty over the rules of engagement on campus. Neutrality, in other words, is not positionless but positions itself, and in two senses. Firstly, and most obviously, it may open the door to voices – over ethnicity, religion, politics and gender – which some would debar from a hearing. Secondly, and more significantly, 'neutrality' positions itself as a claim on discourse, presuming that there is available a neutral space between contestants. Neutrality, therefore, both in its stance and in its discursive consequences, cannot help but be implicated in commitments.

There is no straightforwardly neutral space for the university to inhabit. However and wherever it positions itself, different readings of its positioning will be made. It will have allies and it will have others who are less supportive and who will be forming their own assessments of its positioning. An attempt to be even-handed as an institution may be read as favouring a certain viewpoint or stance, perhaps in relation to industry, to student welfare, to 'equal rights' or to the state itself. The refusal of the University of Oxford to grant an honorary doctorate to the then Prime Minister of the UK was an instance of the impossibility of securing a neutral space: however the University of Oxford acted on that occasion, its stance would have been seen as taking sides.

In a supercomplex world, the university's positioning is not fully of its own making. Others will be trying to determine the university's positioning. It is not so much that the university may have to take sides as that – to repeat – it may inevitably be seen *as* taking sides. Does the university conduct research on pesticides for agricultural use? To do so or not to do so may be judged to be taking a position.

It will be said that, in the teaching domain at least, things are more open. There, the lecturer can open different stances to the students and can invite them to explore the value positions in each stance. The students can even be encouraged to determine and to articulate their own value position on the matter (the use of pesticides in agriculture)[1] and still, it could be claimed, the university is protecting a value-neutral position. But this won't do: in this pedagogical situation, a number of value positions are being taken up in relation to the educational aims, the pedagogical relationship and the educational processes, quite apart from any outcome or value position at which the student will doubtless arrive.

The metaphor of the neutral umpire, then, may be beguiling but it should be treated warily. University life is not a game; it is a serious matter, saturated with value positions and value judgements in all its activities. Further, the rules of its various activities are themselves contested. Characteristically, the actors frame each other and are framed by external parties as favouring certain rules rather than others; and actions are bound to be value-impregnated, however much the actors may strive to be seen as impartial. In short, the metaphor of the neutral umpire runs us into trouble because there are multiple games and the games are taken seriously. They are imbued with intentions, aspirations, hopes and the making of self. Value neutrality, accordingly, is not available either to the university or to those who inhabit it.

Collegiality: hanging together?

Value positions, then, have to be taken up in two senses. Firstly, there is a first-person sense of values being taken up: individuals – whether managers, leaders, administrators, lecturers, researchers or students – are bound to take up value positions, whether they admit it or not; and whether they are aware of their value positions or not. Secondly, there is a third-person sense of values being taken up: individuals will be cast as holding value positions, whether they wish it or not; and whether they would recognize themselves in the value positions ascribed to them or not. Each and every such value position is contested at both levels; the active and the passive levels, as we might call them. Often, value conflict is directly experienced on campus;

however, even when things run smoothly, individuals still understand, deep down, that their value positions are contestable, even if they are not actually contested.

Even if the argument is accepted in principle, some will urge that it is mainly an academic argument. In practice, university life solidifies into communities with their own values. Amid mass higher education, and large-scale multifaculty universities, collegiality may have taken a knock. To talk unreservedly of the university as a community *tout court* is to strain credulity. But the notion of collegiality lingers still; it serves as a regulatory ideal and could be said to characterize engagements within the interstices of the university. Value conflict is apparent when the values of different communities within the university collide. But collegiality – and all that it implies for value consensus and stability – is a concept still with some mileage in it: it is a concept both explicitly called up in university life and one to which many would attach themselves.

But this is to throw too much weight on the concept of collegiality: it cannot straightforwardly offer a way through value conflict on campus. Collegiality is a larger term than community; it refers to a community that is characteristic of a college, at least in its ideal form. It implies, accordingly, an implicit allegiance to the college, or to the institution. It suggests that the institution is more than a series of transactions of an economic or technical kind and points us to a sense of a respect for the traditions of the institution, carried forward in exchanges that have a mutuality to them. Individuals are heard because they are members of the college: their membership confers the right to be heard as an equal. Individuals recognize each other as a member of a particular college.

There are, then, three strands to the concept of collegiality: mutuality, tradition and particularity. As such, it is hardly surprising that collegiality is in some difficulty since all three ideas are themselves in difficulty in the late modern university. Universities have become complex organizations, taking on elements of power and hierarchy, and so making mutuality problematic. They have also become sites of change, being required to live for and even in the future. Tradition is not entirely vanquished: it looks good in the university's prospectus and continues to have market value. But the future calls, even more loudly.

Lastly, it may seem that at least particularity has a place today; indeed, perhaps its time has come. After all, each university in an age of 'diversity' is encouraged to work out its particular 'mission'. But the particularity implied by collegiality had its place precisely within a context of tradition. In an age of uncertainty, each university will want to be as free as possible to determine its own positioning; it will want to maximize its market position. The new particularity is of the moment; it has no durability attached to it. The character, position and ethos of the institution will not be in ten years' time what it is today. Its particularity is always on the move.

'Collegiality', then, does not offer us a way through value conflict on campus. Hanging together, as opposed to hanging separately, is not an option. There is no durability or stability to be sought in that strategy. Supercomplexity on campus is not going to be addressed through collegiality.

Those who fall back on the idea of collegiality – and there are many who do – are not living in the real world. They are not even living in their own worlds, for their own (scholarly) worlds teach them of the difficulties of holding on to boundaries, identities and rules: all these are a matter of convention and are negotiable. The response may be that modern academic life allows precisely for boundaries, identities and rules perpetually to be remade: collegiality, in other words, can and has to be continually remade. New courses are formed and new research is undertaken, calling perhaps for new disciplinary and even multidisciplinary alliances: allegiances are made anew. The students form their own programmes by weaving their own paths through the modules on offer, paths that cut across disciplinary groupings. In the megauniversity (Muller, 1994) of today, there is no identity with the university as such; only attachment to temporary projects within it.

Permanent reconstruction: is this, then, a way of holding on to the idea of collegiality? Only at the price of emasculating the idea of collegiality itself. For that idea speaks to a durability, a continuity, that is no longer available. It speaks, too, to the capacity to recognize individuals as one of a kind. But, as academic groupings splinter and as they are infiltrated by external ideologies (of 'enterprise', of 'transferability'), so academic identity becomes problematic. Permanent reconstruction is the way of post-modern academic life but it can hardly be squared with the idea of collegiality.

The multiversity makes available multiple spaces, multiple identities and multiple communities. The inwardness of pre-modern academic life is now coming to an end. The market, the consumers, the state and the professional bodies: all press their claims. The ability to recognize individuals as of a certain kind is passing rapidly: individuals themselves present multiple identities. Boundaries, rules and community: all are fuzzy and on the move.

In this milieu, the urging for collegiality often turns into a plea to 'leave me alone to do my own thing'. It can represent a disavowal of larger or alternative claims on one's academic identity. The cry 'collegiality', accordingly, stands for a stable state – with secure identities – that is no longer available to the university; *and* it stands for an introversion that pretends that the university can remain an island, free of the claims of the wider world. It can offer us nothing of substance in identifying an ethos for the university in an age of supercomplexity.

Anything goes?

We have, then, to reject both 'the neutral umpire' and 'collegiality' as ways into characterizing the ethos of the university amid supercomplexity. Plural value systems, shifting allegiances and conflicting ideologies: all these constitute the moral context of the late-modern university. For those attracted to the more radical positions of postmodernism, this is all to be welcomed.

Strong postmodernism, after all, endorses difference and denies universal principles. The university, as a progenitor of postmodernism, can hardly remain immune from these sentiments. 'Anything goes' may appear to be a helpful description of the university itself.

In its efforts to enhance its income, indeed to generate new income streams, the university will reach out beyond its traditional positioning. Research and teaching no longer constitute the sole activities of the university. Its new student accommodation will be designed with its potential hotel functions in mind; patents and companies will be established to market its technologies; and its intellectual capital will be harnessed to offer consultancy services. Why – in a post-modern world – should there be any principles that inform such activities? The hope that there should be such principles hankers after a lost world of 'grand narratives', where activities and values could be informed by large, if not universal, stories. Now, the university can reach out in any direction it wishes, unprincipled but guiltless. Strong postmodernism endorses, so it seems, just such unprincipled positions.

But more value-sensitive postmodernisms are also on offer. There are those who argue, even within a postmodern outlook, for 'principled positions' (Squires, 1993). We are told, fairly enough, that:

> revelling in the loss of progress is a Western metropolitan privilege which depends on living in a state of grace, a condition where no one is starving you, no one torturing you, no one even denying you the price of a . . . tube fare to the conference on postmodernism.
>
> (Soper, 1993: 21)

In other words, postmodernism contains within it a degree of parasitism. It takes hold within a context of Western liberalism (a liberalism that has bequeathed institutions, such as the university, which sustain democracy and which have offered the discursive space for postmodernism and for postmodern*ists*). Postmodernism pretends to be outside values but is wholly dependent not just on values but on certain kinds of value. Further, the substance of postmodernism implies a belief *in favour of* liberalism. Postmodernism does not merely draw out difference, but endorses it. As Connor (1993) observes, 'opting for plurality is itself a commitment to plurality'.

'Anything goes', therefore, does not stand outside values but actually invokes values, and a particular set of values (of Western pluralism) at that.[2] For those of this persuasion, of this soft postmodernism, we are led to a new sense of community, albeit of a minimal kind. It is a community in which notions such as plurality, the expression of difference and the opportunity to be heard serve as values.

This may be fine, but the question is: does this set of considerations provide us substantively with a guide to action? As a means of identifying a value basis for the modern university, does it not leave everything pretty much as it is? It alerts us, perhaps, to the incoherence of the university holding to a self-belief in its offering an open forum for debate and adopting strategies or policies that are themselves points of closure. For example, 'competence' and even 'excellence' parade themselves as open for debate, but come contained within ideologies that are hardly up for debate; in turn, criteria and procedures are generated which demand compliance rather than critical examination.[3] Soft postmodernism would rule such moves offside.

The more benign forms of postmodernism can, therefore, accommodate an explicit value position. But it turns out to be a value position with little guidance for action and strategy in the university. It repudiates some obvious and extreme forms of closure; but even there, its impact is uncertain. Would the celebration of an ethos for difference permit or outlaw the use of the university to provide a platform for extreme views, whether political, religious or otherwise? Would the minimal rules of a community that fosters plurality allow for such views? It is unclear.

'Anything goes' is ultimately an incoherent position. That much we can gather from even the more moderate postmodernists. It is a position that depends on value commitments, and of a particular kind. 'Anything goes' does not allow anything to go. But we can get no further forward than that, however matters are dressed up. These softer postmodernists have looked into the nihilism that extreme postmodernism threatens and have shrunk from that spectre. In turn, they look for some bulwark that offers us (or, rather, themselves) protection, some value position that offers a little security. But not wanting to relinquish the insights – as they see it – that postmodernism has brought, they want it both ways: plurality *and* values. They know that, ultimately, these two allegiances run against each other. Either plurality contests values or values repudiate unbridled plurality. The two allegiances cannot be reconciled and still yield cash value.

In an age of supercomplexity, this outcome was inevitable. For this tension between the postmodern celebration of difference and a hankering after some secure value system is another example of supercomplexity. It is an instance of conflicting frameworks by which we orient ourselves to the world and to each other. There can be no resolution of this tension. It is, too, not a tension simply felt within individuals; it is a tension characteristic of contemporary Western culture and, therefore, of its primary institutions such as its universities. We know that 'anything goes' is an incoherent notion but we have no uncontested notion with which to replace it. The university, in an age of supercomplexity, seems still to be without a clear and legitimate ethos.

The self-critical community

A further idea is yet to hand as a touchstone for the university ethos. It is (to return to the second of our 'conditions of realizing the university' in Chapter 7) that of the university as 'a self-critical academic community'. This looks just right for a university in an age of supercomplexity. If nothing is certain, at least the university can be the guardian of uncertainty; indeed, of the virtues of maintaining uncertainty and even of helping us to live at peace with uncertainty. Here, surely, is *the* ethos for the contemporary university.

Under the banner of 'a self-critical academic community', a penumbra of related ideas are called into service. Firstly, the university can content itself that it is authoritative in the identification of critical standards. Secondly, it can persuade itself that it understands what it is to be a self-critical community and that it comprehends how it is that a community can be critical of itself. It knows how to recognize a self-critical community and it can be assured that it, itself, comes up to muster on the designated criteria. Thirdly, through being 'self-critical', the university – as 'an academic community' – can secure a unity and a particularity in and for itself. It may be subject to the slings and arrows that the wider world may throw at it; but, in being a self-critical community, the university can attain a degree of immunity. Lastly, there is in the idea of 'a self-critical academic community' a sense of: trust us to keep the faith. In trusting us, in providing us with the requisite academic freedom, we – the university – will deliver ultimate goods to the wider world.

Perhaps the university as a self-critical academic community can deliver on all these promises. It can determine critical standards with assurance; it can turn itself into a self-learning community; it can preserve an island of rational discourse, independent of the distorted communication of the wider world; and it can repay our trust in it, if we leave it alone. But it has to be a continuing 'perhaps'. Empirically and theoretically, all these hopes are problematic. Critical standards, by definition, remain open to criticism; the academic world – we noted earlier – has been long on the rhetoric of its being a 'self-critical community' but short in realizing the claim (only recently, under some external pressure, has it begun to develop its self-critical capacities in relation to its teaching function); its hopes of being an island of independent rationality have to be understood as more hope than reality; and the thought that trust can be invested in any unitary profession has to be suspect.

It should not surprise us that the notion of the university as 'a self-critical academic community' is problematic. Rather than being a description of the university or a clear set of regulatory standards, the idea has to be seen as a piece of rhetoric, as a means of advancing the interests of the academic class and developing its collective autonomy. Even to talk of the 'academic community' is to presume too much, to imply that the collectivity of academics can be understood as a community. The notion of its being additionally 'self-critical' is to import further question-begging assumptions. We are not helped forward in our search for a suitable ethos for the late-modern university.

There is a curiosity in the argument, as it may seem. Is it being suggested that the university cannot be counted on to constitute itself as a self-critical community? Precisely so. The argument could take either an empirical or a theoretical turn.

Empirically, we could point to the lack of reflexivity within the university as it has developed within modernity. So taken up with the pursuit of its own projects has it become, and so disparate have its internal sub-communities become, that the capacity to reflect critically and collectively on its activities and on its own character has dwindled. Part of the difficulty has lain in its loss of a lingua franca; only information technology, a shared subservience to the state bureaucracies and a common interest in income generation offer weak alternatives to Latin as a means by which each member can recognize another as a member of the same collectivity.

But even more significant are the theoretical considerations. The university's claim to be a self-critical academic community has to be suspect because the idea rests ultimately on there being critical standards of a durable kind. Once that notion is itself shot through, then it is no longer clear what being self-critical amounts to. By what criteria is the university to interrogate its own activities, values and aims? Are the criteria those of scholarship or of impact on the world? But even then, having fallen one way or the other, alternative sets of criteria lie before us, both among the researchers and among those keen on worldy impact. Correspondence *to* the external world and improvement *of* that world: these are contesting criteria but, equally importantly, they are both rhetorical and self-serving clarion calls.

We may be tempted to admit that the criteria are contestable but further to claim that the university will provide a sufficiently open forum by which alternative criteria can come forward and themselves be interrogated. But once we start on this path, there is no end to it. We open ourselves to an infinite regress of having continually to make possible the critical interrogation of the successive critical frameworks. There is no end to that process.

Again, this outcome is inevitable. In an age of supercomplexity, there can be no resting place with regard to critical standards. Here, too, we have a nice example of supercomplexity. The university may content itself that, as a self-critical academic community, it will keep under continuing scrutiny not only its aims and its activities but also the very criteria by which those aims and activities are interrogated. But, deep down, it knows that it will never get to the bottom of its own constitution. The university can never be the transparent critical community that it would have us believe. To a degree, it just has to get on with life, leaving its tacit assumptions, its ideologies and its value systems for later inspection, if at all.

When, therefore, we find ourselves in the presence of the cry that 'we are a self-critical academic community', we should not be taken in. We can retort 'but are you?', looking to empirical evidence that might back up the claim (and that is likely to be thin on the ground). But we can also ask 'to what degree?' However seriously the self-understanding is lived out, there will be limits to the degree of self-criticism. These are *a priori* limits, although not in the sense that they can be readily identified as fixed boundaries which cannot be transcended. On the contrary, wherever the reflexive critical inquiry has reached, there will always be further questions to be asked about this framework, and then that framework and so on. In an age of supercomplexity, there is no resting place with respect to critical standards. The consequence is that the university is always on epistemological thin ice. It can never fully substantiate what it claims and what it does. The self-critical academic community is a fine regulatory ideal but it should not be pressed too hard for the ice is liable to crack.

Collective self-irony

All the main claimants, then, to providing a basis for an ethos for the late-modern university are in difficulty. The neutral umpire, the celebration of difference and the self-critical academic community: none of these turns out to have much substance to it. Nor are they exhaustive of the possible claimants: there are at least two other current ideas, those of excellence and of authenticity. Both can quickly be set aside.

As one author has recently noticed, 'excellence' is a vapid concept (Readings, 1996). By itself, it says nothing. To declare, as many universities do in their 'mission statements', that they are in favour of excellence is to say nothing. Who could be in favour of its opposite, whatever that might be? More to the point, the declaration is empty unless we are told what the university has in mind by 'excellence'. But, having told us that, we are then inevitably into controversial territory. Much as quasi-state bodies in higher education might like to pretend otherwise, what counts as excellence in any setting, together with the criteria for its identification, will be controversial. That is to say, it is always open to legitimate argument. The idea of excellence can and should be put aside.

'Authenticity' could be seen as a response to the idea of excellence. If excellence can be suspected of being a carrier of a state-driven ideology (connected with numerical assessment, efficiency and output), authenticity can be understood as an attempt to wrest back some vestige of personal autonomy. But it, too, runs into difficulties. Authenticity gains purchase from there being a core or stable self to which individuals can be 'authentic'. It is a doctrine of 'to thine own self be true'. The trouble is that, despite recent philosophical attempts to shore up the concepts of self and of person, we can no longer proclaim with any conviction that there is a self to be true to. Authenticity may sound all to the good, and a university may – in its open discursive spaces – appear to be just the place in which to be authentic. Unfortunately, in this postmodern age, we have now to jettison the hope that there remains a stable self to which we might be authentic.[4]

It just may be that there are yet other contenders which we have not encountered and which could still provide an appropriate ethos for the contemporary university. But that we have been able to show the limitations of a number of potential claimants is in itself significant. The thought begins surely to form that there just might not be *any* secure ethos to the university in an age of supercomplexity. If supercomplexity is that cognitive and moral condition in which all our frameworks for understanding the world and each other are contestable, then the point must follow for a would-be ethos. It, too, would be contestable. And this, surely, is just what we see in the contemporary university: different views as to the proper character of the university's ethos.

Where, then, does that leave us? Are we to conclude that the university is without any unitary ethos and that one never could be forthcoming? To believe that is the case is to abandon the university to the many forces that would undermine any sense of community; and such a stance is both unduly pessimistic and premature.

For an ethos for our times, let us embrace positively if not warmly the dominant motifs of our analysis. If nothing is certain, if this is the dominant idea to which the university now has to orient itself, let that become the basis for the ethos of the university. If the university knows, because this is its modern calling, that all its utterances, all its moves, all its activities, all its goals, all its hopes, all its prizes, all its self-beliefs and all its values are challengeable, that there is no security to be had, then surely a collective ethos of self-irony must emerge (cf. Rorty, 1989).

The university might present itself as a source of authoritative insights and of secure frameworks, but it is understood that these are presentational. The reality is that all is insecure.

To repeat, the radical contestability of all that the university does is not something that happens to the university but is largely of the university's making. There would be, therefore, a certain coherence in the university taking seriously the logic of its own functioning. If all is uncertain, if claims and utterances can always be held up to new insights from contending frameworks, it follows that no move can be made with any security. Self-irony is surely a suitable collective quality in this setting.

But self-irony is appropriate not just through the lack of security that accompanies moves and their frameworks. It is also appropriate to the impurity that characterizes the university's activities. Much as the university might wish its activities to be guided solely by the demands of pure reason, it understands that other motives, from both within and without the academic world, are intertwined in all that it does. Instrumental reason and economic reason are combined with the professional self-interests of the academic sub-cultures. Nor is this simply a matter of a conflict between the university's managers and the academics for the academics are themselves being invited to become entrepreneurs, marketing their skills and knowledge. We can legitimately suspect every utterance within the university of being imbued with multiple value systems. There is no space left for pure motives in the university. In such a situation, the ethos of the university cannot be pure. The university knows, deep down, that its fundamental value structure is impure.

There is no way round this situation. It is the condition of the modern university. Our conscience survives only with our tongue in our cheek. Our values remind us of what we wish to be, of what we can sometimes achieve;

but we know that, often, we must fall short of our values. Collective self-irony is the nature of this ethos.

The main conflict in the modern university, accordingly, is not between instrumental and collegial reason, but between those who pretend to be certain and those who demonstrate their awareness of radical uncertainty. The faces around the Planning and Resources Committee might be serious but, deep down, the participants know that there is no absolute authority to be found for any of the positions taken up. They may seem certain, but their certainty is bluff. The seriousness of the one is actually a dismay at the seriousness of the other.

Taken on board as an ethos for the university, collective self-irony will be manifest in a number of ways. It will be evident in a generally relaxed environment since, if we can be certain of nothing at all, we shall be unable to commit ourselves absolutely to any move that we make. Amid self-irony, individuals cannot take themselves too seriously. Much as any act in academic life calls for commitment, still there will always be an existential gap in all that is conducted.

If we cannot be absolutely secure in anything that we say or do, we can be pretty relaxed about things. We can do things and say things and then see what happens. Light the blue touch paper and retire: this is a tempting stance. Self-irony can lead to a lack of any commitment. But this is to allow in mere pragmatism; it is to invite again an allegiance to 'anything goes' and that we have just repudiated. So collective self-irony has to have an edge to it. It calls for endeavours to work things out collectively and openly, but it will be understood that decisions are never final in the sense that they are never entirely grounded. Deadlines may fall; agreements may have to be signed; decisions may have to be made; and preparations for the quality assessors have to come to an end. But there will never be a process of reasoning by which such acts are fully legitimated. There is a radical provisionality in all that is said and done.

Conclusion

For the university in an age of supercomplexity, where no framework of valuing, acting and knowing can be relied upon with any security, a suitable ethos is not to be found by resorting to any idea that itself relies on some sense of security. Accordingly, ideas such as the neutral umpire, excellence, authenticity and a self-critical academic community all have to be rejected. Each in its own way looks to some point of durability or solidity, whether of rules, of criteria, of self or of communication. Since no point of durability or solidity is available amid supercomplexity, all these ideas as a basis for an ethos for the modern university have to be jettisoned. In turn, the post-modern response, whether in its stronger or its weaker variety, also fails. The stronger version – to let anything go – is incoherent; the weaker version

– to ask for minimal rules of engagement while celebrating difference – is even more incoherent.

The result is that, in constructing an ethos for the late-modern university, we have to accept matters as they are: we have to acknowledge that we are faced with multiple uncertainties and that nothing has any solid basis to it.[5] Let us continue to act together and to reason together; but do not pretend that, in the process, we have reached or will reach a position with any security or purity. Let us hold to our values, by all means. But let us not get carried away and attach any absolute quality to them. We all have to be self-ironists now.

Part 4

Realizing the University

10

Constructing the University

Learning or unlearning?

The idea of 'the learning organization' has become a potent idea (Senge, 1990). It embodies the belief that, in a changing world, if organizations are to maintain a ready responsiveness to their environment, they need continually to adapt. In other words, they need to learn, both from their mistakes and from their successes; they will, though, be aware that today's success can be tomorrow's failure. So the idea of learning, which originally worked at the level of individual change and development, comes to be taken up at the level of the organization.

Of course, the idea of a learning organization begs questions. In what sense can we talk of an organization learning beyond the adaptations of the individuals within the organization? Against what criteria can we speak of learning in this context, given that learning means to come up to some kind of standard? In what ways is organizational learning apparent? Intriguing as those questions may be, they are beside the point. The point is that the idea of the learning organization may seem to be potent in our present context, that of conceptualizing the university in an age of supercomplexity. If nothing is certain for the university, then it had better be prepared continually to reflect on itself and to go on learning so as to maintain effectiveness in its environment.

I do not disagree with this line of thinking as such. However, in itself – even allowing for our qualifications about the notion of the learning organization – the idea is inadequate; indeed, it is misleading. Even if the idea of the university as a learning organization has value, we need to couple to it the idea of *unlearning*: the university has to be an unlearning organization. Even if the notion of learning makes sense in relation to organizations, we can only construct universities that are adequate to an age of supercomplexity if we also embrace the notion of unlearning: the contemporary university has to develop the capacities to unlearn what it has already learnt.

Carrying the can

While there is a growing literature that refers to universities as organizations,[1] there is much less of a literature that remarks on this development as such. That is, there is little that is found to be strange nowadays in understanding the university as an organization. We might wonder as to how the university as an organization might be made more effective, be turned into 'a learning organization' or resolve the conflicting agendas that it exhibits. But that the university has become an organization does not appear to warrant much, if any, attention.

The emergence of the university as an organization is worthy of at least a little attention and not only because this development is both sudden and universal, and taken-for-granted. What is of interest, for our purposes, are not its empirical features, its causes, its timing and its precise character, with all the variations across different universities in a mass higher education system. Rather, what is of interest here are matters of principle: what are the general implications of the university becoming an organization for its characteristic functions of knowledge production and knowledge dissemination? Is a greater systematicity in universities a means of attempting to bring a measure of order into a largely chaotic situation? Is there a necessary tension between the university becoming an organization and the capacity of the university to reshape itself amidst a supercomplex environment? Ultimately, these are not empirical matters but are matters of principle and matters of values: we can make judgements about the effects of the university emerging as an organization when we are in possession of a more or less clear set of purposes that we feel a university should fulfil.

Historically, universities were associations or – as Halsey (1992) reminded us – guilds. They were freely associating collectivities of individuals who admitted one another to their ranks. Masters and students were divided only in their progress in the common goal of inquiry. After some several hundred years, to the scholarship of texts was added science; and, in turn, there developed research. Gradually, there came to be more systematicity to research, with teams, hoped-for outcomes and planning of research effort. But the university as such remained, until comparatively recently, largely devoid of large-scale organizational characteristics.

Now universities have become organizations, attempting to manage their resources, both budgetary and staffing. Roles are more precise, responsibilities are more explicit and relationships are clearer. Who does what, who carries the can and who can authorize expenditures are just some of the ingredients of the university becoming an organization. Accountability to the university is inserted as a call upon the staff's self-understanding. Despite assertions as to the university's 'flat' management styles, a hierarchy of decision-making appears. Indeed, the idea of management itself appears, with its tacit assumption that goals can be determined for the university as such. The organized university is a managed university.

What is striking, to repeat, is not that all this has happened in a relatively short space of time but that it gives rise to little comment as a phenomenon. A certain amount of muttering occurs as to the 'managerialism' in university life, but there is no serious protest. That it does not give rise to any great angst is testimony to two things. Firstly, there is a consensus even within universities that, in the contemporary age, they have to be managed and managed well. Staff do not want to be part of a poorly managed institution. This point is easily made, but it represents an extraordinary accommodation on the part of the academics to the realities of university life. Secondly, there is on the part of the large majority of academics a view that they are only too happy for others to be doing the managing. The protests as to the extent of the burden of administration come as much, if not more, from the vice-chancellors themselves (even if many are actually rather pleased not to feel that they have to continue to teach and to publish and so to subject themselves either to the challenge of the students – in their growing heterogeneity – or to the critical scrutiny of their peers in their research and scholarly communities).

Let the managers manage: everyone seems happy, then, with this state of affairs. The managers have fun in managing and the researchers and teachers are left to find what fun they can in their hard-pressed circumstances. This looks like a win-win situation: the university is managed and so is a match for the environment in which it finds itself; and the academics are let off the hook of having to worry about the university's strategic choices and their implementation.

Constructing the university, then, appears to require that a management capability be inserted, so that the university's resources are deployed to their maximum effect. In the more sophisticated of vice-chancellors' suites, there will be talk of everyone in the university having now to manage themselves, it being understood that the day-to-day activities of the university have to be managed by those immediately involved. The dominant view, however, will be that there are those who have a particular responsibility towards the corporate management; and that there needs to be a concentration of the management function.

The question is: to what degree does this make sense for the university in an age of supercomplexity? Are the notions of organization and management in principle helpful to a university in the modern age? The uncertain and unpredictable environment within which universities find themselves seems to call both for a greater level of organization and for a lesser level; it seems to point both to an enhanced management capacity and to a diminished one.

How, then, might the university be organized? How do we give direction where no direction can be determined? How do we make bold pronouncements about strategy and form decisions where no security is available? How do we manage professionals who – especially amid supercomplexity – should have their own autonomy and legitimate insight into their work? The managers are paid to manage, but by what authority? Every one of their utterances, decisions and actions has – especially in a university – to be subject to perpetual questioning. There can be no security in any of these aspects, particularly in a university where everything is contestable.

We need, then, new conceptions of what it is for the university to become an organization. A university – of all organizations – cannot maintain the fiction that any of its aspects are secure. Even the rules and requirements of the national and professional bodies to which the university is subject – brute facts of life as they may be – are themselves subject to change.

The issue before us is not an empirical matter; it is not a matter of finding out what works in practice. For that judgement is dependent on establishing what it is 'to work in practice' and assumes that such a notion of 'working' is itself appropriate. The issue before us is one of conceptual understanding: how can we make sense, at a conceptual level, of the relationships between the idea of supercomplexity (with its embedded ideas of challengeability, contestability, uncertainty and unpredictability) and the ideas of organization and management? The latter carry with them tacit assumptions of stability and reliability, at least at a meta-level; but supercomplexity denies stability and reliability in any sense. How, then, can we make sense of the university as an organization? Is the move that universities have made in this direction a false move: in the long run, in an age of supercomplexity, will the organized university find it hard to survive?

A state of pandemonium?

Is all to be pandemonium, then? If all that the university may do and aim for is challengeable, if any management style and structure that it adopts is contestable and if there can be no security about any form of engagement that the university enjoys with the wider world, perhaps there should be no principles guiding the university. Perhaps the very notion of constructing the university, with its tacit sense of there being some unity to the institution, should be jettisoned. Indeed, perhaps the concepts of management, organization and even leadership should be abandoned since, in an age of supercomplexity, the appropriate construction of the university is no construction at all. A university proper to a chaotic age is a university that is itself chaotic.[2]

This suggestion will seem unacceptable to most; it will be dismissed. The argument *should* be dismissed, not because it plays up the elements of pandemonium and chaos but because *it does not play them up enough*. If a university proper to a chaotic age is a university that is itself chaotic, then there still remains room, indeed a requirement, for management and leadership (although not for organization) because they have a role to play in bringing about conditions of chaos.[3] This new argument will seem bizarre to many. But it needs to be taken seriously.

The university is not merely faced with supercomplexity; it has helped to create it. Indeed, that has become its modern mission: to challenge our taken-for-granted frameworks and demonstrate that there is an infinite number of ways of understanding the world, our activities in it, and our sense of ourselves and our relationships with each other. But that reflection has impact on the construction of the university at three epistemological levels. Firstly, the university has a responsibility to maximize the frameworks with which it lives. Secondly, it should constitute itself as an environment that is likely to generate a flow of new frames of understanding. The university has to be an epistemologically rich environment; indeed, an environment overflowing with its own riches. Thirdly, those frames of understanding will themselves need to be exposed to critique. The university can hardly preach the virtues of critique if it does not offer an environment conducive to critical scrutiny of the frameworks that it is itself generating.

Such an epistemologically rich environment has two repercussions for the construction of the university. Firstly, if all the utterances of the university are to be challengeable, then – it would seem – communication has to be entirely open, devoid of constraint. This, in turn, puts challenges to any form of management that relies on any hierarchy. If communication has to be entirely open, then any injection of roles and relationships in which individuals stand in a hierarchical relationship to each other will be bound to produce a measure of distorted communication.[4] Epistemological creativity and unrestricted critical scrutiny call for an environment that encourages communication from whatever source, in whatever form. Communicative pandemonium is, therefore, positively to be encouraged.

The second repercussion of this 'epistemological pandemonium' thesis is upon the management of the university itself. The injection of a management component into the university was a necessary feature, we might say, of the university becoming a modern institution. It was a necessary concomitant of the university being transformed from a small-scale rural institution into a large-scale – indeed, a mega – enterprise at the centre of the economy and of city life. A strong management function was crucial to this making-public of the university, to its coming into the gaze of public view and being called upon to be a part of the modernization of the nation-state.

But now, as the global economy takes off and with the compression of time and space that it engenders, we have to abandon the organized university, just as it was getting going. The open communicative structure that the emerging 'epistemological pandemonium' calls for in turn means that the management function, if it is to be saved, has to be rethought.

There are two separate considerations. Firstly, if a university is to be a site of unconstrained ideas and associated actions, then its management function has to be curtailed. Rules, regulations and sanctions can have only a limited place in a university in an age of supercomplexity. Secondly, the construction of the university is not immune to the conditions of supercomplexity but is itself subject to those conditions. Any move, any decision, any positioning and any restructuring of the university: all are subject to interrogation from multiple frameworks. There is no escape from this: this is the world of the university, a world that the university itself has helped to bring about. The university cannot remain immune from the very world that it has, in part, brought about.

Constructing the university, then, is looking – at best – as a case of constructing a site of pandemonium. If the world is chaotic, anarchic and ruleless – and the university has helped to bring that world about – then the university had better explicitly adopt those conditions within itself. The management function, accordingly, is a matter of ushering in an environment that is epistemologically and communicatively open. Epistemological pandemonium calls for communicative openness. That in turn calls *not* for the demise of the management function but for a management function that makes itself invisible. It is a management that is intent on constructing epistemological pandemonium.

Sticking to the law

All kinds of holes will be alleged in this argument. Here are just two.

Firstly, the argument runs together a plea for openness and even rulelessness in the domain of knowing and understanding – which I have termed *epistemological pandemonium* – with openness and even rulelessness in relation to the management and organization of the university; that is, *operational pandemonium*. It may be said that epistemological pandemonium does not entail operational pandemonium. The point could be pursued in a practical manner. It could be urged that despite the turbulence in the external environment with which universities are faced, there are features, such as the presence of state agencies and professional and statutory bodies, which supply a certain durability and definiteness: they are a brute fact of institutional life imposing their iron-like requirements with which universities simply have to work. These bodies constitute givens which are even painful at times. So the idea of pandemonium, whatever its validity in the epistemological domain, cannot straightforwardly be transferred to the operational sphere.

A second objection to my 'pandemonium thesis' runs as follows. In a university setting, epistemological pandemonium is a contradiction in terms. Collectively, universities have become a social institution for the systematic production of knowledges. Knowledge production takes place in more or less systematic forms of inquiry. The different fields are institutionalized elaborate conversations, sustained through conferences, collective practices, journals, books, the Internet and other media. Such conversations rely on tacitly understood rules of communication. While the communicative rules differ, while the forms of the conversations move over time and while there will be mavericks who disobey the rules, still the conversations can only work – even in their rough and ready way – if there is a widespread acknowledgement of the rules of communication and validity within each field. Academics, to a large extent, have to be rule-followers.[5] Epistemological pandemonium is not and cannot be a runner.

It would seem, therefore, that talk of pandemonium can only be a rhetorical gambit: neither in its operational nor in its epistemological guise can it bear any weight. However, we should not cave in quite so easily.

It is true that both the managers *and* the disciplinary gatekeepers would often wish to bring about a measure of stability. It is also true that neither any organization (such as a university) nor a set of practices with collective rules of communication and validity tests can exhibit absolute anarchy. Lastly, national and professional bodies exert their own rules, including their timetables, on institutions. Operational and epistemological rules are conditions of getting by on a day-to-day basis. But all this amounts to is that the rules provide a measure of predictability, where otherwise unpredictability and uncertainty would let rip. None of the rules have the durability claimed for them.

In short, the retreat to rules – both epistemological and operational – is for the faint-hearted. The appeal to rules is a sign of modern-day Canutism, an attempt to hold back the tide of uncertainty. It tells us more about their protagonists than about the conditions that they describe.

This is not to deny that patterns are detectable in both the natural and the human worlds. Indeed, the two can hardly be separated: in our Darwinian age, we have to recognize that the hard-wiring in our brains, genetically laid down over generations, predisposes us to engage with the world around us through pattern recognition. Psychologically, we cannot escape the search for order in our self-understanding and in our interactions with the environment. The very idea of society contains the sense of regularities, of individuals taking account of each other, so sustaining predictable patterns of interaction. The presence of patterns in the features of the world or of rules inserted into the world is not, therefore, in question. What is in question is our orientation to such patterns of predictability and to their relationship with expanding pools of uncertainty.

How, then, do we face up to continual uncertainty, unpredictability, challengeability and contestability? How do we construct our universities, in that milieu? It is, we can recall, a milieu of uncertainty that does not just come at the university but is itself partly created by the university. The subject review may be in the diary for next year; that is a matter of certainty. But the actual criteria in use on the day, the ways that professional staff might be brought onside in the preparations and the panel's construal of what it sees: all these are replete with uncertainty.

Universities are famous for their regulations. Historically, the senior administrators came to be the guardians of the regulations. They serviced the committees which paid respect to the historical precedents enshrined in the regulations. But then something happened. The most senior administrators, as the permanent servants of the university, began to travel the world with an eye to new markets. They came to look forward rather than backwards. Their regulations suddenly became an encumbrance, being unable to cope with new practices, such as information technology-based courses, courses run overseas, and intakes of students not possessing 'normal qualifications'. Past understandings were now felt to be inappropriate to the challenges and opportunities opening up to the university as it struggled to position itself amid global uncertainty. In short, when nothing is certain, sticking to the law cannot offer a means to prosperity.

A mosaic on the move

In understanding the challenge of constructing the late-modern university, it may be helpful to imagine the university as a mosaic. Constructing the university is *not* a matter of constructing the mosaic. The mosaic is the university in its given state, as a series of contiguous groups, departments or units. As such, the pieces that constitute the mosaic turn out to be both of different shapes and of different sizes. Some are much larger than many of the others; the different shapes produce unevennesses in the contiguities; and there are even some gaps showing through. The mosaic also turns out, on inspection, to have an energy of itself. The pieces are iridescent, shimmering with changing colours of varying intensity.

If all this is going on, if the university in its given state has this internal energy and complexity, the idea of constructing the university is clearly problematic. It needs no construction, as it may seem. We might say, at most, that the establishment of a *new* university requires construction but, thereafter, it will acquire an internal dynamic of its own. No further construction is necessary.

Those of a postmodern turn of mind will urge the notion of deconstruction; those more in a managerialist mode might urge the notion of reconstruction. But, in an age of supercomplexity, the idea of construction should not be lightly abandoned. For what has to be constructed, it will be recalled, are the university's capacities to respond and to prosper amid radical uncertainty. Since we cannot anticipate the unknown, we cannot know the most effective configuration that the university should assume at any point in the future. The most effective configuration can be known neither in relation to the university's capacity to advance new frames of understanding nor in relation to its capacity to exploit those frames, whether in teaching or in some other activity (such as consultancy or technology transfer). But if the construction of the university has to take place – as it must – in a state of ignorance, its construction has precisely to give the university the best chance of playing its part in conditions of uncertainty. It cannot do so directly; it has, therefore, to do so indirectly.

Returning to our metaphor of the shimmering and moving mosaic: we cannot tell which pieces are likely to glow most brightly. The construction of the university takes on, accordingly, the task of putting all the pieces in such a state that they can respond and shine brightly should the opportunity arise. More than that, the construction of the university has so to arrange the pieces that appropriate new pieces might be created spontaneously.

Added energy and dynamism have to be created but such that the mosaic has the potential to respond in positive ways.

There are three conditions that have to be satisfied in constructing the university to meet this challenging agenda: they are conditions of knowledge, interaction and communication.

The knowledge condition

The more actors understand about their situation, the more they will be able to make judgements and take actions that are likely to anticipate emerging circumstances. Academics have long done this informally. Now, however, that tacit process has to become systematic. An age of supercomplexity demands that actors understand – so far as is practicable – the changing features of their environment, their changing constituencies and their manifold value systems. The academics will say that acquiring that kind of knowledge is the task of 'management'. But they cannot have it both ways; they cannot both plead their professional autonomy (and they are right to do that) and deny responsibility for acquiring the understanding that would enable them to maintain that autonomy.

Knowledge and comprehension have to start at home. In order for a university to maximize its possible engagement with the world, it has to have an informed understanding of itself, especially of its intellectual resources. Extraordinarily, universities, while claiming to be in the business of knowledge, know very little about themselves. It makes sense, therefore, for each university to conduct a detailed epistemological and professional audit of itself. It should mark out the territory that, collectively, the staff cover.

But collective self-understanding has to be actively promoted. The likely success of interventions by the university will be maximized where those conducting the interventions have some understanding of the situation in which the university finds itself. Since the university is the de-coupled organization *par excellence*, this means that all its staff have to go on extending their understanding of the conditions, the discourses and the emerging opportunities that constitute the context of the university.

All universities, in the UK, have staff development policies and programmes. But it is clear that staff development has fundamentally to be reconceived as a continuing programme of events and activities, the main purpose of which is to enable staff to go on expanding their understanding of the conditions of their university. Every member of the academic staff is implicated in this fundamentally educational programme, a programme intended to assist the construction of the opportunistic university. Such a construction calls for a continuing challenging and stretching of the horizon of the possible held by each member of staff. This, indeed, is a key task of management in a supercomplex university: to impart both an understanding of the multiplying challenges before the staff *and* a collective willingness to confront those never-ending challenges. It follows that institutional leaders have to be hands-on leaders.

The interaction condition

The pieces of the mosaic touch only a few of the other pieces. A challenge facing universities is to bring as many of the pieces in touch with each other as possible. Interaction within universities is characteristically limited in scope, both horizontally and vertically. Lecturers may feel uneasy about approaching the vice-chancellor, but they also feel diffident about approaching lecturers working in other domains. The basic units of academic life are not hermetically sealed, but they tend to function by themselves unless encouraged to engage more widely. While interaction remains limited, the university will be ill-equipped to address the conditions of supercomplexity that confront it. The more the basic units are interacting with each other, the more likelihood there is of the frames of understanding that supercomplexity requires themselves proliferating.

Moreover, if units interact that have a history of keeping themselves to themselves, and if interactions occur of a novel kind, it is more probable that novel frames of understanding will result from the university's activities. In universities, cross-disciplinary interaction is relatively weak and, under conditions of supercomplexity, needs to be encouraged.

Interaction can take place without the presence of comprehension. Academics can have their imagination inspired and can suddenly find themselves subject to a train of creative thought as a result of coming into contact with terms and ideas in another discipline which they do not fully understand; or, at least, not as their users understand them.

The counter-argument that ideas, however novel, will have to be understood to a degree in order to generate such creativity should be disregarded. The point here is about comprehension: no comprehension need take place for terms to have a resonance. Further, the meaning imparted in this way may be quite unconnected with the meaning that the terms have in their original context. Interaction may, therefore, be potent even though no comprehension has occurred.

The condition of communication

This might appear to resemble the previous condition on interaction but it picks up a different issue. Communication involves a mutuality of understanding. It would not make sense for B to say that A had communicated with her if her understanding of A's messsage overlapped in no way with that intended by A. As we have just seen, worthwhile interaction can occur without co-understanding among the parties involved.

A key issue, therefore, in constructing the university is the extent to which its members can communicate with each other (given these conditions of mutuality and co-understanding). In turn, a challenge that befalls the university is that of constructing channels of communication such that academics are likely to share to some degree in each other's understandings. Communication can take place at both the operational levels of the conduct of the university and the epistemological levels of the fields of inquiry. Both forms of communication are necessary. The pieces of the mosaic have not merely to spark off each other but – to stretch the metaphor to breaking point – also to do so in illuminating ways.

Energizing a community

This point about communication may seem straightforward but it is controversial for the general thesis I am proposing. Even if the knowledge condition and the interaction condition are both granted, why should it be the case that greater mutuality of understanding should assist the university amid supercomplexity? Why should it matter that the members of the university should understand each other to any significant degree? Is there more here than an outworn hankering after an 'academic community' which has passed into desuetude?

The answer is suggested by the conditions of supercomplexity. The more that there is not just interaction but also communication, the greater will be the intellectual energy and synergy that the university can present in the world. The university does not know the world that it will be in tomorrow (partly because of the multiplication of frames of understanding to which the university itself is party). Consequently, the more that its members can communicate with each other, the closer it will come to maximizing its intellectual capital and so generating the maximum opportunities for collective responsiveness. The argument works both on the epistemological and on the operational levels; that is, in terms of both the potential for teaching and research projects and the possibilities for reordering the university's resources for maximum efficiency.

This is not a plea for a consensus over the intellectual projects of the university or over its ideological positioning or its organizational codes. On the contrary, it is to suggest that – through taking communication seriously – multiple perspectives are more readily made available as resources for collective responses by the university.[6]

The boundaries that mark out the inner life of the university have to be eroded. The natural inwardness of academics has to be addressed. This will not be easy. The forging not just of multidisciplinarity but also of interdisciplinarity,[7] of learning communities and of a culture of collective self-scrutiny has to be worked at continually. Accordingly, university leaders, understanding the challenges of supercomplexity, will inject ever more effort not just in engaging with staff but also in enabling, exhorting and even requiring them to engage with each other.

Different ways will be found, embracing workshops, collective newsletters and the Internet, to encourage the staff of a university to learn and work together so as to transcend the boundaries of academic life and academic identities. 'Do we all know each other's names?' This question is often posed at the start of any meeting in a university, but now it becomes critical to the university's survival and prospering. Individuals have to be encouraged to communicate with each other, not only in the meeting but also outside it. Institutional leaders have to be involved, not just in making decisions or even in themselves communicating with their staff but also in fostering communication *across* their own institutions.

Indeed, as the university becomes an organization, necessarily subject to a managerial interest, the communicative dimensions of the university have to be taken *even more seriously*. Decisions have to be worked through with the staff of the university, so that they are understood; and, in that process, the so-called decisions will have to be modified. In turn, the staff have to be encouraged and given space to work large matters through in their own way. This all takes time and patience, but there is no other way. Without the mutual understanding that develops from communication, there will be no durability to the changes being sought. Vice-chancellors have to deliver, yes; but, amid supercomplexity, they have to deliver advances in process as well as outcomes.[8]

With the triple conditions of knowledge, interaction and communication being met, the pieces of the mosaic which constitute the university do not just spark off each other. Nor do they just do so with mutual understanding and comprehension. The pieces of the mosaic develop a collective energy denied to the sum of the individual pieces. In turn, the mosaic constantly reshapes itself, taking up new configurations, so contributing to and responding to the conditions of supercomplexity which it itself puts into play. It is a mosaic on the move.

Conclusion: leading uncertainty

Under conditions of supercomplexity, the university cannot be constructed directly. This simple but stark point has to be grasped. It does not mean that we can abandon the idea of academic management; still less, that of academic leadership.[9] What it does mean is that we need academic leaders who have a degree of hubris. They will understand that very little can be managed directly, but they can do much to sponsor a new self-understanding in an age of uncertainty: they can help all the members of the university to understand the conditions of uncertainty in which a university finds itself (to repeat, conditions that are partly of the university's own making); they can bring colleagues together from different departments to engage with each other over teaching and research projects but also over cross-university projects; and they can do much to inject a collective will to go on, even amid supercomplexity. They can help to promote a collaborative self-learning that transcends the natural boundaries in which the academics have their identities.

Academic leaders, in other words, can and should be proactive in promoting the capacity of the university to generate and to cope with supercomplexity. They should, therefore, have a close understanding of the activities within the university, and even of its potential activities. But they should also understand that the categories through which those activities are understood are all challengeable; and should work to promote that curious sense of the challengeability of one's own activities throughout the university. Their major task, therefore, is to help to promote that collective understanding of the uncertainties – epistemological and organizational – that characterizes the modern university. Generating a collective clarity about uncertainty, a preparedness among staff to go on addressing the conditions of academic life and a charitable attitude between academics across their different operating units: these are among the main challenges for today's academic leader.

11

Research in a Supercomplex World

In the public eye

The academics are paid to know things; they are trusted to conduct their inquiries with integrity; government task groups turn to them for their acumen; parliamentary committees summon them for their independent advice and learning; all kinds of clients give new livings to the academics in consulting them; column inches in newspapers are extended to them for their articles; and, for some, the television studio becomes more of a home than their own study. In the knowledge society, the academics are on to a good thing.

However, if the academics know one thing, it is that they do not know with any assuredness; they do not know with any certainty. Those who foot the bill for their services know this and so do those who listen to their utterances. It is 'known' that the experts disagree. The generous way of putting this is that academics as experts are accorded respect. Their views are heard without interruption, certainly; but, at the same time, their views are heard with discretion. The age in which academics were treated as sages is over. Now, they are asked to produce soundbites that, in turn, compete with those in the next thirty-second slot. The academics are heard more than ever but receive unquestioned endorsement less than ever.

In the public eye but not of the public: this is the fate of the researcher and the scholar under conditions of supercomplexity. Their knowledge products are wanted more than ever, not for consumption but for evaluation, adornment or legitimation. Those products are not accepted in themselves; their recipients do not claim them for their own but assess them, as they would the product information on an item in the supermarket. The academics have come into the public arena or, at least, are being drawn into it. But their offerings are subject to the critical gaze of a public that feels itself in command of itself. The public feels – and perhaps rightly – that its evaluations are as good as those of the academic's peers. It knows that the academic's peers will dissent; and so the public keeps its critical distance.

Under conditions of supercomplexity, the academics' offerings are subject to evaluations, from numerous quarters and through multiplying perspectives. The academics find that the peer evaluations that they have withstood in the academy are only the beginning of the matter. Now, in the open and public arena, evaluations come thick and fast from many directions. The academics' shields have hitherto barely protected them within the academy. The issue now is whether the academics can forge new shields so that they can engage with their new and increasingly sceptical audiences.

Anxiety among the researchers

For many researchers, this brave new world is too much. They desist from entering it, fearful that their knowledge products will be distorted or contaminated when taken up by others not in the academy. By definition, those others are not knowers. It is not that they are unknowers; rather, they are exploiters. Those different publics will appropriate the research to their own ends. The forty-minute interview turns into a twenty-second comment. The 'off the record' conversation is turned into a headline. A sentence from a press briefing is picked out for its own agenda by an interest group. An unrepresentative extract from a scholarly paper becomes the basis of an ideologically based article in the 'quality' newspapers.

Not surprisingly, the researchers (for the moment, I use the term to embrace 'scholars') turn back to the constituency that they can trust. There may be conflict in the academy and academic conflict is liable to be notoriously fierce, but the rules of that game are more or less agreed. There, the conflicts arise over different perspectives within a form of life. The conflicts are enjoyable: they add spice to life, a relatively stable life. Only very occasionally is the field turned upside down; Kuhnian revolutions are rare events. By and large, the disputes take place within tolerable boundaries. The warring parties can live together; indeed, they take in each other's washing. They gain their identity through their differences with the other camps. There are hardly any losers here: there is space for all. *Vive la différence.*

This inwardness has to be seen for what it is, a flight from instability. Admittedly, it is a matter of degree. Instability is a necessary part of the academic life. Academic conversations positively encourage – in their better moments, at least – the adventurous. The cut and thrust, however, takes place within permissible moves. It is, for the most part, a ritualized dance. The moves are more or less predictable; their novelty lies within an accepted range of tolerance. The boat might rock a little but there is no risk of it sinking.

The academics who shrink from exposing their epistemological wares to public gaze are fearful not so much, therefore, of novelty or of critical rejoinders. Rather, they are fearful of rejoinders or responses that speak of extramural agendas; agendas, that is to say, that are outwith the rules of their particular form of life. They are fearful of risk, even while they talk of 'the risk society'. They seek, therefore, to minimize risk, even though their particular form of life – in its self-understanding – encourages risk. This new riskiness that beckons, the riskiness of going public and of being public, presents a different order of risk. It is a risk seemingly without rules. It is the riskiness of supercomplexity.

Certainly, this diffidence is not a universal stance amongst academics. Many of them welcome the new opportunites for public exposure and self-projection that come their way. Some even act to maximize such opportunities. These more adventurous souls positively embrace supercomplexity; they revel in it. The ringing telephone is picked up willingly for it might herald an invitation to a television or radio studio, even though such opportunities will bring with them their own sources of uncertainty.

For our purposes, what is at issue here are matters neither of psychology, nor of the presentation of academe in the mass media, nor even of the empirical evidence as to the extent of attitudes in either direction. Rather, it is the more theoretical matter of understanding and placing such attitudes under conditions of supercomplexity. The anxiety felt by many may be understandable, but is it an appropriate response? It betokens a retreat to stability, but is stability available? Is this a heads-in-the-sands stance or is it an effective way of maintaining one's intellectual integrity and, thereby, the integrity of one's academic calling as such?

It should be clear that the retreat-to-the-academic-laager cannot offer a satisfactory response to the academic life under conditions of supercomplexity. Much as some would like to pretend otherwise, there is no security available. The academic life is now positioned in the wider world; and, here, world is meant literally. Operationally and discursively, the university is situated globally. It engages in global markets of students and courses, and its knowledge products are not only taken up critically in the wider world but also themselves saturated with extramural interests. The university can no longer even pretend to be able to seal itself from the world. The 'global age' imposes itself on the university as it imposes itself on institutions and practices generally in society.

Anxiety on the part of the academics as they feel the wider world bearing in on them is, then, understandable, but it isn't an adequate response. Amid supercomplexity, there is no hiding place. The threats that supercomplexity presents to the academic world have to be worked through and reinterpreted as challenges. To say this is not to suggest that academics generally have to be reconstructed as 'media dons'. It is rather to move to a higher level of analysis so that we examine the possibilities that are opening for the discursive repositioning of the university. In this way, anxiety might turn to a new sense of challenge and hope.

The uncertainty principle, again

At this point, the uncertainty principle re-emerges (see Chapter 5). Its main constituents will be recalled. The university is a site of organized inquiry for generating and for managing uncertainty. The task of generating uncertainty: that is the university's research function. The task of managing uncertainty, of enabling individuals to live with uncertainty: that is the university's teaching – or, rather, its educational – function.

This is a neat approximation of the uncertainty principle. But it is overneat: amid supercomplexity, each function strays into the other. Research has now to be understood as involving creating and managing uncertainty in the wider society. Teaching has also to be understood as creating and managing uncertainty in the minds of individuals: it becomes a form of inquiry at the pedagogical level. Here, I shall focus on research.

My argument, then, is that research has now to be understood as both the creation and the management of uncertainty in the public domain. Creating and managing uncertainty: these are not just two parallel sets of activity. Rather, there is a synergy between them: they draw strength from each other, they feed each other and they work together. Their sum is greater than their separate efforts.

To take the first of these sets of activity, namely the creation of uncertainty: in one sense, there is nothing new here. As it has grown in the university over the past one hundred years, research has become an institutionalized means of generating uncertainty in our frames of understanding.[1] That, however, is a generous reading of the matter. A more accurate reading is that research has tended to take the form of filling in details in our conceptual or empirical map of the world. Far from promoting uncertainty, research has willingly confined itself to shoring up the existing pillars of knowledge. Research has contented itself in being a force for stability, entrenching existing frames of understanding.

Research claims to be revolutionary but its daily practice is that of the reactionary, of reinforcing what we have learnt from earlier research. That it has this reinforcing character should hardly be surprising: the notion of 're-search' implies a going over of earlier searches. The reactionary elements are necessary to substantiate the revolutionary elements. It is the revolutionary elements that are the motor of knowledge growth through the new frames of understanding that they bring. The reactionary elements are parasitic upon the revolutionary. It is the revolutionary elements of research that impart its crucial reframing quality (Kuhn, 1970).[2]

There is an equivocation attached to that notion of 'crucial', an equivocation that is captured by the distinction between timelessness and timeliness. On the one hand, the term points to the way in which, ultimately, research gains its legitimacy by telling us something *new*. There is an accompanying expectation that the newness should also be significant. Individual projects may confirm or qualify what we already know and still be worthwhile. But the institution of research gains its point through its sponsorship of new frames of understanding that are likely to have some durability. Their very newness takes us forward in some way. Unless research is fulfilling this reframing criterion, it cannot be a serious contender for the title of 're-search'. Let us call this the *timelessness character* of 'reframing' research. It is a timelessness in that this research is intended to and, in part, does contribute to the ever-continuing accumulation of understanding of the world, whatever the discontinuities en route.

On the other hand, supercomplexity poses a more contemporaneous sense in which reframing research is crucial. That research should have reframing qualities is simply to say that academic research should recognize that reframing is part of the global age.[3] The global age spawns continuous reframing in culture, work and life more generally. It is this continuous reframing that produces supercomplexity in which all our frames of understanding are challengeable. In such circumstances, research is faced with two possibilities: it can seek to commentate on the changing and conflicting frames of understanding in the wider world, and it can also seek to proffer to the world its own new frames of understanding. (These are compatible roles.)

Both roles have their virtues and both are, to an extent, problematic. The first of these roles, the commentating role, can enable us to live at ease with the perplexity that results from the supercomplex age. It can open for us a way through the discursive maze, helping us to understand the positions of the different factions in contemporary disputes; it can help us to come to informed views on significant matters in our social and ecological environment; and it can enable us to live up to the challenges of global citizenship. However, it can end up by placing the researcher in the role of endorser. I use the term 'endorser' in a general way; for example, to include the comments of the professor of the economics of the motor-car industry on the activities of the motor-car industry itself.

The second of these roles, the reframing role, can all too easily turn into promoting a utopian ideology, cut adrift from political realities. But this second role – amid conditions of supercomplexity – is the more significant role. Left to itself, the commentating role could leave us prey to the dominant ideologies (made dominant by the power of the media, money or force). The commentating role can easily act as cement for the distorted communication present in the world. It will claim that it is not in hock to any influence, that it is unbiased. But the way to demonstrate that fully is not to be content with a commentating role but to develop an independent voice. And, for that, a distinct position is called for, a position that offers a new and distinctive reframing to the world.

This is not to abandon the commentating role but it is to go beyond it. Through understanding the academic role in this way, new resources of hope can be extended to the world (Williams, 1989). We are not just trapped in the presenting stories which are themselves bearers of ideologies through distorting media. The development of research as reframing, therefore, is crucial to the repositioning of research under conditions of supercomplexity. Let us call this the *timely character* of 'reframing' research.

We emerge, then, with the following classification of research in the supercomplex age.

	Projection within academe	Projection beyond academe
Endorsing	(i) Paradigm-endorsing	(ii) Commentating
Creative	(iii) Revolutionary	(iv) Reframing

For the most part, academics content themselves with role (i), projecting themselves and, implicitly, their disciplines within academe and, thereby, remaining as endorsers of the dominant conceptual apparatus. Where researchers and scholars venture beyond that role, perhaps increasingly they turn to (ii), the commentating role in the world rather than attempting to take on (iii), becoming revolutionaries within the fold. Largely left untackled is role (iv), that of assisting in the reframing of forms of understanding in the public consciousness. Space has recently opened for the scientists to claim this role, projecting their thinking as to the building blocks of man, matter and the universe. It is a space into which, apparently, the humanists and the social scientists are more cautious of entering.[4] Unless, however, researchers and scholars come to understand this role as a responsibility, research and scholarship will be overtaken and displaced by other producers of more popular ideas and frameworks.

A triple imperative

We can return to the uncertainty principle. Amid supercomplexity, the university is faced with radical contestability in all that it does. Its knowledge products are in the public domain and are taken up by different interest groups, put to conflicting ends and given contrasting 'spins'. It is an uncertain world to which the university has contributed through its own knowledge products of an extraordinarily rich diversity. The university is now called into this world, to contribute to this world as it makes its way amid radical uncertainty.

Faced with this uncertain world – despite it being a world partly of the university's making – different positions open, as we have just seen, for the reconstruction of research. Many researchers attempt to remain in the academic laager, the majority working to conserve and strengthen the dominant paradigms. Only a few embrace uncertainty and attempt to offer a significant reframing of their fields of inquiry. Others eye up the external world and accept the role of commentator on it, attempting to forge a hybrid role (in and out of the world). Yet others eagerly identify opportunities for whole-hearted engagement in the world, through setting up companies for technnology transfer or in patenting their knowledge 'products'.

In this world, research products – data, theories and ideas – are produced in the world and are of the world. The position of other-worldly research, maintaining barriers between academe and the wider world, rests on an inadequate reading of the contemporary situation. The search for security – and, indeed, for purity – is understandable but misguided. More than that, it reduces the potential scope and value of research amid supercomplexity. The commentators can be helpful in promoting civic understanding, but are liable to surrender the public understanding to the dominant forces governing the circulation of ideas. The activists – at least – wear their ideologies on their sleeves and take the newly minted shilling wheresoever it is to be found.

Against this background, the uncertainty principle develops a normative aspect. It describes how things are: as a matter of fact, the university is one of the prime institutions for developing and for transmitting uncertainty. But in the supercomplex age, a new responsibility develops. It is that of enabling the wider world to live at ease with uncertainty. It can do this in part by adopting a commentating role but, ultimately, as we have seen, that role is problematic. Accordingly, the university can better assist the wider world in living at ease with supercomplexity by itself becoming an institution for the creation of new frames of understanding. It faces uncertainty best by deliberately contributing to uncertainty. There is no way out; anything else surrenders the university to dominant forces that have interests other than public enlightenment.

The uncertainty principle yields, therefore, a triple imperative on the university: to increase the proportion of 'revolutionary' research as against norm-endorsing research; to refine its commentating role so that it possesses, as one of its goals, increased public understanding for global citizenship; and to develop its reframing role, so that it seeks to offer new frameworks for understanding and for acting in the world. In the supercomplex world, research has to be a site for the production and management of uncertainty in the public, that is, the supercomplex, realm.

For research to be so understood, the national research assessment exercises to which researchers are subject will themselves have to embrace wider criteria of research. Impact, yes, but it will have to include the growth of public understanding. What is now marginal has to become central in the framing of research if research is to advance its role of public enlightenment.

Scholarly footnotes

Scholarship is the research of scholars; of the schoolmen. The term has its origins in the scholasticism of the clerks of the Middle Ages, who aligned themselves to one or other of the schools of philosophy of the times. Their task – in a pre-printing age – was to understand thoroughly the texts in question so as to be able to spread the messages contained therein. Their scholarship was creative; it was interpretive. Although the Mediaeval Schoolmen engaged in fierce disputes with each other, their activities were embedded in an oral tradition of a wider engagement, of attempting to reach out to disseminate the fruits of their intellectual labours so as to enlighten those without access to such education.

Modern scholarship has turned all this on its head. Whereas the Mediaeval Schoolmen attempted to reach out to wider communities, modern scholarship speaks only to itself, in inwardly academic conversations so arcane as to surpass the Mediaevals for all their debates over nominalism and substance. Whereas the Mediaevals anchored their efforts in an oral tradition, the modern scholars confine themselves to the production of their own texts. Whereas the Mediaevals saw themselves as having a wider role of public enlightenment, the moderns are happy just to speak to each other.

The deformation of scholarship is the result of the institutionalization of scholarship within the universities. This scholarship is the research of the humanities. This is why academics in the humanities take unkindly to the current debate – in the UK and elsewhere – about the relationship of scholarship to teaching and to research. For them, the idea that scholarship can be distinguished from research is incomprehensible and is simply an indication of a debate being driven by the dominant interests of the empirical sciences, where such a distinction is at least tenable. For academics in the humanities, their scholarship is their research. Their raw materials are the existing texts in their intellectual fields, whether of a historical or a contemporary character.

To repeat, what we have here is the institutionalization of scholarship, a process that is *pari passu* with the formation over the last one hundred years of the higher education system. In a situation where livings came to be dependent on the state and where the empirical sciences demonstrated their apparent worth in tangible outcomes, the humanities were obliged to develop symbols of their worth and substance. The bibliography is the most obvious of these, in which academics are able to demonstrate the intellectual company they keep. However, it is the footnote that is the arch-symbol of the institutionalization of scholarship. In the footnote, scholar speaks unto scholar. It is a conversation of the cognoscenti, of those in the know, of those who recognize each other as members of the same community. The footnote is the socially legitimate aside behind the hand at the academic dinner party.

The footnote is not just a sign of a conversation internal to the academic community; not just a sign that the academics believe that they can circumscribe their world and place symbols to mark out its borders. It is a sign of a search for stability and for intellectual security on the part of the academics. The practice of supplying footnotes, in other words, is *not* a game that academics play to mark out their territories. It appears to be frivolous but it is deadly serious. It is a means of projecting to the world that something of substance is going on; it is a means of developing academic identities; and it is a means of defending the borders of one's epistemic community.

We may not yet be seeing the passing of the footnote in the humanities. We are, though, seeing the end of its ubiquity and a lessening of its pervasiveness. Mainstream publishers and journals, while not outlawing them as such, discourage their use. This development says much for our particular purposes. Just as the footnote is the arch-symbol of the institutionalization of scholarship, and reflects a time when the academics held the greater control over their own means of production, the diminution of the footnote is symptomatic of the unstoppable slide of the university into the supercomplex age.

Its diminution reflects a number of things. Firstly, it reflects the dissolution of the boundaries between academe and the wider world. The knowledge products of the majority of academics are now in the wider world, promoted by publishers that are increasingly part of large international conglomerates (Agger, 1990). Secondly, it reflects the arrival of the discursive global age. Academics have to make themselves and realize their identities in the wider world, their knowledge products being simply part of the discourses of the global age.[5] Thirdly, it reflects the arrival of supercomplexity, in which all discourses have to take their chances and be interrogated potentially by all others. The footnote betokens an age of borders, known epistemic communities and secure identities. All have gone; and with their passing, in turn, the footnote loses its point. And so – notwithstanding the rearguard actions of those who crave stability even as they preach the language of postmodernism – it passes away, the symbol of another age.

Reshaping research

The concept of research seems invariably to be elastic. Technology transfer, action research, consultancy, establishing patents, the solving of social and technological problems, and the creation of software: all these activities – and the list could be multiplied – remind us of the widening but increasingly uncertain scope of research in the modern world. The category of research is a contested concept, with groups in the professional and artistic domains struggling to bring their own knowledge products under the formal definitions held by the research councils and the funding councils. The definition of research is a political matter: its borders are policed, with sanctions falling on those whose knowledge products fall outside the formal definitions. What counts as research, accordingly, is elastic, contested *and* policed.

Effort might be made to locate criteria that could legitimize this ruling in and ruling out, which could salve the consciences of the dominant groups determining the rules. Peer review and being public are the two favoured criteria. But those in fine art departments producing their paintings, or those in professionally oriented departments engaged in action research on client behaviour, or those in health departments producing materials for use in health settings, or those in teacher education producing curriculum materials: these academics can point to both the public character of their products and that they have been subject to peer review. Often, too, those knowledge products will have been trialled and evaluated; or they will have gone through a process of continuous evolution leading, for example, to rigorous scrutiny in a public exhibition.

Such processes of lengthy gestation, of evaluation and of public test-ability put to shame precipitous announcements on cold fusion or on a new 'wonder' cancer drug in the so-called rigorous disciplines. The pres-sures to 'go public' are understandable in those fields subject to priority disputes, especially where very large sums of money are at stake. The point is not that this or that behaviour should be better policed and outlawed. Rather, it is, to repeat, that the category of research is no longer secure. There are no criteria that will rule in one group of activities and exclude others. The marginalized turn out often to be closer adherents to the favoured criteria than those supposedly dominant within the 'research' community.

All this is inevitable in an age, as we might term it, of institutional migra-tion. In the post-modern age, the borders between social institutions become porous. Different institutions take in each other's agendas. For example, policing, social work, health service, education, transport and town plan-ning: all these shade into each other. More locally to our present discussion, universities, industry, the professions, research institutes, military establish-ments, think tanks and management consultants: all are involved in research or quasi-research activities. Accordingly, the research community is no longer confined to academe; on the contrary, the universities constitute just a part – even if a significant part – of the research community.

What is at issue here is, as just hinted, a global migration of knowledge production. Accompanying that migration, in which knowledge production is distributed widely across institutions and interest blocks, there are no boundaries to research and no definite forms that it might take.[6] In the global age, epistemologies are not just social but are also themselves global in character, always on the move and always being reshaped. Research, accordingly, has no fixed abode. It is a label affixed to socially desirable epistemic activities.

It follows that, in the late-modern age, research is a category devoid of meaning in itself. 'Research' evaporates. All that is left are inquisitive inquiries searching for an audience or a patron or both. The research life offers no security in any sense. It is a life of radical uncertainty. In the late-modern university, research approaches a shapeless form. But super-complexity invites research to take on *responsibilities* both to expand our frameworks for understanding the world *and* to help us live with the ensuing uncertainty. Supercomplexity would give new point and shape to research.

Reframing the researchers

There is a triple reframing at work. Firstly, in a supercomplex world, re-search becomes an activity charged with redrawing the frameworks through which we comprehend the world. Secondly, research itself is reframed, as it is opened to multiple actors, modes, locations and audiences. But thirdly, the researchers have themselves to be able to handle multiple frames, not just of thought but also of action, of self-understanding and of communication. In short, they have to undergo a process of reframing themselves.

The point deserves some elaboration. Research, we have seen, migrates across domains. Different activities demand to be accorded the title of 'research'. But, at the same time, complexity enters into any act that would claim to be a research act. In a supercomplex age, each research act is itself subject to interpretation and evaluation by multiple audiences, it is subject to interrogation by different ideologies and it is liable to be taken up by conflicting stakeholders; and all this both within and beyond the academic world (although, as we have noted, that distinction is now barely credible). In short, the research act itself dissolves as a coherent act. It is fragmented, according to the discourses in which it is placed, its interrogators and its recipients.

Accordingly, *being* a researcher calls for multiple forms of being even in the one research act. By way of example, we can take the matter of communication. In a supercomplex world, the successful researchers will be those who have a bold self-understanding, who can engage with state bureaucracies, and who can inhabit the discourses of the policy-makers and the bureaucrats, speaking to them in a language that they can understand (that is to say, in a way that latches onto their own discourses). Academics have to live in the world: they have to become communicators.

The discursive complexity of the research act in a supercomplex world does not stop there. It involves projecting the research to multiple audiences in multiple media. Indeed, in the UK, the research councils – no less – now demand a statement on 'impact' to back up research proposals put before them. Consequently, the researchers are encouraged to take training workshops to develop their skills at presenting their research to the mass media, whether for print, radio or television, where they will lose any control over the final outcome. It may even involve the researchers taking their putative projects and embryonic ideas to the financiers, who will interrogate the proposed activities for possible income generation over the short to medium term. In this milieu, the research plan has to be reconstructed as a business plan.

Here, we are returned to our opening observations in this chapter: some 'researchers' will shrink from this multiple exposure. This is hardly surprising, amid the unfolding epistemology of research. In a supercomplex world, in a world replete with multiple reframing, what counts as knowledge expands and, in the process, the scope of research itself is bound to expand. But there are – as we might put it – ontological dimensions at work too. The authority and legitimacy of researchers have now to be tested and reconstructed continually, day by day, as they engage with their different audiences. This calls for a certain humility on the part of the new researchers; but it calls also for a certain degree of courage, in engaging with their different audiences and in projecting their work even against the ideological currents of the age.

An implication of this discursive implicatedness of research is that we have to abandon the notion of 'problem solving' as a metaphor for research. There can be no facile presentation of solutions to problems for there are *no* solutions to problems (Rouse, 1994). There are only stories of understanding problems which are themselves disputable.

Academics as researchers, therefore, have to become adept at handling disputes, disputes that are framed by rival discourses and opposing power blocks. Academics have to become public persons, even politicians (Barber, 1997), but of a particular kind. Yes, they have to engage in the art of the possible; but they have also to push back the horizon of the possible so that more things come into view (Castoriadis, 1997). Their task is not just to give us new frames of comprehension but to do so in ways that are comprehensible to the widest range of publics.[7]

Conclusion: the art of the possible

Academics as researchers have to become practising epistemologists and practising ontologists. They have to widen the frames of knowing *and* they have to engage with the widest range of audiences; they have to *become* different beings as researchers. This means not just projecting oneself in one's academic community but also making oneself as an academic in the wider world. Academics have to confirm their legitimacy in knowing things. They have to practise the arts of communicating, of negotiating their knowledge with the conflicting interest groups.

Research in the supercomplex world becomes the art of the possible in giving the client – whether research community, national body, transnational company or local community – something of what the client is asking for, but much else besides. It becomes a matter of supplying frames of understanding that the clients cannot envisage for themselves. In turn, those value-added frames of understanding have to be negotiated with the client and conveyed to even wider audiences. Research has to become a self-consciously political act.

It is in this sense that we can deploy such constructions as the university as 'the conscience of society' (cf. NCIHE, 1997) and as a promoter of civil society. The metaphysical connotations of such expressions have to be discarded. Provided that researchers come to accept their responsibilities to the wider polity (a polity that ensures their livings), research can expand the stories that we have in the world and of the world. It can widen the frameworks both through which society understands itself and through which its members comprehend the world. Through the continuing expansion and critique of public frames of understanding, the university becomes anew a liberal institution.[8]

In this way, research can justifiably be seen as enabling the university to be the conscience of society in that such publicly projected research calls to account current stories of our age; and it promotes civil society by injecting contesting frames of understanding in society. The university has no monopoly in either role. But supercomplexity presents it with this dual responsibility that is bequeathed *to no other social institution.* This is a particularly daunting set of responsibilities: we should not expect that the university will be rushing to take it on.

12

Teaching for a Supercomplex World

Universalizing supercomplexity

Under conditions of supercomplexity, teaching and learning are in difficulty. If every utterance, every frame of understanding, every action, every
value system and every state of human being are challengeable and *are*
challenged – and they are – the activities that pass as teaching and learning
in higher education are problematic. What, under these circumstances, is it
to educate at the highest level? What is it to be educated under conditions
of radical uncertainty and challengeability?

   The response that, in a mass higher education system, there will be a diversity of educational aims pursued is true but facile: it does not get to grips with
the problem just posed. The problem that a supercomplex age poses is
general; indeed, it is global. Under these conditions, the plea for diversity is
at best disingenuous. Certainly, local educational strategies will be pursued,
strategies that make sense in the context of the discipline in question, the
market position of the institution and its history, the wider bureaucratic
environment and the developing higher education policies of the state. But,
whatever the configuration of these local conditions and the strategies that
present to address them, the wider problematic of supercomplexity remains.

   Supercomplexity presents the university with a universal educational challenge and responsibility, namely that of educating for the formation of human
being that is going to be adequate to conditions of supercomplexity. Within a
mass higher education system that has many features of a market, and in a
democracy, diversity of provision for the education of adults is inevitable and
appropriate. But unless the challenges of supercomplexity are faced, universities will not be addressing the educational challenges now falling upon them.

Discontinuity *and* continuity

If it can be shown that supercomplexity does indeed present all 'universities' with a particular set of educational challenges and responsibilities,

how might we place those responsibilities against the traditional value back-ground of the Western university? Do the responsibilities generated by supercomplexity amount to a radical break with that heritage? Are we look-ing, in effect, to the birth of a new conception of higher education or is it a conception that can be understood within that traditional heritage? Are we in the presence of continuity or discontinuity?

We are in the queasy position of experiencing both situations at once. We do have to re-understand higher education; we do have to reach out and embrace a new conception of it. That conception calls for higher education in its pedagogies to be understood as a threefold educational process. Firstly, it has to create epistemological and ontological disturbance in the minds and in the *being* of students: it has to pose cognitively and experientially the radical uncertainty presented by supercomplexity. Students have to come to *feel* in every sense the utter insecurity of the post-modern world. Secondly, higher education has to enable students to live at ease with this perplexing and unsettling environment.[1] Thirdly, it has to enable them to make their own positive contributions to this supercomplex world, while being sensitive to the unpredictability and uncontrollability of the consequence of what they say and do.

Living effectively amid supercomplexity: this has to represent a break with the conceptual and value heritage of the Western university. It is an education that anticipates a future in which nothing can be anticipated. It is an education, therefore, that calls for the detraditionalization of the universities, institutions that – above all – repose on tradition. But, gener-ously interpreted, this new set of responsibilities can be seen to keep faith with that heritage. The new university for the twenty-first century can both represent a new conceptualization of higher education and retain some of the traditional heritage that has produced what we know as the Western university.

Nothing ventured, nothing gained

If higher education is to be adequate to the supercomplex age, it has to bring into its pedagogies something of the radical uncertainty that char-acterizes the supercomplex age itself. If every framework that students take on is itself susceptible to critique, we do students no proper service if we do not expose them to the unsettling character of that critique. For example, students taking chemistry and who later hold posts within the chemical industry are going to be exposed to critiques not just of the chemical industry but also of chemical processes as such. Higher education, then, faces up to the challenging of frameworks that characterizes supercomplexity by enabling students to sense that the frameworks through which we seek to understand the world are themselves challengeable. To repeat, *this* handling of uncertainty is a matter of living effectively not so much with cognitive uncertainty as with experiential uncertainty.

Part of the responsibility of higher education in a supercomplex age, therefore, is that of creating disturbance in the minds *and being* of the students. *Both* a cognitive and an experiential disturbance are called for. The chemistry graduate in the chemical industry is actively going to have to contend with and make her own experiential accommodation to those critiques. To generate the necessary dispositions and experiential resilience, students have to be unsettled in their minds *and* in their being. For this is the world to which they will be exposed, a world of continuing disturbance and unsettling, and in which they are going to have to make their way.

But this responsibility to unsettle that now comes the way of the university is only part of the story; in fact, it is only one-third of the story. For, if it were left at that point, higher education would have produced just disturbed and anxious persons. They would be persons, each with his or her centre of independence, but they would be liable to be plagued with anxiety. Accordingly, higher education has the second task of enabling students to live at ease with this unsettling. The unsettling cannot be displaced entirely. A characteristic of an age of supercomplexity is that one never knows the direction, or character, of the next instance of unsettling. The unsettling character of the world has to be lived with and lived through.

But even being confronted with alternative frameworks and being enabled to live with something approaching ease in their presence does not exhaust the pedagogical challenge to higher education. Left at that point, the subjectivities that higher education would be producing among its students would be simply voyeuristic. They would be watching, perhaps with wry amusement, the world go by; they would not be participating in it. By extension, too, they would not be extending their own offerings, their own contributions, to the world.

The voyeuristic stance is not totally without its point. At least, it limits the vulnerability of the human subject. But this is a 'nothing ventured, nothing gained' philosophy. Either it betrays an understandable anxiety about the world (its apparent ease is skin-deep) *or* it ends up being parasitic upon the world that it surveys. A third goal, therefore, opens up for higher education under conditions of supercomplexity.

A higher education

The third goal is that of enabling students, as graduates, to act purposively in the world. Two sets of questions open up in relation to the suggestion of such a goal as that of purposive action. Firstly, its character: can anything be said in general terms about it and its relationship to the individual's understandings? Secondly, its justification: what is particular, if anything, about purposive action under conditions of supercomplexity? In taking each of these questions in turn, I shall develop an argument about our understanding of higher education in such an environment.

On the first issue, that of the general character of purposive action, the action taken should be beneficial in its intentions. What counts as 'beneficial effect' will, of course, be subject to dispute. But there should, at least, be the plausible prospect that actions may be brought within the horizon of the ethical and be willing to be tested as such. Given the unpredictability inherent within a supercomplex world, it would be an over-strong condition to require that actions be beneficial in their effects: under supercomplexity, consequences cannot be predicted with assurance. Accordingly, we should limit our first condition simply to that of intent: actions should be conceived in part under categories that could be said to be ethical in intent.

Bringing actions within the horizon of the ethical is a necessary but an insufficient criterion of appropriate action. Action has also to be conceptually connected with an espoused framework or set of frameworks. As Argyris and Schön implied (1974), the theory in action should correspond to the espoused theory; but, we can add, the theory should also contain some ethical anchoring. Unless the action has some ethical anchoring, we are liable to develop just the kind of non-integrated subjectivity captured graphically by Steiner (1984) in pointing to the Nazi who would listen to Schubert by night and participate in the work of the concentration camps by day.

Certainly, the notion of integration is problematic in a postmodern age, for integration suggests some kind of subordination to some overarching narrative; and that, for strong postmodernism, is no longer seriously available to us. Integration is in difficulty because the sense that things can or do hang together is an illusion. It both implies a discreteness to the entity in question and glosses over the multiple readings of situations which, in turn, would jeopardize any effort to sustain an integrated structure. Orderliness, coherence and unity: these notions have to be highly suspect, if not repudiated altogether.

And yet the hope that there might be *some* connecting tissue, however flimsy, to a student's developing subjectivity surely must be retained, if only as a pedagogical lifeline. That there are persons in front of one, rather than disembodied units of experience, is a necessary presupposition of effective teaching. In turn, too, the hope that there are in front of one the makings of an integrated person, if only to some degree, may itself be a harbinger to that end.

We now turn to the second issue, that of the particularity of purposive action under conditions of supercomplexity. This issue is even more pertinent for our purposes and its essence can be easily stated: why should purposive action be particularly important in conceptualizing higher education under conditions of supercomplexity? Why cannot higher education rest with the dual aim of sensitizing students to the radical uncertainty present in the modern age of supercomplexity and of enabling them to live at ease with the ensuing perplexity? Why should a higher education in an age of supercomplexity be especially drawn to the third aim of enabling students to act purposively amid the radical uncertainty that they are faced with?

Ultimately, the supercomplex world presents not challenges of knowing but of *being*. *This* is the fundamental educational problematic of supercomplexity and it is one from which the university shrinks. The academics have contented themselves with the thought that their formal intellectual offerings were sufficient: arming the graduate with a repertoire of well-understood intellectual frameworks was itself sufficient to carry him or her forward into *life*. In their heart of hearts, they knew that not to be the case, and many courses incorporated elements of industrial, professional or community experience. The student's propositional knowledge never could carry him or her fully and satisfactorily into experiential situations; the is–ought gap never was susceptible to a technical solution. The epistemological gap between formal knowing and acting can only be bridged, if at all, through taking the plunge, through personal commitment to and in presenting situations.[2]

The challenges of personal commitment and action multiply in a supercomplex world. In a relatively stable world, in a world where graduates were going to engage with other graduates of a Western university, and in a world characterized by an educated community,[3] intellectual understandings could perhaps carry one forward. But in a global age, in a world where one's assumptions are challenged daily, that earlier world of met expectation is gone.

Fate deals unexpected cards, day after day. Professional life, especially, brings forth a melange of communication styles, of ideologies and of projected identities. Multiprofessionalism, changing professional–client relationships, changing standards and the globalization of problems dislodge any felt security over one's inner frameworks. This is the supercomplex world that confronts graduates as they develop their careers. Professions give way to professionalism, as individual members of a profession can no longer fall back on the profession's corpus of 'knowledge' and self-understandings but, instead, have to remake themselves anew with the dawning of each day.

The education of human beings has, then, to recognize the three domains of knowing, self-identity and action as irreducible to each other. Accompanying these three domains are three elements: communication, emotion and a sensitivity to the ethical. Knowing, self-identity and action each in turn call for communication, emotion and a sensitivity to the ethical: the latter three are vehicles for the realization of the former three achievements of human being. The first three, therefore, take priority. Of the first three, self-identity is itself gained through one's knowing efforts and in one's attempts to act in the world.

	Domains of:	**Knowing**	**Self-identity**	**Action**
Modes of realization				
Communication				
Emotion				
The ethical				

The structure of a higher education in a supercomplex age

It follows, from these reflections, that a higher education has to attend to action. Especially in a supercomplex world, the domain of action presents human being with challenges in itself. A 'higher education' limiting itself to the domain of knowing would leave graduates vulnerable in the sphere of action. Even, in addition, developing a student's 'self-identity' will still result in an insufficient pedagogic strategy. Under conditions of super-complexity, frameworks are contested in action; they need, therefore, to be confronted in action. Higher education would be falling short of its respons-ibilities if it did not incorporate, to some extent, this dimension.

The responsibility in question is threefold. Firstly, it is to students, who are going to have to make their way in the world. Higher education has now a responsibility to assist students to embark on the formation of their 'reflexive biographies' (Scott, 1995). But a reflexive biography is made largely in and through action, through purposive engagement with the world. Secondly, the responsibility is to the wider society which, in an age of supercomplexity, is calling for citizens who possess a dual capacity for engagement *and* disengagement. Individuals are embarked on a permanent shuttlecock of a shifting identity: now it is stable and secure, now it isn't. The supercomplex world requires individuals, especially those in profes-sional life where the dislocations are structural, to be able to act positively in such a milieu of dislocation. Thirdly, the responsibility is to the academic world itself. The academic world now has a new calling thrust upon it, that of making a direct difference to the emerging world of supercomplexity. It does this by embracing supercomplexity in its pedagogies.

With this conception of higher education, the adjective 'higher' is given a new justification, a justification not dependent on the social status of the university, on the chronological age of its students or on the cultural signific-ance of higher education. In none of those senses does the new higher education justify its 'higher' attribution. Instead, a genuine higher learning is apparent when the student is enabled to understand the contestability of all the frameworks that she encounters and comprehends *and* to confront that contestability in all its presenting forms. Since much of that contest-ability will be in the sphere of action, the student's higher education will be bound to embrace that domain.

This is a logical and an educational sense of 'higher'. It is logically higher in that it reveals the contestability of the higher-order frameworks in which we seek to understand the world. The understanding called for is a second-order or meta-level of understanding. It is also educationally higher in that those involved are called upon to develop as human beings capable of assimilating and accommodating this higher-order uncertainty in a new state of being. Such a human development will be expressed through meta-levels of self-reflection and of action. These powers are the necessary powers of the making of a 'reflexive biography', as distinct from having one's biography made for one by the manifold forces that dominate this supercomplex world.

A pedagogy for supercomplexity

In a supercomplex age, teaching in the university is characterized by three forms of uncertainty. Firstly, academics – as academics – will be imbued with the uncertainties of living with supercomplexity, having a sense of the continuing challengeability of all the frameworks that they might hold. Secondly, teaching generates in the minds and the beings of students an awareness of that uncertainty. Both these points are apparent from our preceding discussion, but a further form of uncertainty presents itself in relation to teaching. Thirdly, the pedagogical situation itself has to exhibit the characteristics of uncertainty. Students will not gain an awareness of uncertainty of any depth from a pedagogical situation that is itself entirely predictable. Accordingly, a pedagogy for supercomplexity has to become a pedagogy that is itself characterized by uncertainty, unpredictability, contestability and challengeability.

In turn, it follows that we have to give up the notion of teaching as such; at least, to give up a narrow view of teaching. We have to dispense with there being a tight connection between teaching and knowledge (Chapter 3). In a university built on the uncertainty principle, teaching as a means of disseminating research findings and scholarly understandings has to be displaced. Instead, new modes of teaching, which focus on the student's being and which produce the challenges of coping with uncertainty, have to be developed. The necessary transformation of the student's being requires nothing less.[4]

University teaching should see the severest attenuation of the formal lecture, if not its total abandonment. The formal lecture is a refuge for the faint-hearted, both lecturer and students. It keeps channels of communication closed, freezes hierarchy between lecturer and students and removes any responsibility on the student to respond. Even though these points might be granted, it may be said that lectures can still provoke a sense of uncertainty, unpredictability, contestability and challengeability. All these components of supercomplexity can be made apparent. But even if present – a large claim, empirically – the medium of the lecture ensures that the unsettling that such elements can provoke is barely skin deep. That is to say, the students remain as voyeurs; the lecture remains a comfort zone. The hierarchy and the monological character of the communication it represents ensure that the students' unsettling is held at a distance. The disjunction offered by the lecture is muted.

The total pedagogical environment of the lecture hall is a safe environment. The student watches a performance and is not obliged to engage with it. It is like watching a horror film: one knows that, however disturbing it is at the time, soon the lights will go on and its fictionality can be embraced, with nothing much dislodged.

The challenge of a pedagogy for supercomplexity, accordingly, is to place students into situations in which they are *required* to handle conflicting ideas and perspectives and uncertain situations (Collier, 1993). There must be no escape. Challenges that yield alternative legitimate responses must be obligatory. The responses, too, should be personal *and* interpersonal for that is the character both of academic life amid supercomplexity and of the wider world: both call up the personal and the interpersonal. Debates and structured workshops of all kinds should be explored so as to generate contained arguments among the students.[5] The disputations favoured by the mediaeval university may have something to offer us after all (Bjorkland, 1995).

A pedagogy for supercomplexity, then, cannot be construed as a matter of procedures or of delivery systems. It cannot be a matter of passing on knowledge or of acquiring skills for such definitions reek of certainty. It cannot even just be a matter of purposive action on the student's part. No; teaching for a supercomplex world has to become the generation of disjunction in the mind and in the being – in the self-understanding and in the actions – of the student (Jarvis, 1992).

As we saw, the pedagogical challenge presented by supercomplexity is not just that of becoming intimately aware of and sensitive to uncertainty and contestability. It is also that of handling that uncertainty such that one can engage purposively and effectively in its midst. But such reflections have, in turn, profound implications for the pedagogical situation. Enabling students to handle their own disturbance calls for a pedagogical transaction in which the student has the pedagogical space to develop her own voice.[6] In turn, too, the student can only develop her own voice if those in positions of power and potentially dominating influence – her lecturers and professors – step aside to some extent. Her lecturers have their professional responsibilities as educators, but the dispositions and qualities that supercomplexity calls for cannot be properly developed if the pedagogical processes are dominated by those in power over her.

This is not a call for democracy nor even for a Habermassian 'ideal speech situation'.[7] Equality is not at issue. What is at issue is the need for students to have the space to develop their own voice, their own sense of themselves and their own being: a human *being* that is likely to be adequate to the challenges of the radical contestability of all the students' frameworks and understandings, which will confront them beyond the university.

Lecturers may sense here a call for them to surrender something of their own authority in the pedagogical situation. That suspicion has to be repudiated. The lecturer has now to widen his or her authority, for the pedagogical situation has itself to widen. But in a pedagogy for supercomplexity, the lecturer's authority cannot be assumed; it has to be made and remade. Since supercomplexity has come into the pedagogical situation, the lecturer's position itself will be subject to continuing questioning. In part, therefore, the plea for pedagogical space for the student is pragmatic in character: injecting spaces for students to insert and to develop their own claims on the pedagogical situation is a form of bargaining. The students as adults in an increasingly individualized society (Beck, 1992) will grant an authority to the lecturer, provided that they are given space in which to develop their own selves according to the definitions that they bring to the pedagogical situation.

But the granting of pedagogical space is not just a pragmatic response to supercomplexity in the university's teaching settings. It is an educational requirement of supercomplexity itself. Supercomplexity does not deny that there are legitimate responses to problems and situations; what it does deny is that responses are unproblematic. Accordingly, students have to begin to understand that they have to imbue their responses with themselves; they have to take responsibility for their responses and their responses have to be theirs. Such personal responses call for pedagogical space to be accorded to students. They have to be granted and to feel that they have been granted space to make their own offerings, to formulate hesitantly their own insights, to contribute their own suggestions, to create their own products, to develop their own concepts and to engage in their own actions.

More than this, supercomplexity requires that students – of 'universities' – develop the wherewithal to contribute to the supercomplexity of the world in which they are going to be making their way. A pedagogy for supercomplexity, accordingly, requires space and encouragement for students to be audacious, daring and creative. Their ideas, their formulations, their insights and their creations matter; and they will feel and understand that they matter.

For such pedagogical space, the lecturer has to displace herself for her presence invades the space of the students. In such self-displacement, the lecturer will be fearful of losing control and of inviting undue risk into the pedagogical situation. But the lecturer has not just a right but also a duty to remain in such a position that control can be assumed; and assumed immediately. Yet, unless some element of control is ceded to the students, they can never develop the subjectivities appropriate to handling continuing assaults on their own understandings in their engagements with the wider world. Nor will they develop the confidence to form and to put forward their own offerings.[8] And nor will they find the space in which to be genuinely creative and audacious.

The ceding of authority is conditional on its being used by the students to good effect; the lecturer stands ready to withdraw that pedagogical space at any time. This is not to say that the space is conditional upon good behaviour. Rather, it is conditional upon its sustaining a value-added to the pedagogical situation.

Under conditions of supercomplexity, therefore, the lecturer's responsibilities are widened and moved laterally. Supercomplexity presses pedagogical challenges and so the claim of higher education to develop 'critical minds' has to be recast. Doubtless, the domain of knowledge must be retained but, in a world that is radically unknowable, its character has now to be problematized. The lecturer has also to widen her educational purview so as to bring into the reckoning the development of the student's capacities in the domains of action and of self-understanding. The educational task, therefore, widens as it shifts. Only in this widening and displacing of the educational task, so as to embrace the student's being, will students be enabled to acquire and to develop their own resources for living with the radical uncertainty posed by supercomplexity.

Teaching and research: a holy alliance

The relationship between teaching and research is an issue over which there is much angst, partly because it appears to be irresolvable. Its apparent intractability derives from the conceptual as much as the empirical nature of the matter. Even identifying a correlation between research and teaching 'outcomes' is challenging enough; setting up test conditions in which any causal relationship might be determined is even more problematic. But these empirical challenges arise partly out of more deep-seated conceptual difficulties. As we noted in the last chapter, what counts as 'research' in a supercomplex age is itself controversial.

Despite all that, we can see in the argument of this book an 'answer' to this long-standing problem. In a supercomplex world, research, I have argued, has to be understood as the promotion of supercomplexity in our public understandings. In its research function, it is the task of the university to contribute to the complexity of the life-world itself. If lecturers can be persuaded to take on the role of public intellectuals, the citizens of society will have their frames of understanding tested, stretched and multiplied. To that extent, their supercomplex world will be compounded. Research here takes on a dual pedagogical function at the level of society: the university conducts itself in public spaces, contributing to supercomplexity but providing the means by which society can take more informed views on issues. In that way, the university distinguishes itself from a research institute: the university in its research function takes on an educational role towards society as a whole.

Teaching, on the other hand, has to be construed as the production of supercomplexity in the private space of the minds of students and as the development of the capacity on the part of students to handle the resulting dislocation. In research for supercomplexity, the university is contributing to the growth of supercomplexity in the public sphere and to the growth of public understanding of that supercomplexity. In a pedagogy for supercomplexity, teaching produces the capacity of the students themselves to contribute to supercomplexity. It gives them the capacity to be inventive, the courage to be iconoclastic and the daring to produce bold formulations of ideas.

Given this recasting of the research and teaching functions of the university around the notion of supercomplexity, their relationship in turn becomes clear. Research, as the public production of supercomplexity, is a necessary condition of teaching in higher education. Teaching, as the production of supercomplexity in the student's mind, is the private act corresponding to the public act of enhancing supercomplexity in the wider polity. The frameworks produced for the wider public disturbance are the very frames to be brought into the pedagogical situation, even if the manner of their bringing-in must be problematic.

The lecturers are able to bring into the pedagogical situation an unsettling dimension, the unsettling that comes through coping with supercomplexity, for that is the world in which the researchers are having to make and remake themselves on a daily basis. Or, at least, that must be the hope. Unfortunately, lecturers too often possess a concept of teaching that places students in a subservient position such that they are the recipients of a curriculum instead of largely making it themselves. The issue, then, is whether the conditions of supercomplexity will prompt the lecturers themselves to adopt teaching approaches that are likely to foster student experiences that mirror the lecturers' experience as researchers.

The probability is to the contrary: precisely under the perplexing conditions of supercomplexity, lecturers will fall back on teaching approaches that appear to offer, in their pedagogical relationships, a degree of security and predictability. Indeed, the students themselves, faced with the corresponding challenge of a pedagogy for supercomplexity, are likely to resort to more orderly and predictable pedagogical situations. They will opt for dependency. In short, a conspiracy for safety develops between lecturers and students precisely when such curricular approaches should be jettisoned as the pedagogy of another age.

Nonetheless, at least theoretically, I believe that the idea of supercomplexity solves – or, rather, dissolves – the prickly issue of the relationship between research and teaching. With research construed as the public production of supercomplexity in the wider discourses of society and teaching construed as the private production of supercomplexity in the minds of students, the relationship is clear. The activities are separate and distinct and are not to be confused. However, research is a strong condition for teaching: being engaged in research of a frame-developing kind and projecting those frames to wide publics is a strong – although not exactly necessary and certainly not sufficient – condition of teaching that is aimed at bringing about supercomplexity in the minds of students and enabling them to live effectively amid their own personal sense of supercomplexity.

Not only the institutions but also the students have the right to expect that their lecturers are engaged in research. But, for the expectation to have bite, both the learning and the research have to be appropriate to the conditions of supercomplexity. They have to contain moments of public projection, of external engagement and communication, and of purposive action.

It is hardly surprising that academics will choose to pursue the life of research in preference to that of teaching. Even though research is becoming more challenging, teaching is becoming more challenging still. For the academic who comprehends research as the promotion of supercomplexity has also to compound that complexity by promoting radical uncertainty in the minds of his or her students *and* of enabling them to cope with that uncertainty. This kind of teaching requires a continuing commitment to the students, a continuing relationship. The academic has to be continually *there* for the students, to give them encouragement, self-belief and a sense of their future achievements.

Give me the easy life, give me research; let me not be troubled by teaching. Such an attitude is understandable, even if it is not easily forgivable.

Conclusion

In a supercomplex world, the key challenge is not one of knowledge but one of being. Accordingly, the main pedagogical task in a university setting is not that of the transmission of knowledge but of promoting forms of human *being* appropriate to conditions of supercomplexity. Teaching becomes the discomforting of minds *and* beings; but it becomes also the comforting of minds and beings. Students are embarked on a never-ending process of self-doubt and self-reflection, but also of determinate action, of living purposively with wry acceptance amid half-sensed precariousness.

Ever since Heraclitus, philosophers – whether directly or indirectly – have borne testimony to the challengeability of fundamental frameworks of comprehension and self-understanding. However, now, with the coming of supercomplexity and the global age, for the first time the challenge to cognitive and action frameworks becomes a societal and structural matter. This supercomplexity, this contestability of fundamental frameworks, no longer is a matter just for the literate classes persuaded by the philosophical texts but now enters directly and inescapably into the life-world of every person.

Understood in this way, university teaching attains – *for the first time* – the promise of a *higher* education. Now, under conditions of supercomplexity, higher education is obliged both to produce a dislocation among its students and to enable them not just to tolerate this dislocation but to live effectively through it. The dislocation has now to embrace the three dimensions of being: knowing, self-identity and action. This is a complete education, in that it extends across the full dimensions of human being. But it is also a genuine *higher* education, in that it calls for the highest order of self-reflexiveness, a self-reflexiveness that understands that, at best, only a precarious stability is attainable. This is a self-reflexiveness that does not delude itself with the soft option of *any* grand narrative – of truth, justice, economic competitiveness, virtue, community and the like – but accepts, even if resignedly, that there is no security to be had.

What is on offer, then, and for the first time, is the realization of a fully educated human being in the sense that human being in a supercomplex world has to attain a self-monitoring and self-critical capacity and yet be able to live through the resulting fragility of human being. Nothing like this has been needed before; and, as such, nothing like this has seriously been possible. The new conditions of supercomplexity make it possible for and, indeed, require higher education to live up to its rhetoric for the first time. Now, at last, a higher education can be realized.

Conclusions

Hats and rabbits

One conclusion that may be drawn on the argument presented here is that the rabbit has been pulled out of the hat. The first section of the book was spent rejecting the proposition that there could be a set of ideas that carried the university forward. Then, hey presto, the idea of supercomplexity arose and, suddenly, there appeared before us a universal set of ideas after all. Is this ingenuity or disingenuity?

The immediate answer is that that is how things are. We have to give up the idea that there can be a single set or – by extension – a complex of ideas of the conventional kind that can place the university in the late-modern age. It is not so much that large ideas are suspect as that they are contested. Our age is one of contestation. For every idea, there are a multitude of interpretations, improvisations and extensions. Of the increase of ideas, there shall be no end.

This is a situation, to repeat a point made in our study, that is partly of the university's own making. The surfeit of ideas, of possibilities and of new orderings is partly the result of the university doing its own thing. If it appears that the university's foundations have been undermined, that is partly due to the university's own handiwork on itself. The infinite production of ideas, imaginings and interpretations is precisely what the university is in business for.

But how, then, does it come about that 'supercomplexity' can furnish us with what appear to be foundations after all? How can it be that super-complexity can offer a universal set of ideas to carry forward the idea of the university when just such a project seems to have been ruled out?

There are two responses. The first is that 'supercomplexity' is a short-hand for the state of affairs in which we find ourselves. It is that state of affairs which is characterized, at its heart, by uncertainty, unpredictability, challengeability and contestability. It is precisely such a state of affairs that led us to conclude that any determinate set of ideas – built around such concepts as knowledge, work, democracy or emancipation – has to be entertained only with large provisos. Beware, all who enter here, has to be the entry sign. 'Supercomplexity' is, therefore, a metaconcept: it works as a descriptor at a higher level than those against which we cautioned. It is that state of affairs that gives backing to our cautions. If there is substance in our cautions, it is due to supercomplexity. Buy the cautions, buy supercomplexity. It is a package deal.

The second response is that supercomplexity is a cleaner concept than the others. The others – work, knowledge, democracy, emancipation and so on – come with their values on their sleeves. They say: be in favour of us. Understand yourselves, organize yourselves and declare yourselves in favour of us. And many do. Those terms are, in the strict sense, ideologies: they conjoin description and exhortation. Supercomplexity, by contrast, is more neutral. It says simply: this is how the world is. It does not demand that its observers strike up for it.

Some will do so, warmly embracing the challenges of supercomplexity; others will shrink from it. Sooner or later, supercomplexity will press its claims – on individuals, organizations (such as universities), nation states and transnational organizations. Especially in activities requiring any complexity of understanding, the challenge to frameworks that lies at the centre of supercomplexity will be felt. There is a ubiquity to, and an insistence within, supercomplexity that cannot be evaded. Head in the sand cannot be a proper response in this situation, a situation – to repeat – that is much of the university's own making.

A new responsibility

Metaconcept, fact more than values, its ubiquity and its ultimate insistence: these, then, are the features of supercomplexity that distinguish it from the other discarded sets of ideas. But how, then, emerge with a definite set of ideas that is so mega that it provides a new universal for the university, such that we can continue to talk of 'the university' *tout court*? Isn't there a sleight of hand here? Now you see it (the university), now you don't; and then, *voila*, now you see it again.

There are two charges here: a smuggled-in is/ought jump and an unwarranted universality. Firstly, the smuggled-in is/ought jump: how do we get from observations about supercomplexity to supercomplexity becoming a new banner to guide our efforts in developing our universities? Supercomplexity is the world into which the graduates of universities will go; it marks out the experiences that they will face of continual challenge and insecurity. It is not knowledge that will carry them forward but their capacity to embrace multiple and conflicting frameworks and to offer their own positive interventions in that milieu. What counts is not their knowledge but their mode of being. Supercomplexity wills its own pedagogical 'ought': a university that shrank from this challenge would be failing its students.

The second charge is that of an unwarranted universality. Continuing talk of 'the university' merely retains an allegiance to an outworn sense of a unity within and across universities. Universities are actually required to exhibit diversity among themselves. However that may be, the charge misses the point. The case being argued here is not one about the extent to which, empirically, universities exhibit diversity. It is a case in favour of a set of regulatory ideas; even, regulatory ideals. We can continue to use the language of 'the university' not because there is a continuing claim but because there is a new set of universal claims on those institutions that would take the title of 'university'. Supercomplexity is a universal phenomenon and one that every 'university' should acknowledge.

We can, therefore, to return to our starting point (in the Introduction), talk of responsibility reposing on the university. The two go together: retention of the idea of 'the university' and a sense of there being a general responsibility. The responsibility in question – that of attending to super-complexity – is new, however. It follows that 'the university' sketched out here is a new university; or, at least, that there is a new set of ideals for institutions that would term themselves 'university'.

Enlightenment lives

But isn't there still a separate sleight of hand at work here? How can we be given a new idea of the university on the one hand and yet – so the argument has wanted to urge – still retain a link with the idea of enlightenment? The argument claims to be offering a new way of framing the university and yet also claims a continuity with earlier notions of the university. The phrase 'the Western university' has, after all, been on display as a sign of some continuation in the value background. How, then, meet the charge – identified in the opening of the first chapter – that there is here a reluctance to disavow the past that has more to do with the values of the text than the logic of the argument?

The charge has been addressed on several occasions in the text itself. Much of the metaphysical baggage of 'the university' has to be ditched. Talk of knowledge, truth, justice and even emancipation have to be abandoned as carriers of the university. They require so many conditions and provisos to give them any substance that they end up, at best, as lumbering vehicles. These would-be upholders of the faith can be set aside.

However, even as the university is enjoined to take on the new faiths of impact, performance, outcomes and standards, so there are parallel, if quieter, voices that call up earlier ideas of the university. On the one hand, the university is reminded of its calling as 'the conscience of society'; on the other hand, it is reminded of its own educative aspirations to promote such personal qualities as 'breadth' of mind, self-reliance, flexibility and adaptability. In these urgings, we see the press of supercomplexity. In its public projection of itself – through research and consultancy – the university is reminded of its claim to hold up to society new and counter frames of understanding; in its more personal pedagogic activities, it is urged to deliver on its claims to develop human qualities and modes of being that are able not just to tolerate continuing challenge but also to generate positive interventions in such an uncertain world. In short, supercomplexity is requiring from the university the production and projection of new ideas, the resilience to challenge and the potential for daring interventions that are associated with the university as a beacon of enlightenment.

Universities are faced with a babel of voices. The many tongues speak different languages and some are louder and more insistent than others. The voice of performativity speaks more loudly than the voice of enlightenment. Universities are not seriously in danger of giving way wholesale to the call of performativity and of abandoning their enlightenment heritage. The history of universities is that, collectively, new strata of functioning are laid down on top of the earlier callings. But there is the prospect of the enlightenment capacities of the university being underplayed and downvalued just at the point when they are becoming needed by the wider world more than ever before.

Enlightenment lives on in the university, but only just. We can continue to speak of 'the Western university' as a living idea. But the idea is fragile. Its institutional base is weak.

So what?

A further rejoinder to the argument in this book might take a quite different form. It might take the form of 'so what?'. Doesn't the argument ultimately amount to a plea that all is right with the world or, at least, with universities? They engage with the wider world in new ways, they respond to diverse constituencies, and they continue to carry their traditions into a new age. End of story.

Nothing could be further from the truth. The argument has been that universities misunderstand their responsibilities in helping the world to address the conditions of supercomplexity that beset it. There is a collective doubt that there could be an idea of the university that might hold across a diverse mass higher education system. The possibility that there could be a collective responsibility, that we might continue to speak of an idea of the university, albeit a new idea, is not seriously entertained; indeed, is often dismissed. Insofar as it is entertained, the collective responsibility amounts to a switch to the performative university. As a result, universities are falling short of their wider contemporary responsibilities. Because – fortuitously – there turn out to be resonances between earlier ideas of the University and the new calling to advance and to promote daring ideas, universities by chance fulfil their task to some extent. But, with this new calling hardly noticed, it is in danger of being under-represented.

A yet further response may be that the detail of the argument turns out to be familiar stuff. The working through of the argument into the management and leadership of universities, and for their research and teaching activities, yielded little of substance, or so it might be alleged. Such a charge is, I believe, doubly wrong. Firstly, as we have noted, in many areas universities are falling well short of their rhetoric. For example, most research and scholarship are safe, confined to filling in the details of dominant paradigms: they do not, for the most part, take the form of adding significantly to our frames for understanding the world. In teaching, again, relatively safe pedagogic methods are chosen that give both lecturer and student an easy time: they fail systematically to promote self-reliance. And in university governance, systems of critical self-evaluation are only weakly developed: the forms of continual critical self-scrutiny appropriate to supercomplexity are hardly in evidence. In the first place, therefore, supercomplexity requires that the university live up to its self-pretensions. In doing so, it would be transformed into a much more vibrant place and be more in command of itself.

But, as we have seen, supercomplexity calls for much more in the way of responses from the university. It calls for the university to approach its self-description as an academic community, not in there being an allegiance to an over-arching ideal of 'community' on campus but in the sense that academics holding different values, having different relationships with the wider community and working in different disciplines will be prepared to interact with and to gain from each other. In turn, this consideration calls for a university leadership that actually concerns itself with the knowledge structures of the university and the knowledge policies that that configuration represents. Securing such transdisciplinary interactions cannot be a matter of fiat but has to be actively worked for. Academics will not lightly engage with those apparently different from themselves. They have to be brought to do so, painstakingly, resolutely and carefully. This will involve epistemological and ontological turmoil. It is the task of the university's leadership to create and to orchestrate that necessary turmoil.

In the area of research, as we saw too, fundamental developments are required if the university is to respond to supercomplexity with any adequacy. New frameworks of understanding have to be not only produced in-house but also made available for consumption in the wider society. In an age of supercomplexity, research can no longer rest with an internal audience. The university has a civic role to play, both in expanding the frames of understanding in the wider world and in assisting their assimilation. This would constitute a transformation not only in research but also in the role of researcher.

Lastly, a transformation in the pedagogies of the university is also required by supercomplexity. The key problem of supercomplexity is not one of knowledge; it is one of being. Accordingly, we have to displace knowledge from the core of our pedagogies. The student's being has to take centre stage. Feeling uncertainty, responding to uncertainty, gaining confidence to insert oneself amid the numerous counter-claims to which one is exposed, engaging with the enemy, and developing resilience and courage: these are matters of *being*. Their acquisition calls for a revolution in the pedagogical relationships within a university. Students can only gain control of themselves amid unceasing uncertainty if they are given the necessary pedagogical space. The conventional pedagogical relationship has to be inverted.

In its internal forms of engagement, in its external forms of engagement, in its definitions of research and scholarship and in its educational purposes and pedagogical relationships: a world of supercomplexity demands nothing less than an inversion of much of our present thinking and practices in our universities. Universities that take seriously their responses to supercomplexity have to be a different kind of place.

All's well . . .

What, then, are the prospects for the university to be realized in this way? What is the likelihood that concerns with teaching performance might give way to a serious debate about the curriculum and the need to transform it into an experience for new modes of being? What is the likelihood, given narrow definitions of research productivity, that we will see a transformation in the definitions of research and the research role to encourage not just revolutionary ideas but also their public projection and assimilation? What is the likelihood, amid the inevitable drive to see financial independence and high scores on league tables, that institutional leadership will come to concern itself with the epistemological disposition of a university and work actively to sponsor academic interaction where it would not otherwise have occurred?

The problem is that all will seem well without any of this happening. That this is possible says much about the emerging criteria of success. There are two concluding points to be made.

Firstly, the dominant criteria of success focus on outcomes, demonstrable impact and the bottom line. There is nothing amiss with these criteria in themselves but they are insufficient to sponsor a university that is meeting its responsibilities – pedagogic, civic and epistemic – in an age of supercomplexity. For that, attention has to be paid to processes: institutional processes, pedagogic processes, research processes and communicative processes. Processes do not show up on the balance sheet, except perhaps as opportunity costs. The sheer effort, time and resources required to transform processes and to sustain that transformation over time would be daunting to institutional leaders and heads of department at the best of times. That such actions are implicitly discouraged in the emerging performance indicators says little for their being pursued with much seriousness. In a climate of performativity, processes receive low marks.

The second reason that the conditions of realizing the supercomplex university are in some difficulty is perhaps even more telling and it follows from the first. It is that the current performance indicators evoke a totally safe environment. Staff may wince at the claims on their time, at the pressure to publish, at the call to raise income and at the need to comply with the demands of powerful external bodies. But all this, pressured as it undoubtedly is on occasions, amounts to a predictable environment. It might be tough but the parameters are well-known. A university for supercomplexity, in contrast, is one in incessant turmoil, where all the basic assumptions as to one's self-identity as researcher, scholar and teacher are kept perpetually in the air. As we saw, supercomplexity, taken seriously, calls for continual pandemonium.

The signs, however, are not entirely unfavourable. As we have noted, more muted though they may be, voices in the wider world are calling on the university to retain some of its enlightenment heritage. On the analysis here, this is inevitable; and those calls are likely to become louder. Supercomplexity requires of its universities, if they are to have a societal role to play, that they become sites for the continual production of revolutionary ideas, that graduates are able to live effectively amid radical uncertainty, and that the wider society is enabled to understand its condition and make ever more insightful evaluations of the large issues in front of it.

Some universities are reading at least some of the tea-leaves. 'The entrepreneurial university' is a kind of half-way house to the supercomplex university. Its undeclared motto of 'seize the main chance' requires something of the internal spontaneity and flexibility and something of the communicative reach that supercomplexity calls for. But the pedagogical transformation, the widening of the role of researcher to embrace that of public intellectual and the transdisciplinary interactions are, at best, likely to be present only embryonically. On the other hand, again as we noted, universities are having to win friends and influence people. They are having to latch on to wider public aspirations. Their researchers are widening their roles. Their research is assessed for its impact, even if 'impact' is narrowly drawn.

The jury has to be out, therefore, on whether the supercomplex university will be realized in the near future. In the longer term, I believe that universities will move in the required direction because, as we have seen, there is a societal, and even a global, call for it to come about. The writing is on the wall. However, universities will have choices as to the extent to which they will pursue the agenda set out here and it is likely that many will opt for the safer definitions of the role: operational enlightenment before communicative enlightenment.

In the mediaeval beginning of the university were text and spoken word: outcome and process went together. An age of supercomplexity compels that that twin set of activities be reinterpreted and reinvigorated. Amid supercomplexity, the university has the dual responsibility not only of compounding uncertainty but also of helping us to live with uncertainty; even to revel in it. This is the task in front of the university. In a world where everything is uncertain, there is no other task.

Notes

Chapter 1   Death and Resurrection (pp. 11–22)

1. 'At this very postmodern moment that finds the University learning what may be its end . . . the Institute may just be beginning' (Lyotard, quoted in Peters, 1995: 22).
2. Peter Scott (1997: 11) sees such language as 'obviously a rhetorical deceit'. Webster (1998: 69) considers that 'There has been too much comment of late that refers to the death of the university'. Obviously, as an institution, the university continues and even flourishes. I am arguing a different thesis, namely that the legitimacy of the university is now at an end; it has been delegitimized. However, a new legitimacy awaits.
3. In 1995, there were approaching 82 million students in higher education worldwide, split roughly equally between the developed and developing worlds. See UNESCO (1998: 7, Table 2.3). See also Sadlik (1998).
4. The University of Cambridge was itself born out of a migration of scholars from Oxford after a particularly violent affray in which the townspeople pitched upon the clerks following a 'quite accidental' killing of a townswoman by one of the scholars (Rashdall, 1895: 348).
5. The attractiveness of the site of the then new University of Essex was, for its first Vice-Chancellor, a particular feature of note and one 'which gives physical and visual expression to the academic ideas [behind the formation of that University]' (Sloman, 1964: 64).
6. Admittedly, the term 'mass' has to be qualified. For Trow, a system moved from being 'élite' in character to 'mass' when it had merely reached an age participation rate of 15% (Trow, 1973). While the meaning of 'higher education' and the populations included are not exactly clear, UNESCO figures are nevertheless indicative: they show participation rates in 1995 for the developed world of 60% (ibid.: Table 2.2: 6).
7. On the 'new public management', see Bottery (1996).
8. On 'life-world becoming', see Chapter 12 of my book, *The Limits of Competence* (Barnett, 1994).
9. The Report, in the UK, of the National Committee of Inquiry into Higher Education (the 'Dearing Report') allows room for 'academic freedom' but only within forms of 'accountability' and 'responsibility' both within institutions and

to the wider society. In comparison with the treatment of the topic in the 'Robbins' Report' of the comparable Committee on Higher Education (Robbins, 1963), we are certainly offered here an 'attenuated' view of academic freedom.

10. On universities and globalization, see Currie and Newson (1998); Scott (1998b). 'Globalization' is a fraught concept and its relationships to universities awaits a clear and full exposition.

11. See Daniels (1998).

12. This is especially so in 'The Network Society', in which differential influence accrues in a new political geography focused on the nexus between knowledge production and technological innovation (Castells, 1996).

13. The names refer to fictional characters who appear from time to time in a satirical back-page column by Laurie Taylor in the London weekly *Times Higher Education Supplement*.

14. One attempt to implement such strategies is that of the UK's Quality Assurance Agency as set out in its newsletter, *Higher Quality*, especially Nos 3 and 4.

Chapter 2   The End of Enlightenment? (pp. 23–34)

1. See para. 11.103 of the Report of the National Committee of Inquiry into Higher Education in the UK (the 'Dearing Report') (NCIHE, 1997).

2. cf. Derrida: '. . . we might say that the difficulty [of inserting a university responsibility] will consist . . . in determining the best lever, what the Greeks would call the best *mochlos*.' (Derrida, 1992: 31).

3. For a recent typification of skills, held up to the university sector and to which the sector is likely to declare its allegiance, see the 'Dearing Report' (NCIHE, 1997).

4. Lyotard implies just this in various of his writings. See, for example, his examination of *The Postmodern Condition: A Report on Knowledge* (1984).

5. I take the notion of a 'horizon of values' from Taylor (1991).

6. See, for instance, the 'Dearing Report' (NCIHE, 1997).

7. The notion of 'higher education as transformation' is fast becoming a mantra but is, it should be clear from this account, a weasel term. The term should invite the questions: what kinds of transformation? In whose interests? Coloured by some of the dominant interests of our age, it all too easily takes on an ideological programme of transforming students so that they are themselves capable of exerting transformations on their environments. It is an education for fabrication that supplants an education for understanding. See Harvey and Knight (1996).

8. For just one such more subtle voice, see Coldstream (1999). Patrick Coldstream, it is worth noting, was the first Director of the UK's Council for Industry and Higher Education.

9. See Gergen (1994) and also the Introduction by Simons and Billig in that book; but the implication – that postmodernism spells the end of ideology – is also present in Lyotard's now classic text (1984).

10. Jurgen Habermas has argued a 'colonization' thesis, namely that instrumental reason will – without countervailing strategies – tend to colonize the life-world (which should otherwise be subject to other claims and interests of open communication and engagement): 'The thesis of internal colonization states that the subsystems of the economy and state become more and more complex as a

consequence of capitalist growth, and penetrate ever deeper into the symbolic reproduction of the lifeworld' (Habermas, 1989: 367).

Chapter 3   The Ends of Knowledge (pp. 35–46)

1. There are developing sets of dynamic interrelationships between the global economy, technologies and curricula in higher education. As a study on *The Changing Pattern of Undergraduate Curricula* in which the author is involved has revealed, a sub-field such as optoelectronics can just as quickly disappear from the curriculum as it had appeared, as the perceived 'need' for certain technological competences waxes and wanes.
2. Devoid of its Marxian/Arendtian flavour; cf. Arendt (1958).
3. Again, drawing on the above study (Note 1), it turns out that even in the élite universities, where curricula might – on the surface – seem stable, in their epistemological interstices movement can usually be detected, and usually in the direction of performativity. Partly, this is due to a greater performativity creeping into the concepts and topics of inquiry in the research endeavours of different disciplines.
4. 'It was Nietzsche who first explicitly suggested that we drop the whole idea of "knowing the truth". His definition of truth ... amounted to saying that the whole idea of "representing reality" by means of language, and thus the idea of finding a single context for all lives, should be abandoned' (Rorty, 1989).

Chapter 4   The Fading Constellations (pp. 47–58)

1. A notable example of a carrier of this discourse is that of the UK Report of the Inquiry into Higher Education (NCIHE, 1997).
2. The presence of a discourse around participation, particularly in relation to social class, within that national report (Note 1) *alongside* the more instrumental agendas of skills and of the productive capacities of universities is notable: the Report is a mix of multiple discourses and agendas. How far they hang together in an integrated 'vision' is a further matter.
3. Alasdair MacIntyre has drawn attention to the 'achievement [of the Scottish nineteenth university academics] in creating and sustaining an educated public'; in other words, democracy, insofar as it entails an educated public, followed the birth of the liberal university; it did not precede it.
4. Among recent returns to *Bildung* particularly pertinent to the argument here see Rothblatt (1993) and Readings (1996). But see also Rorty (1980: 359–62) who urges that we understand and practise philosophy as a means of *Bildung* or, as he prefers to put it, 'edification' through the project of 'finding new, better, more interesting ways of speaking' (ibid.: 360).
5. See, for example, Dearden (1972); Crittenden (1978); Christman (1989).
6. Admittedly, Ayer's thesis has been criticised. For example, Gettier (1963: 145) has pointed out that 'it is possible for a person to be justified in believing a proposition that is in fact false'.
7. Jurgen Habermas' specification of the validity claims inherent in any truth-oriented discourse implies something of this notion of commitment, but does not seriously address this existential component. Crudely, for Habermas, there are three validity claims embedded in a rational discourse, which reflect in turn

claims as to truthfulness, appropriateness and sincerity. It is this last that comes closest to the notion of commitment but falls short of it, focusing as it does on the truthfulness of communications: e.g., there is here a communicative intent on the part of the speaker 'that he express *truthfully* his beliefs, intentions, feelings, desires and the like . . .' (Habermas, 1991: 397).

8. Basil Bernstein suggests that the trivium of the mediaeval university provided a means of sustaining a 'distinct modality of the self' (even while it was 'dislocated' from the consciousness of the world provided by the quadrivium). However, as he points out, the new market principle represents a new dislocation in which knowledge is pursued just for its use value and the self, in the process, is disconnected from knowledge altogether (B. Bernstein, 1996: Chapter 4).

   In general, however, the sociologists currently seem relaxed about if not actually intent on dissolving the self while the philosophers seem more intent on saving it. Compare, for instance, Giddens (1991) with Taylor (1992). Admittedly, the 'postmodernists' from *both* philosophy and sociology share a particular concern about the problematic nature of the self: see Haber (1994) on Lyotard, Rorty and Foucault.

9. Even back in 1969, Galbraith (1969: 378) spoke of the university sector as having become excessively 'accommodated' to the economy.

10. See the Report of the UK National Inquiry into Higher Education (NCIHE, 1997, especially 1.22; Table 18.1: 283).

11. More recently, Ulrich Beck has argued for a self-reflexive science (Beck, 1992: 179): 'An *alternative* science is always possible.'

12. It is also a set of ideals that I have promoted in earlier explorations, for example, in *The Idea of Higher Education* (Barnett, 1990).

13. There is an extensive literature on Critical Theory that develops this point. See, for instance, Held (1983), Jay (1996), Laclau (1996).

14. Even a national body can be found to pin its view of higher education to the mast of the ship, Emancipation (CVCP, 1996).

Chapter 5   The Constellation of Fragility (pp. 61–71)

1. For such a defence, see MacIntyre (1985).

2. The Dearing Inquiry indicated that the UK higher education system required an expenditure of £400m either immediately or in the very short term in order to sustain activities, infrastructure and services of a proper quality (NCIHE, 1997: 17.23). In addition, a further £400–500m per annum was needed for research purposes (ibid.: 17.21).

3. For a treatment of scientific research through concepts such as uncertainty, ignorance, risk and complexity, see Funtowicz and Ravetz (1993) and Ravetz (1993): science 'encompasses the management of irreducible uncertainties in knowledge and ethics'.

4. Castoriadis (1997: 44): '. . . the historical being goes beyond the simply living being because it can provide new responses to the "same" situation or create new situations'. Also, Beck (1998: 21): 'Many theorists do not recognize the *opportunities* of risk society . . . [one of the strategies available to us is that we pose] questions of organized irresponsibility.'

5. 'There is no theory-independent way to reconstruct phrases like "really there"' (Kuhn, 1970: 206).

Chapter 6   Supercomplexity: the New Universal
(pp. 72–83)

1. From Plutarch, according to Heraclitus: 'One cannot step twice into the same river, nor can one grasp any mortal substance in a stable condition, but it scatters and again gathers' (Kahn, 1987: 53, LI). 'To the extent that there are laws in history, those laws are valueless and history is valueless' (from *The Use and Abuse of History*). 'Over all things stands the contingency of heaven' (from *Thus Spake Zarathustra*); see chapter on Nietzsche in Roberts (1990: 226–27).
2. 'O brave new world that has such people in 't', *The Tempest*, V.i.183.
3. cf. Beck (1992: 180–81): 'It would be up to [the social scientists] to encourage the emancipation of science from its self-inflicted fate of immaturity and blindness with respect to risks . . . What is sought is a *pedagogy* of scientific rationality. . . .' (UB's emphasis.)
4. From an empirical research project in which the author is currently involved, it is apparent that there are tendencies in the humanities (notably in history) explicitly to build reflexive strategies into the curriculum; for example, to have a module focusing on historical methods as such, partly in the hope of illuminating their embedded 'transferable skills'.
5. cf. MacIntyre (1985).
6. As I think Bertrand Russell once put it.
7. As is well known, the phrase 'a will to power' is Nietzsche's (1988 edn), but as I read him, he is warning against a will to power that is embedded in much language and thought, including that of the philosophers themselves.

Chapter 7   The Conflict of the Faculties (pp. 84–95)

1. In a series of books over a thirty-year period, Ernest Gellner argued that reason contained within itself both a philosophical and a sociological precariousness. Reason provokes critique of itself and yet can never completely shore up itself: ultimately, an act of faith is called for. At the same time, the sociological conditions of the birth and of the sustaining of reason are not well understood but are clearly continuously stretched. The emphasis contained in Western reason on it being possessed and tested by individuals is both a strength and a weakness. In his earlier writings, Gellner seemed to be optimistic that the ratchet could never fall back; in his later writings, he appeared to be less sanguine. For just some of the key Gellner texts on these themes, see his 1964, 1974, 1991, 1992, and his last book, published posthumously, 1998. We await a book that examines the implications of Gellner's writings for our understanding of the birth, development and legitimation of the Western university.
2. For example, Plumb (1963) and, more recently, Berube and Nelson (1995).
3. cf. Wyatt on 'keystone' disciplines (Wyatt, 1994).
4. Kuhn (1970) spoke of 'incommensurability' but within his story lurked the sense that, ultimately, the choice of a paradigm was not purely a-rational. There was some logic to theory choice, even if the choice was in part a form of social logic. Supercomplexity, on the other hand, presents us literally with incommensurable frameworks, in the sense that we are offered competing frameworks that do not yield value-free preferences.
5. The discourse of skills exercises a 'double-whammy': it terms both human activities and transactions 'skills' when they are little of the kind; and it attempts to

exercise a kind of discursive hegemony, attempting to widen its scope *ad infinitum*, such that everything that might be done in an educational setting might come under its label. See Barrow (1990).
6. See O'Hear (1988) for a stout defence of valuelessness in the university.
7. Their associated speech acts, accordingly, are – technically – illocutionary acts (Austin, 1962).
8. cf. Gellner on Feyerabend (Gellner, 1992: 100–111).
9. A way of putting this point more formally is that the sub-cultures within the university hold allegiance to differing social epistemologies. (For a recent examination of this latter notion, see Schmitt (1994).)

Chapter 8   Conditions of the University (pp. 99–110)

1. There is, admittedly, a double sense in which the term 'conditions' is being used here. On the one hand, there are the empirical conditions of the university, the conditions under which universities labour and in which they have to survive; on the other hand, there are the conditions of realizing an idea of the university, the conditions at issue here.
2. On 'critical interdisciplinarity', see my *The Idea of Higher Education* (Barnett, 1990: 182–88).
3. 'On its own account' has to be taken with a large grain of salt: the humanities become introspective, examining and displaying their inner virtues because they feel themselves to be under scrutiny, if not under threat; the sciences, by and large, do not because they are confident in themselves (even if this self-confidence expresses a certain naïvety).
4. For an early reference to 'the evaluative state', see Neave (1990). For a recent revisiting of the idea, see Neave (1998). See also Power (1997) on 'the audit society'.
5. See the Report of the Committee of Enquiry chaired by Sir Norman Lindop which analysed and made recommendations on 'The Academic Validation of Degree Courses in Public Sector Higher Education' (Lindop, 1985). The Report made great play with the idea of academic institutions being 'a self-sustaining and self-critical academic community' (ibid.: 105): this was the test by which an aspiring polytechnic might be adjudged sufficiently 'mature' to become a university (ibid.). This, of course, was question-begging big-time: it assumed that those institutions on which had already been bestowed the status of 'university' fulfilled this criterion.
6. See Ramsden (1998).
7. The prospect of border transactions and also nomadism arises especially in a postmodern world. See, for example, Giroux (1991); Ladwig (1995); McClaren (1995).
8. This dual structure parallels but is somewhat different from that of Becher and Kogan (1992).
9. cf. Wyatt (1994).
10. It should be clear that, on the argument here, such an institution should forfeit the right to the title of 'university' since, for a university to be realized, it has a responsibility directly to challenge and to enable students to live effectively amid supercomplexity.
11. What is required is not so much communicative competence or even communicative tolerance but communicative dexterity. See Reid (1996) for an indication of the complexities of serious communication in the modern university.

12. *The Times Higher Education Supplement* of London now carries a regular column allowing 'whistle-blowers' anonymously to air their grievances.

Chapter 9   A Suitable Ethos (pp. 111–123)

1. The general case for a pedagogy that would assist the handling of controversial issues was made by Lawrence Stenhouse (1967: Chapter 11). Subsequently, the more specific case in relation to higher education was made extensively by Gerald Collier (to whom this book is dedicated). See, among his many papers on the subject, 'Learning moral judgement in higher education' (Collier, 1993).
2. A pluralism that, as Lyotard reminds us, includes Auschwitz (Lyotard, 1992: 91).
3. See, for example, the emerging policies of the UK Quality Assurance Agency, set out in its Bulletins, 3 and 4 (1998). No. 3 was a 'Consultative Document' with No. 4 setting out the agreed policy. Almost all of the main planks of the proposed policy in No. 3 were retained, even though it was admitted that there was considerable resistance to them from within the higher education sector.
4. Notably, Nietzsche attempted to develop a concept of authenticity amid an unsettled world, although his concept of authenticity was not entirely unambiguous (Cooper, 1983).
5. See Berman (1995) *All That is Solid Melts into Air*. Berman indicates that the conditions of uncertainty and insecurity that I am trying to draw out are not especially postmodern but have their origins in modernism. However, I contend that they are now developing apace so as to produce both the conditions of postmodernity and of the *Weltanschauung* of postmodernism.

Chapter 10   Constructing the University (pp. 127–139)

1. For some illustrative sources, particularly pertinent to the argument here, see Muller (1996a); Winter (1995); Maassen and Van Vught (1996, especially Part II on Governance); Trowler (1998: especially 24–30); Currie and Vidovich (1998).
2. For a somewhat ironic treatment of pandemonium in an organizational setting, see Burrell (1997).
3. In their (1992) paper, Middlehurst and Elton excoriate 'transactional' models of university leadership for not being sufficiently radical in the face of conditions of 'external shock' and performance critique and, instead, propose a 'cybernetic' model, in which a proactive leadership produces 'useful change' (ibid.: 254–255). However, it is unclear whether a cybernetic model is going to be adequate to the situation that they describe since the very point of a cybernetic model is, in fluctuating circumstances, to return the entity in question to a state of equilibrium. Under conditions of supercomplexity, no such state is available.
4. The idea of 'distorted communication' I take from Habermas. For an examination of the educational implications of the idea, see Young (1989: 106ff.).
5. The idea of 'rule-following' was central to Richard Peters' philosophy: '*Man is a rule-following animal*' (Peters, 1960 edn: 5). But if Peters overdid his case, both empirically and idealistically, the presence of rules, especially in systematic epistemic activities, is inescapable. In his concept of 'paradigm', Kuhn (1970) is underlining the extent to which science is, in fact, a matter of following rules. Of course, iconoclasts such as Foucault (1977) and Feyerabend (1978) have inveighed against the tyranny of rules: in both cases, rules represented illegitimate

power and ideology but, again, the stridency of their different arguments were testimony to the intractability of rules. Rather than whether we can or cannot do without rules, the key question is: how shall we live with them?

6. 'Universities should nurture within themselves and justify publicly a climate in which the unthinkable can be thought' (Williamson and Coffield, 1997: 127). Or, as it might be put, the university becomes a site for the production of 'variation': 'variation in the future can only be mastered *through* variation' (Marton and Marton, 1997, my emphasis).

7. For an argument that exactly parallels the case I am making here for institutional leaders to understand that they have responsibilities towards assisting the collaboration and negotiation of epistemic communities in their universities and that they should, therefore, concern themselves with the 'knowledge policies' of those institutions, see Fuller (1998).

8. For many vice-chancellors, it is less a case of 'back to the rough ground' than of cultivating it in the first place (cf. Dunne, 1993).

9. The relationships between the concepts of leadership and management are complex. Crudely, we might say, 'leadership' is an achievement concept whereas 'management' is a task concept: leadership implies 'followership'. On such matters, and for a detailed analysis of the literature, see Middlehurst (1993).

Chapter 11   Research in a Supercomplex World
(pp. 140–152)

1. The idea of the university as a site of organized research is relatively recent, being not much more than one hundred years old. As Peter Scott once observed, in this sense the university is relatively a modern institution (Scott, 1984).

2. Those of a Popperian persuasion would argue that the growth of research is neither revolutionary nor reactionary in character but is evolutionary (see, for example, Muntz (1985)). Revolution arises through micro changes. Quite apart from its doubtful historical accuracy, the problem for our task here is the matter of responsibility: the evolutionary story allows researchers to duck their responsibilities in producing transformations of our understandings, both for their internal peers and, more importantly, for the wider supercomplex world. The evolutionary story encourages conformity, safety and inwardness.

3. The idea of 'the global age' I take from Albrow (1996).

4. This was not always the case. In the Victorian age, scholars generally saw it as their duty to project their views and findings generally across society. The 'extension movement' at Oxford and Cambridge was as much a vehicle for the nineteenth century academics to promote themselves and the fruits of their academic labours as it was a response to a 'demand' for learning from a public that had not enjoyed a higher education. See Gordon and White (1979); Heyck (1982). See also MacIntyre on the 'collective achievement' in 'creating and sustaining an educated public' in Scotland (1990: Chapter X, 223).

5. See Currie and Newson (1998); Scott (1998b).

6. As we have noted, in trying to unravel this knowledge production messiness, Gibbons and his associates (1994) talk of Modes 1 and 2; essentially, knowledge produced in the academy separately from its use; and knowledge produced in-use, especially in problem-solving in the world of work. However, as others are now observing, there are not just two but many knowledges (Gokulsing and

DaCosta, 1997). Key concepts within 'theoretical' domains take on a practical character. Categories of purity and – by implication – impurity are no longer helpful in demarcating forms of research.

7. For many, there will seem to be a strange and even heretical silence in this chapter: there is no mention of it being among the tasks of researchers that they pursue knowledge and truth. The silence in itself will seem to amount to an attack on the 'Western Rationalistic Tradition' which, as John Searle (1994) sees it, is a crucial part of the traditional conception of the university. But Searle's argument does not hold. Reason understood as disinterested enquiry, as the collaborative search for the better argument, and as the promulgation of innovative and challenging ideas (Searle is rather silent himself on this last) can still be part of the self-understanding of the university without invoking metaphysical notions such as knowledge and truth.

8. On these matters, although he has had little to say about the university as such, I believe that the writings of Rorty are pertinent. See especially his *Philosophy and the Mirror of Nature* (1980) and his *Contingency, Irony and Solidarity* (1989).

Chapter 12   Teaching for a Supercomplex World

(pp. 153–165)

1. Sinclair Goodlad (1976) talks of higher education as a process of developing 'authoritative uncertainty' but it should be clear that under conditions of supercomplexity, uncertainty cannot be authoritative.

2. cf. Niblett (1974: 64): 'If we lose the capacity for learning of a more directly "felt" experiential kind we shall sacrifice more than we can possibly afford.' See also Trigg (1973: especially Chapter 3) for whom commitment involves belief. My point here is the reverse: namely, that belief involves commitment.

3. It was, for Leavis (1969; 1979 edn), one of the tasks of the university – particularly through the 'English School' – to develop that educated community. Recently, Paul Filmer (1997) has implied that, while the Leavis project – requiring, as it would, an 'élite intellectual culture' and representing an anti-industrial spirit – has 'failed' (page 49), the embedded notion within Leavis' conception of a university of 'sustaining the continuity of cultural tradition' (page 52) is one that retains legitimacy.

4. There is much talk currently of higher education having to be a site of 'transformation' but, unless we are careful, the idea of transformation will come to have a double instrumental connotation: firstly, that students develop the skills with which to transform their environment; and secondly, that higher education should be practised as a set of procedures to produce those skills and so effect that transformation in students. (See Harvey and Knight, 1996.) It should be clear that such an interpretation of 'transformation' is going to be entirely inadequate to the conditions of supercomplexity, quite apart from anything that might be termed 'higher education' as such.

5. Admittedly, mass higher education, with its high student:staff ratios, presents challenges in realizing these aims but they are not insuperable. Imaginative and creative educational situations have to be designed. These could include large group workshops, action learning sets, and interactive (that is, student–student) use of the Internet. See Bourner and Flowers (1997). For a more general argument articulating the university as a place of constrained disagreement in which

a central responsibility would be 'to initiate students into conflict', see Goodlad (1995). We could call this 'benevolent disputations' (Dunne, 1993: 23, quoting Plato).

6. For a parallel argument, which includes challenging students to cope with stress, see Eliot Jacques' proposals for 'Learning for Uncertainty' (Jacques, 1970).

7. The concept of the 'ideal speech situation' is one over which Habermas has been subject to much critical comment, especially on its status. In an interview (Dews, 1986: 174), Habermas offered a clarification: 'The ideal speech situation is . . . a description of the conditions under which claims to truth and rightness can be discursively redeemed.' In other words, the ideal speech situation is not purely an ideal but is already presupposed in rational language and, since – as Habermas recognizes – these claimed-for conditions are 'unproblematic', we must presume that the ideal speech situation is *actually* present. It follows that it is entirely legitimate to enquire as to how such conditions can be systematically produced in a pedagogical situation. However, the extent to which such an 'ideal speech situation' is appropriate to a pedagogy for supercomplexity, which is characterized by conditions of power and *incommensurable* conflict, has to be in doubt. The character of such a pedagogical situation requires a different tack altogether, one that takes into account the expressive and experiential character of the conditions of its realization.

For careful discussions of the application of the notions of democracy and the 'ideal speech situation' to the construction of the university as such, see Myerson (1997) and Blake (1997).

8. The quality of students' learning is dependent on their own feelings of self-confidence and self-worth (Abouserie, 1995). It follows that a major, if not the first, responsibility on lecturers as educators is to imbue their students individually with that self-confidence. Unfortunately, pedagogical transactions are all too often characterized by processes and rituals that undermine students' self-confidence. Equally, many lecturers simply do not take into their own self-understandings that they should take the time and effort to give students that self-confidence.

Bibliography

This bibliography contains a limited number of sources that are not cited either in the text or in the notes but which are pertinent to the argument and which constitute additional reading.

Abouserie, R. (1995) Self-esteem and achievement motivation, *Studies in Higher Education*, 20(1): 26.

Adorno, T. and Horkheimer, M. (1979) *Dialectic of Enlightenment*. London: Verso.

Agger, B. (1990) *The Decline of Discourse: Reading, Writing and Resistance in Postmodern Capitalism*. Basingstoke: Falmer.

AGR (Association of Graduate Recruiters) (1995) *Skills for Graduates in the 21st Century*. Cambridge: AGR.

Albrow, M. (1996) *The Global Age*. Cambridge: Polity.

Alexandra, J.C. (1995) *Fin de Siecle Social Theory: Relativism, Reduction and the Problem of Reason*. London: Verso.

Apple, M. (1995) Cultural capital and official knowledge, in M. Berubé and C. Nelson (eds) *Higher Education under Fire: Politics, Economics and the Crisis of the Humanities*. London: Routledge.

Arendt, H. (1958) *The Human Condition*. Chicago: University of Chicago Press.

Argyris, C. and Schön, D. (1974) *Theory and Practice: Increasing Professional Effectiveness*. San Francisco: Jossey-Bass.

Austin, J.L. (1962) *How to do Things with Words*. Oxford: Oxford University Press.

Aviram, A. (1992) The humanist conception of the university: a framework for postmodern higher education, *European Journal of Education*, 27(4): 397–414.

Ayer, A.J. (1956) *The Problems of Philosophy*. London: Penguin.

Barber, M. (1997) *How to do the Impossible: A Guide for Politicians with a Passion for Education*. Inaugural Lecture. London: Institute of Education.

Barnes, B. (1977) *Interests and the Growth of Knowledge*. London: Routledge and Kegan Paul.

Barnett, R. (1990) *The Idea of Higher Education*. Buckingham: Open University Press.

Barnett, R. (1992) *Improving Higher Education: Total Quality Care*. Buckingham: Open University Press.

Barnett, R. (1994) *The Limits of Competence: Knowledge, Higher Education and Society*. Buckingham: Open University Press.

Barnett, R. and Griffin, A. (eds) (1997) *The End of Knowledge in Higher Education*. London: Cassell.

Barrow, R. (1990) *Understanding Skills: Thinking, Feeling, and Caring.* Ontario: Althouse.

Bates, A.W. (1997) Restructuring the university for technological change. Paper presented to conference on *What Kind of University?* London, Higher Education Quality Support Centre, Open University.

Baudrillard, J. (1987) The evil demon of images, extract reprinted in T. Doherty (ed.) (1993) *Postmodernism: A Reader.* Hemel Hempstead: Harvester Wheatsheaf.

Baumann, Z. (1991) *Modernity and the Holocaust.* Cambridge: Polity.

Baumann, Z. (1997) Universities: old, new and different, in A. Smith and F. Webster (eds) *The Postmodern University? Contested Visions of Higher Education in Society.* Buckingham: Open University Press.

Becher, T. (1989) *Academic Tribes and Territories.* Buckingham: Open University Press.

Becher, T. and Kogan, M. (1992) *Process and Structure in Higher Education.* London: Routledge.

Beck, U. (1992) *Risk Society: Towards a New Modernity.* London: Sage.

Beck, U. (1998) Politics of risk society, in J. Franklin (ed.) *The Politics of Risk Society.* Cambridge: Polity in association with IPPR.

Beck, U., Giddens, A. and Lash, S. (1995) *Reflexive Modernization: Politics, Tradition and Aesthetics in the Modern Social Order.* Cambridge: Polity.

Berman, M. (1995) *All That is Solid Melts into Air.* London: Verso.

Bernstein, B. (1996) *Pedagogy, Symbolic Control and Identity.* London: Falmer.

Bernstein, R.J. (1991) *The New Constellation.* Cambridge: Polity.

Berubé, M. and Nelson, C. (eds) (1995) *Higher Education Under Fire: Politics, Economics and the Crisis of the Humanities.* London: Routledge.

Bjorkland, S. (1995) *A University Constitution for Disputation.* Studies of Higher Education and Research. Stockholm: Council for Studies of Higher Education.

Blake, N. (1996) Between postmodernism and anti-modernism: the predicament of educational studies, *British Journal of Educational Studies*, 44(1): 42–65.

Blake, N. (1997) Truth, identity and community in the university, in R. Barnett and A. Griffin (eds) *The End of Knowledge in Higher Education.* London: Cassell.

Blake, N., Smith, R. and Standish, P. (1998) *The Universities We Need: Higher Education after Dearing.* London: Kogan Page.

Bloland, H.G. (1995) Postmodernism and higher education, *Journal of Higher Education*, 66(5): 521–59.

Bottery, M. (1996) The challenge to professionals from the new public management: implications for the teaching profession, *Oxford Review of Education*, 22(2): 179–97.

Bourdieu, P. (1998) *Practical Reason.* Cambridge: Polity.

Bourdieu, P. and Passeron, J-C. (1979) *The Inheritors: French Students and Their Relation to Culture.* London: University of Chicago.

Bourdieu, P., Passeron, J-C. and de Saint Martin, M. (1996) *Academic Discourse.* Cambridge: Polity.

Bourner, T. and Flowers, S. (undated, but 1997) *Teaching and Learning Methods in Higher Education: A Glimpse of the Future.* Brighton: University of Brighton.

Burgen, A. (ed.) (1996) *Goals and Purposes of Higher Education in the 21st Century.* London: Jessica Kingsley.

Burrell, G. (1997) *Pandemonium: Towards a Retro-Organization Theory.* London: Sage.

Cameron, J.M. (1978) *On the Idea of a University.* London: University of Toronto.

Carr, W. and Hartnett, A. (1996) *Education and the Struggle for Democracy.* Buckingham: Open University Press.

Castells, M. (1996) *The Rise of the Network Society.* Oxford: Blackwell.

Castoriadis, C. (1997) *The Imaginary Institution of Society.* Cambridge: Polity.

Christman, J. (ed.) (1989) *The Inner Citadel: Essays on Individual Autonomy.* New York: Oxford University Press.

Clark, B.R. (1998) *Creating Entrepreneurial Universities.* Oxford: Pergamon.

Coffield, F. (1997) *Can the UK become a Learning Society?* Fourth Annual Education Lecture. London: King's College.

Coffield, F. and Williamson, B. (eds) (1997) *Repositioning Higher Education.* Buckingham: Open University Press.

Coldstream, P. (1999) *A Responsible Conversation . . . : What universities and industry have to say to each other.* Professorial lecture. London: Institute of Education.

Cole, J.R., Barber, E.G. and Graubard, S.R. (eds) (1994) *The Research University in a Time of Discontent.* London: Johns Hopkins University.

Collier, G. (1993) Learning moral judgement in higher education, *Studies in Higher Education* 18(3): 287–97.

Connor, S. (1993) The necessity of value, in J. Squires (ed.) *Principled Positions: Postmodernism and the Rediscovery of Value.* London: Lawrence and Wishart.

Cooper, D.E. (1983) *Authenticity and Learning: Nietzsche's Educational Philosophy.* London: Routledge and Kegan Paul.

Cowen, R. (1996) Performativity, post-modernity and the university, *Comparative Education,* 32(2): 245–58.

Crittenden, B. (1978) Autonomy as an aim of education, in K. Strike and K. Egan (eds) *Ethics and Educational Policy.* London: Routledge and Kegan Paul.

Currie, J. and Newson, J. (eds) (1998) *Universities and Globalization: Critical Perspectives.* London: Sage.

Currie, J. and Vidovich, L. (1998) Micro-economic reform through managerialism in American and Australian universities, in J. Currie and J. Newson (eds) *Universities and Globalization: Critical Perspectives.* London: Sage.

Cuthbert, R. (1996) *Working in Higher Education.* Buckingham: Open University Press.

CVCP (Committee of Vice-Chancellors and Principals) (1996) Vision Statement and Main Recommendations. Vol. 1 from *Our Universities, Our Future* (4 Vols). Submission to the National Committee of Inquiry into Higher Education public consultation. London: CVCP.

Daniels, J. (1998) *Mega-Universities and Knowledge Media.* London: Kogan Page.

Davie, G. (1961) *The Democratic Intellect.* Edinburgh: Edinburgh University Press.

Davie, G. (1986) *The Crisis of the Democratic Intellect.* Edinburgh: Polygon.

Davies, P. and the Board and Society of the United American Methodist Church (1974) *The Truth about Kent State: A Challenge to the American Conscience.* New York: Noonday.

Dearden, R. (1972) Autonomy and education, in R.F. Dearden, P.H. Hirst and R.S. Peters (eds) *Education and Reason,* Part 3 of Education and the Development of Reason. London: Routledge and Kegan Paul.

Delanty, G. (1998a) The idea of the university in the global era: from knowledge as an end to the end of knowledge, *Social Epistemology,* 12(1): 3–25.

Delanty, G. (1998b) Rethinking the university: the autonomy, contestation and reflexivity of knowledge, *Social Epistemology,* 12(1): 103–13.

Derrida, J. (1991) Of Grammatology, extract in P. Kamuf (ed.) *A Derrida Reader: Between the Blinds.* Hemel Hempstead: Harvester.

Derrida, J. (1992) Mochlos; or, the Conflict of the Faculties, in R. Rand (ed.) *Logomachia: The Conflict of the Faculties.* London: University of Nebraska.

Dews, J. (1986) *Habermas: Autonomy and Solidarity.* London: Verso.

Dickman, H. (ed.) (1993) *The Imperilled Academy.* New Brunswick: Transaction.

Dickson, D. (1988) *The New Politics of Science*. London: University of Chicago.

Doherty, T. (ed.) (1993) *Postmodernism: A Reader*. Hemel Hempstead: Harvester Wheatsheaf.

Dunne, J. (1993) *Back to the Rough Ground: 'Phronesis' and 'Techne' in Modern Philosophy and in Aristotle*. Notre Dame: University of Notre Dame.

Feyerabend, P. (1978) *Against Method*. London: Verso.

Feyerabend, P. (1982) *Science in a Free Society*. London: Verso.

Filmer, P. (1997) Disinterestedness and the modern university, in A. Smith and F. Webster (eds), *The Postmodern University? Contested Visions of Higher Education in Society*. Buckingham: Open University Press.

Foucault, M. (1977) *Discipline and Punish*. London: Allen Lane.

Fox, C.J. and Miller, H. (1996) *Postmodern Public Administration: Toward Discourse*. London: Sage.

Franklin, J. (ed.) (1998) *The Politics of Risk Society*. Cambridge: Polity in association with IPPR.

Fukuyama, F. (1993) *The End of History and the Last Man*. New York: Avon.

Fuller, S. (1998) The Position: Interdisciplinarity as Interpenetration, in W. Newell (ed.) *Interdisciplinarity*. New York: The College Board.

Funtowicz, S. and Ravetz, J. (1993) Science for the Post-Normal Age, *Futures*, 25(7): 739–55.

Galbraith, J.K. (1969) *The New Industrial State*. Harmondsworth, Middlesex: Penguin.

Gellner, E. (1964) *Thought and Change*. London: Weidenfeld and Nicolson.

Gellner, E. (1974) *Legitimation of Belief*. Cambridge: Cambridge University Press.

Gellner, E. (1991 edn) *Plough, Sword and Book*. London: Paladin.

Gellner, E. (1992) *Reason and Culture*. Oxford: Blackwell.

Gellner, E. (1998) *Language and Solitude*. Cambridge: Cambridge University Press.

Gergen, K.J. (1994) The Limits of Pure Critique, in H.W. Simons and M. Billig (eds) *After Postmodernism: Reconstructing Ideology Critique*. London: Sage.

Gettier, E.L. (1963) Is justified true belief knowledge? in A. Phillips Griffiths (ed.) *Knowledge and Belief*. Oxford: Oxford University Press.

Gibbons, M. (1998) *Higher Education Relevance in the 21st Century*. Washington: World Bank.

Gibbons, M., Limoges, C., Nowotny, H., Schwarzman, S., Scott, P. and Trow, M. (1994) *The New Production of Knowledge: The Dynamics of Science and Research in Contemporary Societies*. London: Sage.

Giddens, A. (1991) *The Consequences of Modernity*. Cambridge: Polity.

Giddens, A. (1992) *Modernity and Self-Identity: Self and Society in the Late Modern Age*. Cambridge: Polity.

Giddens, A. (1994) *Beyond Left and Right*. Cambridge: Polity.

Giddens, A. (1995) Living in a Post-Traditional Society, in U. Beck, A. Giddens and S. Lash (eds) *Reflexive Modernization: Politics, Tradition and Aesthetics in the Modern Social Order*. Cambridge: Polity.

Giroux, H. (1991) *Border Crossings*. London: Routledge.

Gokulsing, K. and DaCosta, C. (eds) (1997) *Usable Knowledges as the Goal of University Education*. Lampeter: Edwin Mallen Press.

Goodlad, S. (1976) *Conflict and Consensus in Higher Education*. London: Hodder and Stoughton.

Goodlad, S. (1995) *The Quest for Quality*. Buckingham: Open University Press.

Gordon, P. and White, J. (1979) *Philosophers as Educational Reformers*. London: Routledge and Kegan Paul.

Gorz, A. (1989) *Critique of Economic Reason.* London: Verso.

Gouldner, A. (1979) *The Future of Intellectuals and the Rise of the New Class.* London: Macmillan.

Green, A. (1997) *Education, Globalization and the Nation State.* Basingstoke: Macmillan.

Grundy, S. (1987) *Curriculum: Product or Praxis.* Lewes: Falmer.

Gutman, A. (1987) *Democratic Education.* Princeton: Princeton University Press.

Haber, H.F. (1994) *Beyond Postmodern Politics: Lyotard, Rorty, Foucault.* New York: Routledge.

Habermas, J. (1972) *The Rational Society.* London: Heinemann.

Habermas, J. (1978 edn) *Knowledge and Human Interests.* London: Heinemann.

Habermas, J. (1989) *The Theory of Communicative Competence: The Critique of Functionalist Reason.* Volume 2. Cambridge: Polity.

Habermas, J. (1990) *The Philosophical Discourse of Modernity.* Cambridge: Polity.

Habermas, J. (1991) *The Theory of Communicative Competence: Reason and the Rationalization of Society.* Volume 1. Cambridge: Polity.

Hague, D. (1991) *Beyond Universities: A New Republic of the Intellect.* London: IEA.

Halsey, A.H. (1992) *Decline of Donnish Dominion.* Oxford: Clarendon.

Handy, C. (1990) *The Age of Unreason.* London: Arrow.

Harker, B. (1995) Postmodernism and Quality, *Quality in Higher Education,* 1(1): 31–40.

Harvey, L. and Knight, P.T. (1996) *Transforming Higher Education.* Buckingham: Open University Press.

Heidegger, M. (1985) The Self-Assertion of the German University. Address (1933), delivered on the solemn assumption of the Rectorate of the University of Freiburg. *Review of Metaphysics,* 38, 467–502.

Held, D. (1983) *Introduction to Critical Theory.* London: Hutchinson.

Heyck, T.W. (1982) *The Transformation of Intellectual Life in Victorian England.* Beckenham: Croom Helm.

Horton, R. (1971) African Traditional Thought and Western Science, in M.F.D. Young (ed.) *Knowledge and Control.* London: Collier-Macmillan.

Hutton, W. (1995) *The State We're In.* London: Jonathan Cape.

Jacques, E. (1970) *Work, Creativity and Social Justice.* London: Heinemann.

Jarvis, P. (1992) *Paradoxes of Learning: On Becoming an Individual in Society.* San Francisco: Jossey-Bass.

Jaspers, K. (1960) *The Idea of the University.* London: Peter Owen.

Jay, M. (1996) *The Dialectical Imagination.* London: University of California.

Kahn, C.H. (1987) *The Art and Thought of Heraclitus.* Cambridge: University of Cambridge.

Kant, I. (1992) *The Conflict of the Faculties.* Trans. Mary J. Gregor. London: University of Nebraska.

Karseth, B. (1997) How to Become a Proper University Discipline: The Conflict of Knowledge in Nursing Science. Paper presented at conference on *What Kind of University?* London: Higher Education Group, Open University.

Kells, H.R. (1992) *Self-Regulation in Higher Education: A Multi-National Perspective in Collaborative Systems of Quality Assurance and Control.* London: Jessica Kingsley.

Kerr, C. (1972) *The Uses of the University.* Massachusetts: Harvard University.

Kerr, C. (1994) *Higher Education Cannot Escape History: Issues for the Twenty-first Century.* Albany: State University of New York.

Kuhn, T. (1970) *The Structure of Scientific Revolutions.* London: University of Chicago.

Laclau, E. (1996) *Emancipation(s).* London: Verso.

Ladwig, J. (1995) Educational intellectuals and corporate politics, in R. Smith and
    P. Wexler (eds) *After Postmodernism: Education, Politics and Identity*. London: Falmer.
Leach, E. (1968) *A Runaway World?* London: BBC.
Leavis, F.R. (1969) *English Literature in our Time and the University*. London: Chatto
    and Windus.
Leavis, F.R. (1979 edn) *Education and the University*. Cambridge: Cambridge Univer-
    sity Press.
Lindop, Sir N. (1985) *Academic Validation in Public Sector Higher Education*. The Report
    of the Committee of Enquiry into the Academic Validation of Degree Courses
    in Public Sector Higher Education, Cmnd 9501. London: HMSO.
Lukasiewicz, J. (1994) *The Ignorance Explosion*. Ottawa: Carleton University Press.
Lyotard, J-F. (1984) *The Postmodern Condition: A Report on Knowledge*. Manchester:
    Manchester University Press.
Lyotard, J-F. (1992) *The Postmodern Explained to Children: Correspondence 1982–1985*.
    London: Turnaround.
Maassen, P.A.M. and Van Vught, F.A. (eds) (1996) *Inside Academia: New Challenges for
    the Academic Profession*. Utrecht: De Tijdstroom.
Macfarlane, B. (1994) Issues concerning the development of the undergraduate
    business studies curriculum in UK higher education, *Journal of European Business
    Education* 4(1): 1–14.
MacIntyre, A. (1970) *Marcuse*. London: Fontana/Collins.
MacIntyre, A. (1985) *After Virtue: A Study in Moral Theory*. London: Duckworth.
MacIntyre, A. (1990) *Three Rival Versions of Moral Enquiry*. London: Duckworth.
Marcuse, A. (1968) *One-Dimensional Man: The Ideology of Industrial Society*. London:
    Sphere.
Marcuse, A. (1969) *An Essay on Liberation*. London: Penguin.
Marton, F. and Marton, S. (1997) *The University of Learning or the University of Politics?*
    Paper presented at conference on 'What Kind of University', London: Higher
    Education Quality Support Centre, Open University.
McCarthy, E.D. (1996) *Knowledge as Culture*. London: Routledge.
McClaren, P. (1995) *Critical Pedagogy and Predatory Culture*. London: Routledge.
Middlehurst, R. (1993) *Leading Academics*. Buckingham: Open University Press.
Middlehurst, R. and Elton, L. (1992) Leadership and Management in Higher
    Education, *Studies in Higher Education*, 17(3): 251–64.
Midgley, M. (1989) *Wisdom, Information and Wonder*. London: Routledge.
Moberly, Sir W. (1949) *The Crisis in the University*. London: SCM.
Montefiore, A. (ed.) (1975) *Neutrality and Impartiality: The University and Political
    Commitment*. London: Cambridge University Press.
Muller, S. (1994) Presidential leadership, in J.R. Cole, E.G. Barber and S.R. Graubard
    (eds) *The Research University in a Time of Discontent*. London: Johns Hopkins
    University.
Muller, S. (1996a) The Advent of 'The University of Calculation', in S. Muller (ed.)
    Universities in the Twenty-First Century. Providence: Berghahn.
Muller, S. (ed.) (1996b) *Universities in the Twenty-First Century*. Providence: Berghahn.
Muntz, P. (1985) *Our Knowledge of the Growth of Knowledge: Popper or Wittgenstein?*
    London: Routledge and Kegan Paul.
Myerson, G. (1997) A New University Space: A dialogue on argument, democracy
    and the university, in R. Barnett and A. Griffin (eds) *The End of Knowledge in
    Higher Education*. London: Cassell.
Nash, A.S. (1945) *The University and the Modern World*. London: SCM.

NCIHE (National Committee of Inquiry into Higher Education) (1997) *Higher Education for a Learning Society*. London: HMSO.

Neave, G. (1990) On preparing for markets: trends in higher education in Western Europe, 1988–1990, *European Journal of Education* 25(2): 105–23.

Neave, G. (ed.) (1998) *The Evaluative State Revisited*. Issue of *European Journal of Education*, 33(3).

Newman, J.H. (1976) *The Idea of a University* (ed. I.T. Ker). Oxford: Oxford University Press.

Niblett, W.R. (1974) *Universities Between Two Worlds*. London: University of London.

Nietzsche, F. (1988 edn) *Beyond Good and Evil*. Harmondsworth, Middlesex: Penguin.

Nisbet, R. (1971) *The Degradation of the Academic Dogma*. London: Heinemann.

Norris, C. (1996) *Reclaiming Truth: Contribution to a Critique of Cultural Relativism*. London: Lawrence and Wishart.

Nowotny, H. (1996) *Time: The Modern and Postmodern Experience*. Cambridge: Polity.

O'Hear, A. (1988) Academic freedom and the university, in M. Tight (ed.) *Academic Freedom and Responsibility*. Milton Keynes: Open University Press.

Ortega y Gasset, J. (1946) *Mission of the University*. London: Kegan Paul, Trench, Trubner & Co.

Perry, W.G. (1988) Different worlds in the same classroom, in P. Ramsden (ed.) *Improving Learning: New Perspectives*. London: Kogan Page.

Peters, M. (ed.) (1995) *Education and the Postmodern Condition*. Connecticut: Bergin and Garvey.

Piper, D. (1997) Authentic teaching and learning in cyberspace: a Heideggerian perspective, *Westminster Studies in Education*, 20, 75–87.

Plumb, J.H. (ed.) (1963) *Crisis in the Humanities*. Harmondsworth, Middlesex: Penguin.

Polanyi, M. (1966) *The Tacit Dimension*. New York: Doubleday.

Popper, Sir K. (1963) *Conjectures and Refutations*. London: Routledge and Kegan Paul.

Popper, Sir K. (1966) On the sources of knowledge and of ignorance, in J.N. Findlay (ed.) *Studies in Philosophy*. London: Oxford University Press.

Popper, Sir K. (1975 edn) *Objective Knowledge*. Oxford: Oxford University Press.

Popper, Sir K. (1977) Normal science and its dangers, in I. Lakatos and A. Musgrave (eds) *Criticism and the Growth of Knowledge*. Cambridge: Cambridge University Press.

Power, M. (1997) *The Audit Society: Rituals of Verification*. Oxford: Oxford University Press.

Quality Assurance Agency (1998) *Higher Quality*. Nos 3 & 4. Gloucester: Quality Assurance Agency.

Ramsden, P. (1998) *Learning to Lead in Higher Education*. London: Routledge.

Ransom, S. (1994) *Towards the Learning Society*. London: Cassell.

Rashdall, H. (1895) *The Universities of Europe in the Middle Ages*. Oxford: Clarendon Press.

Ravetz, J. (1993) A leap into the unknown, *Times Higher Education Supplement*, 19–20.

Readings, B. (1996) *The University in Ruins*. Massachusetts: Harvard University Press.

Reich, R. (1992) *The Work of Nations: Preparing Ourselves for 21st Century Capitalism*. New York: Vintage Books.

Reid, I. (1996) *Higher Education or Education for Hire? Language and Values in Australian Universities*. Rockhampton: Central Queensland University.

Ritzer, G. (1997) McUniversity in the Postmodern Consumer Society, Chapter 12 in his *The McDonaldization Thesis: Explorations and Extensions*. London: Sage.

Roberts, J. (1990) *German Philosophy: An Introduction*. Cambridge: Polity.

Robbins, Lord L. (1963) *Higher Education.* Report of the Committee appointed by the Prime Minister. Cmnd. 2154. London: HMSO.

Robinson, F.N. (1957 edn) *The Works of Geoffrey Chaucer.* Oxford: Oxford University Press.

Rorty, R. (1980) *Philosophy and the Mirror of Nature.* Oxford: Blackwell.

Rorty, R. (1989) *Contingency, Irony and Solidarity.* Cambridge: Cambridge University Press.

Rothblatt, S. (1988) *The Idea of the Idea of a University and its Antithesis.* Seminar on the Sociology of Culture, La Trobe University, Australia.

Rothblatt, S. (1993) The limbs of Osiris: liberal Eden in the English-speaking world, in S. Rothblatt and B. Wittrock (eds) *The European and American University Since 1800: Historical and Sociological Essays.* Cambridge: Cambridge University Press.

Rothblatt, S. (1997) *The Modern University and its Discontents.* Cambridge: Cambridge University Press.

Rouse, J. (1994) *Knowledge and Power: Toward a Political Philosophy of Science.* Ithaca: Cornell.

Ryle, G. (1949) *The Concept of Mind.* Harmondsworth, Middlesex: Penguin.

Sadlik, J. (1998) Globalization and concurrent challenges for higher education, in P. Scott (ed.) *The Globalization of Higher Education.* Buckingham: Open University Press.

Schmitt, F.E. (ed.) (1994) *Socializing Epistemology: The Social Dimensions of Knowledge.* Maryland: Rowman and Littlefield.

Schön, D. (1971) *Beyond the Stable State.* London: Temple Smith.

Schön, D. (1987) *Educating the Reflective Practitioner.* London: Jossey-Bass.

Scott, P. (1984) *The Crisis of the University.* Beckenham: Croom Helm.

Scott, P. (1995) *The Meanings of Mass Higher Education.* Buckingham: Open University Press.

Scott, P. (1997) The changing role of the university in the production of new knowledge, *Tertiary Education and Management,* 3(1): 5–14.

Scott, P. (1998a) The Postmodern University?, in A. Smith and F. Webster (eds) *The Postmodern University? Contested Visions of Higher Education in Society.* Buckingham: Open University Press.

Scott, P. (ed.) (1998b) *The Globalization of Higher Education.* Buckingham: Open University Press.

Searle, J. (1994) Rationality and realism: what is at stake?, in J. Cole, E. Barber and S. Graubard (eds) *The Research University in a Time of Discontent.* Baltimore: Johns Hopkins University Press.

Senge, P. (1990) *The Fifth Discipline: The Art and Practice of the Learning Organization.* London: Century Business.

Sloman, A. (1964) *A University in the Making.* London: BBC.

Smith, A. and Webster, F. (1997) An affirming flame, in A. Smith and F. Webster (eds) *The Postmodern University? Contested Visions of Higher Education in Society.* Buckingham: Open University Press.

Smith, D. and Langslow, A. K. (1999) *The Idea of a University.* London: Jessica Kingsley.

Smyth, J. (ed.) (1995) *Academic Work.* Buckingham: Open University Press.

Soper, K. (1993) Postmodernism, subjectivity and the question of value, in J. Squires (ed.) *Principled Positions: Postmodernism and the Rediscovery of Value.* London: Lawrence and Wishart.

Squires, J. (ed.) (1993) *Principled Positions: Postmodernism and the Rediscovery of Value.* London: Lawrence and Wishart.

Standish, P. (1997) Heidegger and the technology of further education, *Journal of Philosophy of Education*, 31(3): 439–59.

Stehr, N. (1994) *Knowledge Societies*. London: Sage.

Steiner, G. (1984) *George Steiner: a Reader*. Harmondsworth, Middlesex: Penguin.

Stenhouse, L. (1967) *Culture & Education*. London: Nelson.

Strike, K.A. (1978) Liberality, neutrality and the modern university, in K.A. Strike and K. Egan (eds) *Ethics and Educational Policy*. London: Routledge and Kegan Paul.

Strike, K.A. and Egan, K. (eds) (1978) *Ethics and Educational Policy*. London: Routledge and Kegan Paul.

Stryker, L. (1996) The Holocaust and Liberal Education, in B. Brecher, O. Fleischmann and J. Halliday (eds) *The University in a Liberal State*. Aldershot: Avebury.

Taylor, C. (1991) *The Ethics of Authenticity*. London: Harvard University Press.

Taylor, C. (1992) *Sources of the Self*. Cambridge: Cambridge University Press.

Trigg, R. (1973) *Reason and Commitment*. London: Cambridge University Press.

Trow, M. (1973) *Problems in the Transition from Elite to Mass Higher Education*. Berkeley, CA: Carnegie Commission on Higher Education.

Trow, M. (1994) *Managerialism and the Academic Profession: Quality and Control*. Higher Education Report No 2. London: Open University Quality Support Centre.

Trowler, P.R. (1998) *Academics Responding to Change*. Buckingham: Open University Press.

UNESCO (1998) *Statistical Outlook on Higher Education*, 1980–1995. Report for UNESCO Conference on 'Higher Education in the Twenty-first Century: Vision and Action'. Paris: UNESCO.

Usher, R. and Edwards, R. (1994) *Postmodernism and Education*. London: Routledge.

Velody, I. and Williams, R. (eds) (1998) *The Politics of Constructivism*. London: Sage.

von Krogh, G. and Roos, J. (1996) *Managing Knowledge: Perspectives on Cooperation and Competition*. London: Sage.

Weber, M. (1991 edn) Science as a Vocation, in H.H. Gerth and C. Wright Mills, *From Max Weber: Essays in Sociology*. London: Routledge.

Webster, F. (1998) The idea of the university: a response to Delanty, *Social Epistemology* 12(1): 67–72.

Weil, S. (1997) Postgraduate education and lifelong learning as collaborative inquiry in action: an emergent model, in R. Burgess (ed.) *Beyond the First Degree*. Buckingham: Open University Press.

Weil, S. (1998) *Recreating Universities for 'Beyond the stable state': from 'Dearingesque' systematic control to post-Dearing systematic learning and inquiry*. Mimeo. Northampton: Nene College.

White, J. (1997) *Education and the End of Work*. London: Cassell.

Williams, R. (1989) *Resources of Hope*. London: Verso.

Williamson, B. and Coffield, F. (1997) Repositioning higher education, in F. Coffield and B. Williamson (eds) *Repositioning Higher Education*. Buckingham: Open University Press.

Winter, R. (1995) The university of life plc: the industrialization of higher education?, in J. Smyth (ed.) *Academic Work*. Buckingham: Open University Press.

Winter, R. (1996) New liberty, new discipline: academic work in the new higher education, in R. Cuthbert (ed.) *Working in Higher Education*. Buckingham: Open University Press.

Wittgenstein, L. (1978) *Philosophical Investigations*. Oxford: Blackwell.

Wolff, R.P. (1997 edn) *The Ideal of the University*. New Brunswick: New Jersey.

Wyatt, J. (1990) *Commitment to Higher Education.* Buckingham: Open University Press.
Wyatt, J. (1994) 'Maps of knowledge: do they form an atlas?', in R. Barnett (ed.) *Academic Community: Discourse or Discord?* London: Jessica Kingsley.
Young, R. (1989) *A Critical Theory of Education: Habermas and our Children's Future.* Hemel Hempstead: Harvester Wheatsheaf.

Index

Particularly significant references are in bold type; references to endnotes (pp. 173–82) are in italics.

Abouserie, R., *182*
academic autonomy, 1, 55
academic class, 36
academic community, 16, 105–6, 114, 117–18, 137, 170
　academic community, a self-critical, 106, 117–18, 122
academic freedom, 14–15, *173*
academic illiteracy, 44
access, 50
accountability, 17, 128, *173*
action, 90, 155–8, 162–4
action learning, 18, 37
action research, 42
adult students, 78
　see also mature students; students
Agger, B., 148
Albrow, M., *180*
anything goes, 31, 38, 99, **116–17**, 122
Arendt, H., 49, *175*
Argyris, M., 68, 156
arts, 23, 90
astronomy, 87
audit of universities, epistemological, 135
audit society, 15, 23, *178*
Auschwitz, 25, 46, 69, *179*
Austin, J., *178*
authenticity, 120, 122, *179*
authority, 160–1
autonomy, 53–4, 129

Aviram, A., 77
Ayer, A., 53, *175*

Barber, M., 151
Barnes, B., 24
Barnett, R., 20, *173, 176, 178*
Barrow, R., *178*
Baudrillard, J., 76
Baumann, Z., 25
Becher, T., 80, 86, *178*
Beck, U., 46, 71, 161, *176, 177*
benchmarking, 20
being, 154–5, **157**, 164, 167, 170
　being, modes of, 169, 171
　see also human being
Berman, M., *179*
Bernstein, B., *176*
Bernstein, R., 48
Berubé, M., *177*
Bildung, 53, *175*
Billig, M., *174*
biochemistry, 93
biology, 89
biotechnology, 17, 41, 95
Bjorkland, S., 160
Blake, N., *182*
borders, 107
　see also boundaries
Bottery, M., *173*
boundaries, 16, 27, 38–9, 80, 102, 107, 115, 148

Bourdieu, P., 13, 50
Bourner, T., *181*
brave new world, 21, 43, 62, 78–9, 141, 177
breadth, 30, 168
Burrell, G., *179*
business studies, 24, 37, 41

Cambridge, University of, *173*, *180*
Cameron, J., 72
capital, cultural, 20
   capital, discursive, 105
   capital, financial, 20–1
   capital, intellectual, 20–1, 32, 101, 116
   capital symbolic, 21
Carr, W., 50
Castells, M., *174*
Castoriadis, C., 151, *176*
challengeability, 63, **65–6**, 67–8, 74, 139, 153
chaos, 63, 130
Chaucer, G., 23
chemistry, 37, 154–5
Christman, J., *175*
citizenship, 50, 146
civic role, 170
civil society, 151
Clark, B., 99
Coffield, F., 13, 52, *180*
Coldstream, P., *174*
collegiality, 28, 58, 113–15
Collier, G., 160, *179*
commitment, 53, 122, *175*
commodification, 15
communication, 74, 136–8, 150, 157
   communication, distorted, 131, *179*
communicative dexterity, *178*
community, 16, 50, 116
competence, 27, 49, 117
complexity, 6, 29, 76
Connor, S., 116
'conscience of society', 30, 151, 168
consultancy, 17, 36, 68–9, 116
consumerism, 28
consumption, universities as sites of, 13
contestability, 63, **65–6**, 67–8, 74–5, 158, 160
control, 161
conversation, 92–3, 107

Cooper, D., *179*
corporate universities, 31
Council for Industry and Higher Education, *174*
courage, 81
Cowen, R., 14
creativity, 69, 89
critical dialogue, 57, 83, 102
critical self-reflection, 54, 56
critical theory, 56, 81, *176*
critique, **54–6**, 57, 69–70
Crittenden, B., *175*
culture, 13
curriculum, 28, 35, 171
Currie, J., *174*, *179*, *180*
CVCP, 32, *176*

DaCosta, C., 14, *181*
Daniels, J., *174*
Davie, W., 51
Davies, P., 55
Dearden, R., *175*
Dearing Report
   see NCIHE
death of the university, 11–13, 22
Delanty, G., 30, 76
democracy, **50–2**, 57, 116
Derrida, J., 2–3, 79, *174*
design, 87
detraditionalization, 5, 28, 58, 62, 77–8, 154
Dews, J., *182*
Dickman, H., 112
disciplines, 21, 31, 36, 80, 85–9, 91, 93, 95, 149
disinterestedness, 29
disjunction, 159–60
disputations, 160
dissolving university, 17–18, 20, 94, 148
diversity, 31, 114, 168
Dunne, J., *180, 182*
Durkheim, E., 16

ecology, 87, 112
economic development, 49
economics, 37
Edwards, R., 54
Elton, L., *179*
emancipation, 32, 38, **56–7**, *176*
emotion, 157

engagement, 110, 145
engineering, 37, 41–2
English, 86
enlightenment, 47, 72, 95, 168–9, 172
enlightenment, the, 23–4, 31–4, 38,
    69, 71
enterprise society, 23
entrepreneurial university, the, 99,
    121, 172
epistemologies, 37, 41–2, 45, 94, 149
equality, 38, 50
essentialism, 4, 47–8
Essex, University of, *173*
ethical dimension, 157
ethics committees, 81
ethos, **Chapter 9**
'evaluative state', 1, 105, *178*
excellence, 2, 99, 117, 120
exchange value, 15, 39
experiential learning, 42

Feyerabend, P., 75, *178*, *179*
Filmer, P., *181*
fine art, 148
Flowers, S., *181*
footnotes, 146–8
forms of knowledge, 18
'forms of life', 38
Foucault, M., 80, *179*
foundations, lack of, 4, 45, 56, 58, 100
foundations of universities, 1–3, 7,
    62–3, 84
fragility, 63–4, **65–6**, 67, 69, 71, 78, 84
frameworks, 56, 63, **75–7**, 82, 119, 131,
    149, 154, 158, 163–4, 167
  frameworks, conflict between, 75–6,
    88
  frameworks, multiplication of, 6,
    137, 151
freedom, 56
French, 93
Fukuyama, F., 77
Fuller, S., *180*
Funtowicz, S., *176*

Galbraith, J., *176*
Gellner, E., 36, *177*, *178*
Gergen, K., *174*
German universities, 25
Gettier, E., *175*

Gibbons, M., 17, 36, 108, *180*
Giddens, A., 28, 42–3, 71, *176*
Giroux, H., *178*
'global age', 1, 15, 31, 73, 90, 142,
    144, 148, 153, 157, 164, *180*
global economy, 55, 77–8, 106, 131
globalization, 3, 15, 39, 58, 133, 142,
    174
goals of universities, 1
  see also university, purposes of
Gokulsing, M., 14, *180*
Goodlad, S., *181*
Gordon, P., *180*
Gouldner, A., 36
grand narratives, 56–8, 61, 75, 164
Gutman, A., 50

Haber, H., *176*
Habermas, J., 26, 32, 52, 55, 74, 80,
    160, *174–5*, *175–6*, *179*, *182*
'habitus', 13
Hague, D., 35, 108
Halsey, A., 128
Handy, C., 49–50
Hartnett, A., 50
Harvey, L., *174*, *181*
health studies, 148, 155
Held, D., *176*
Henry VIII, 18
Heraclitus, 77, 164, *177*
Hesse, H., ix
Heyck, T., *180*
higher, concept of, 158, 164
higher education, 49–50, 154, 158–9
higher learning, 29, 78, 83, 158
history, 81
Horton, R., 80
human being, 153, 160, 164
  see also being
humanities, 23, 53, 87, 90, 105, 147,
    178
Humanities and Arts Research
    Council, 23
Humboldt, W., 2
Hutton, W., 50
Huxley, A., 78
hyper-complexity, 76

ideal speech situation, 160, *182*
identity, 54, 58, 68, 87, 158

identity, academic, 106, 108, 115, 148
see also self-identity
ideologies, 16, 19, 33–4, 70–1, 115, 144, 146, 150, 167
ideology, 33, 40, 75, 81, 88, 120, 144, *180*
ideology, end of, 30, 32, *174*
ignorance, 43–5, 63–4
impact, 20, 34, 39, 150, 172
impartiality, 29, 112
incommensurability, *177*
infomatics, 17
information society, 23
information technology, 3, 15, 23, 58, 89, 119
see also Internet
instability, 58, 78, 141
instrumentalism, fork of, 90
interdisciplinarity, 104, 137
interdisciplinarity, critical, 104–5, *178*
see also multidisciplinarity
international relations, 90
Internet, 17–19, 21, 31, 48, 92, 137
see also information technology
'intimacy' of higher education, 53
irony
see self-irony
is–ought gap, 157
ivory tower, 17, 41

Jarvis, P., 160
Jaspers, K., 5
Jay, M., *176*
justice, 1, 50–1, 75

Kahn, C., *177*
Kant, E., 2, 85, 95
Kells, H., 101
Kent State University, 55
Kerr, C., 5, 14, 48
Knight, P.T., *174*, *181*
knowing, 157, 164
knowledge, 1, 21–2, 24, **Chapter 3**, 37–8, 40, 43, 45, 47–8, 52, 68–9, 77, 85, 95, 157, 159, 164, 167, 170, *181*
knowledge, absolute, 70
knowledge acquisition, 39

knowledge as contemplation, 37
knowledge as praxis, 37
knowledge creation, 39
knowledge, definitions of, 57
knowledge, ideas of, 68
knowledge-in-use, 17–18
knowledge, its own end, 14, 17, 24–5
knowledge networks, 21
knowledge policies, 170, *180*
knowledge processes, 18, 21–2
knowledge production, 17, 43–5, 51, 66–7, 108, 132, *174*, *180*
knowledge, propositional, 18, 157
knowledge resources, 46
knowledges, 14, 17, 35, 38, 43
knowledge society, 14, 17, 23, 27, 34, 36, 44, 55
knowledge, universal, 72
see also epistemologies
Kogan, M., *178*
Kuhn, T., 141, 143, *176*, *177*, *179*

labour market, 89
Laclau, E., *176*
Ladwig, J., *178*
languages, 39
Lash, S., 71
Leach, E., 71
leadership in universities, 106–8, 110, 130, 137–9, 170–1, *179*, *180*
learning, 128
learning, higher, 78
learning organization, 128
learning organization, university as, 128
learning society, 23, 52
Leavis, F., 80, 86, *181*
lectures, 159
legitimation crisis, 30, 61, *173*
leisure studies, 37
liberal education, 25
liberalism, 116
liberation, 56, 72
life chances, 51
lifelong learning, 89
life-world, 39, 162, *174*
life-world becoming, 14, *173*
Lindop, Sir N., *178*
Lukasiewicz, J., 43

Lyotard, J.-F., 14, 38, 40, 42–3, 75, *173, 174, 179*

Maassen, P., *179*
Macfarlane, B., 24
MacIntyre, A., 55, *175, 176, 177, 180*
management studies, 95
management, university, 111, 128–32, 138, 170, *180*
managerialism, 58, 111, 129
'manufactured risk', 42–3
Marcuse, H., 55
market in higher education, 14, 20, 23, 26, 38–9, 42–3, 52, 99, 101, 112, 142, 153, *176*
Marton, F., *180*
Marton, S., *180*
mass higher education, 5, 13, 19, 48, 52, 54, 92, 101, 114, 153, *173, 181*
mature students, 39
    see also adult students; students
McClaren, P., *178*
McDonaldization, 102
media dons, 142
mediaeval universities, 12, 16, 72, 147, 172, *173*
medicine, 6, 17, 66
megauniversity, 115
metanarratives, 75
Middlehurst, R., *179, 180*
Midgley, M., 44
mind, 162
mind, critical, 161
minds, 164
mission statements, 94, 106, 120
mission, university, 114
Moberly, Sir, W., 5
modernity, 3–4, 20, 25
modern society, 23, *179*
modern university, the, 14–16, 20, 28–30, 35, 50, 57–8, 61, 67, 86
    cf. post-modern university
Montefiore, A., 112
moral virtues, 27, 29
    see also virtue; virtues of the university
Muller, S., 115, *179*
multidisciplinarity, 31
'multiversity', 14, 48, 115

Muntz, P., *180*
Myerson, G., *182*

Nash, A., 25
Nazi regime, 25, 156
NCIHE, 30–1, 34, 50, 109, 151, *173, 174, 175, 176*
Neave, G., *178*
negotiability, 74
Nelson, C., *177*
network society, *174*
neutrality, 112–13, 115, 122
Newman, J.H., 5, 14, 25
'new public management', 14
Newson, J., *174, 180*
Niblett, W.R., *181*
Nietzsche, F., 45, 77, 82, *175, 177, 179*
Nisbet, R., 25, 68
Norris, C., 45
Nowotny, H., 87
nursing, 36
nursing studies, 37, 41

objective knowledge, 18, 43, 56
Office for Science and Technology, 23
O'Hear, A., *178*
opposition, higher education as, 54
optoelectronics, 37, 40–1, *175*
Ortega y Gasset, 5
Oxford, University of, 113, *173, 180*

Pacific Rim, 101
pandemonium, 130–2, 172
paradigms, *179*
participation, 50, *175*
Passeron, J.-C., 50
pedagogical aims, 57
pedagogical challenge, 161
pedagogical environment, 159–60
pedagogical relationship, 99, 163, 171
pedagogical situation, 161
pedagogical space, 160–1, 171
pedagogies, 158
pedagogy for supercomplexity, 159–60, 162, *182*
pedagogy for value conflict, *179*
peer observation of teaching, 15
peer review, 148
performance indicators, 39, 49, 89, 172

performativity, 5, 14–15, 23–4, 28–30, 32–4, **38–43**, 45, 169, *174*
performativities, 46
personal dimension, 160
personal fulfilment, 52, 54
Peters, M., *173*
Peters, R., *179*
pharmaceutical industry, 37
philosophy, 85–6, 91
Plato, 24, *182*
Plumb, J., *177*
Plutarch, *177*
political correctness, 112
political science, 90
Popper, Sir K., 43–4, 56, 72, 84, *180*
positioning of the university, 19, 29–30, 101, 107, 113, 116, 133, 142
    see also repositioning of the university
positioning, ideological, 137
Post-Fordist age, 15
postmodern, the, 4, 18–19, 39, 172
postmodernism, 3–4, 26, 38, 42, 52, 58, 73, 115–16, 122–3, 156, *179*
postmodernists, 25, 73–4, 84, 116–17, *176*
postmodernity, 4, 15, 18, 58, 74, 87, *179*
postmodern story, 74
post-modern age, 48, 54, 56, 79, 116
post-modern society, 3–4, 83, 111
post-modern university, the, 4, 17, 19–22, 28, 65, 69, 71, 88–9, 95, 99, 108, 115
power, 19–20, 38, 109, 160
Power, M., 15, *178*
practical interest, 37
pragmatism, 122
premodern university, 16, 20
problem-solving, 42, 151
professional education, 36
professional life, 6, 157–8
professions, 17–18, 70, 157
progress, 77
public intellectuals, 162, 172
purity, 146

quality, 99
Quality Assurance Agency, *179*

radically unknowable, the world as, 63, 77
Ramsden, P., *178*
Ransom, S., 52
Rashdall, H., *173*
rationality, *177*
rational society, 70
Ravetz, J., *176*
Readings, B., 2, 99, 106, 120, *175*
realizing higher education, 165
realizing the university, 103, 171
reason, 2, 23, 25, 31, 55, 72, 74, 84, *177*
    reason, collegial, 122
    reason, critical, 33, 84
    reason, dialogic, 58, 103
    reason, economic, 24, 121
    reason, instrumental, 40, 57, 92, 121–2
    reason, life of, 78, 81
    reason, performative, 34
    reason, pure, 85
    reason, technical, 58
    reason, universal, 74
reflexive biographies, 158
reflexivity, 81, 105, 119
reframing, 143–5, 149
Reich, W., 50
Reid, I., *178*
relativism, 45
repositioning of the university, 13, 33, 142, 144
    see also positioning of the university
research, 15, 23, 28, 31, 34, 36–7, 43, 54, 67, 69–70, 79, 116, 138, **Chapter 11**, 162, 164, 170–1, *180*
Research Assessment Exercise, 43
researchers, 141, 145, 150
respect for persons, 27
responsibilities of universities, 2, 51, 82, 105, 149, 154, 158, 161, 169, 171–2
responsibility of the university, 1–5, 70, 76, 78–9, 146, 152, 155, 167–9, *173*, *174*, *178*, *180*
resurrection of university, 11
risk, 141
'risk society', 46, 142
Ritzer, G., 102

Robbins Report, *174*
Roberts, J., *177*
Robinson, F., 23
Rorty, R., 121, *175, 181*
Rothblatt, S., *175*
Rouse, J., 151
ruins, 2–3
rules, 113, 132–3, 141, *179, 180*
runaway world, 77
Russell, B., *177*
Ryle, G., 78

Sadlik, J., *173*
Schmitt, F., *178*
scholarship, 23, 43, 54, 67, 70, 79, 119,
    146–8, 170–1
Schön, D., 29, 68, 156
Schubert, 156
science, 17, 55, 65–6, 105, *178*
Scott, P., 13, 17, 21, 37, 48, 158, *173,*
    174, 180
Searle, J., *181*
self, **52–4**, 56–7, 65–6, 120, *176*
    self-critical capacity, 164
    self-enlightenment, 69
    self-regulation, 101
    self-identity, 157–8, 164
        see also identity
    self-irony, collective, 121–3
    self-reflection, organizational, 80
    self-reflexiveness, 164
    self-understanding, 162
semiotics, 41
Senge, P., 109, 127
Simons, H., *174*
skills, 24, 35, 44, 57, 90, *177*
    skills, key, 34, 49, 91
Schubert, 156
Shakespeare, W., 78
Sloman, A., *173*
sociology, 87
Soper, K., 116
Squires, H., 26, 116
state, the, 55, 70
'stable state', 110, 115
staff development, 135
standards, 20, 118
standards, critical, 119
Stehr, N., 14, 36
Steiner, G., 156

Stenhouse, L., *179*
Stryker, L., 25
student, 160
students, 11, 49–50, 53–4, 99, 113,
    115, 133, 142, 154, 157–61,
    163–4, 167, 171
subjectivity, 156
supercomplexity, 6–7, **Chapter 6,**
    75–7, 80–3, 84, 88, 91, 95,
    101–3, 106–7, 111–13, 117, 127,
    129–31, 134–5, 142, 144, 146,
    148, 152, 153, 155, 160–3, 168,
    170, 172, *177*
supercomplexity, conditions of,
    92–3, 108, 155–6, 164–5, 169,
    179
supercomplexity, idea of, 166–7
    see also pedagogy for
        supercomplexity
supercomplex management, 111
supercomplex university, 108–9, 135,
    171–2
supercomplex world/age, 6, 104, 109,
    119–20, 122, 149, 155–6, 158,
    162
surveillance, 15

Taylor, C., *174, 176*
Taylor, L., *174*
teacher education, 36, 41, 148
teaching (in universities), 15, 34, 39,
    69–70, 79, 107, 116, 138,
    Chapter 12, 170
    see also pedagogy
technology, 65–6, 84
technology transfer, 23, 145
tolerance, 26, 109, 141
traditions of the university, 6, 62, 114
transdisciplinarity, 170
    see also interdisciplinarity;
        multidisciplinarity
transferable skills, 15, 28, 35, 91
transformation, human, 32, *174, 180,*
    181
transport studies, 41
Trigg, R., *181*
Trow, M., 58, *173*
Trowler, P., *179*
truth, 14, 21–2, 38, 45, 47–8, 53, 57,
    69, 73, 81–2, *181*

truth criteria, 40
truth-telling, 53

UK, 13, 23, 43, 100, 135
uncertain age, 58, 71
uncertainty, 63, **65–6**, 67–9, 73, 82, 95,
    114, 118, 123, 129, 138, 143,
    145–6, 159, 170
  uncertainty, authoritative, *181*
  uncertainty, cognitive, 154
  uncertainty, creation of, 143
  uncertainty, epistemological,
    99–101, 103–4, 139
  uncertainty, ontological, 99–101,
    103–4
  uncertainty, organizational, 139
  uncertainty, radical, 154
uncertainty principle, 69–71, 142–3,
    145–6, 159
UNESCO, 173
universality, 72, 74, 85, 166
universals, 73–4, 79, 82, 167
university, 26
  university as meta-institution, 79
  university as organization, 128,
    138
  university, attenuated, 14–16
  university, conditions of, 4, **103–9**,
    178
  university, death of, 11–12, *173*
  university, democratic, 52
  university, elusive, 21
  university, idea of, 11–12, 72, 78, 86,
    99–100, 127, 168–9
  university, late-modern, 114–15, 118,
    123
  University of Industry, 31
  university, people's, 51
  university, performative, 33, 169
  university, purposes of, 64
  university, the, 2, 5, 18–19, 94
  university, the attenuated, 14–16
  university, title of, 18, 27, 31,
    102–4, 167–8
unpredictability, 63, **65–6**, 67–8, 73,
    129, 156, 172
Usher, R., 54

USA, 5
use value, 17, 34, 39–40

validity claims, 80, *175*
value added, 30, 33, 83, 151
value background, 1, 22, 26–8, 30,
    61–2, 82–3, 154
value component, 64
value conflict in universities, 28–9,
    113–14
value fork, 27
value for money, 90
value freedom, 25, 111
value neutrality, 113
value positioning of universities, 2
values, 23, 25–9, 33, 61–2, 82, 94,
    112–14, 117, 121, 123
  values, horizon of, 27, 33, *174*
Van Vught, F., *179*
vice-chancellors, 22, 40, 91–2, 101,
    104, 108, 110, 129, 138, *180*
Vidovich, L., *179*
virtual university, 16, 21, 31, 93
virtue, 28–9
virtues of the university, 79–81
vision of higher education, *175*
voice, 160

Webster, F., *173*
Weil, S., 80
western university, the, 1–2, 5, 11, 24,
    37, 40, 42, 53, 57, 62, 72, 79,
    81, 84, 92, 102–3, 154, 157,
    168–9
whistleblowers, 109
White, J., 49, *180*
whole person, 79
Williams, R., 144
Williamson, B., 13, *180*
will to power, 81–2
Winter, R., *179*
Wittgenstein, L., 38
Wolff, R., 25
work, 17, 49–50, 89, 91
Wyatt, J., *177*, *178*

Young, R., *179*

The Society for Research into Higher Education

The Society for Research into Higher Education exists to stimulate and coordinate research into all aspects of higher education. It aims to improve the quality of higher education through the encouragement of debate and publication on issues of policy, on the organization and management of higher education institutions, and on the curriculum and teaching methods.

The Society's income is derived from subscriptions, sales of its books and journals, conference fees and grants. It receives no subsidies, and is wholly independent. Its individual members include teachers, researchers, managers and students. Its corporate members are institutions of higher education, research institutes, professional, industrial and governmental bodies. Members are not only from the UK, but from elsewhere in Europe, from America, Canada and Australasia, and it regards its international work as among its most important activities.

Under the imprint *SRHE & Open University Press*, the Society is a specialist publisher of research, having over 70 titles in print. The Editorial Board of the Society's Imprint seeks authoritative research or study in the above fields. It offers competitive royalties, a highly recognizable format in both hardback and paperback and the worldwide reputation of the Open University Press.

The Society also publishes *Studies in Higher Education* (three times a year), which is mainly concerned with academic issues, *Higher Education Quarterly* (formerly *Universities Quarterly*), mainly concerned with policy issues, *Research into Higher Education Abstracts* (three times a year), and *SRHE News* (four times a year).

The society holds a major annual conference in December, jointly with an institution of higher education. In 1996 the topic was 'Working in Higher Education' at University of Wales, Cardiff. In 1997 it was 'Beyond the First Degree' at the University of Warwick and in 1998 it was 'The Globalization of Higher Education' at the University of Lancaster. The 1999 conference will be on the topic of higher education and its communities at UMIST.

The Society's committees, study groups and networks are run by the members. The networks at present include:

Access	Mentoring
Curriculum Development	Postgraduate Issues
Disability	Quality
Eastern European	Quantitative Studies
Funding	Student Development
Legal Education	Vocational Qualifications

Benefits to members

Individual

Individual members receive:

- *SRHE News*, the Society's publications list, conference details and other material included in mailings.
- Greatly reduced rates for *Studies in Higher Education* and *Higher Education Quarterly*.
- A 35 per cent discount on all SRHE & Open University Press publications.
- Free copies of the Procedings – commissioned papers on the theme of the Annual Conference.
- Free copies of *Research into Higher Education Abstracts*.
- Reduced rates for the annual conference.
- Extensive contacts and scope for facilitating initiatives.
- Free copies of the *Register of Members' Research Interests*.
- Membership of the Society's networks.

Corporate

Corporate members receive:

- Benefits of individual members, plus:
- Free copies of *Studies in Higher Education*.
- Unlimited copies of the Society's publications at reduced rates.
- Reduced rates for the annual conference.
- The right to submit applications for the Society's research grants.
- The right to use the Society's facility for supplying statistical HESA data for purposes of research.

Membership details: SRHE, 3 Devonshire Street, London W1N 2BA, UK. Tel: 0171 637 2766. Fax: 0171 637 2781. email: srhe@mailbox.ulcc.ac.uk
World Wide Web: http://www.srhe.ac.uk./srhe/
Catalogue: SRHE & Open University Press, Celtic Court, 22 Ballmoor, Buckingham MK18 1XW. Tel: 01280 823388. Fax: 01280 823233. email: enquiries@openup.co.uk

IMPROVING HIGHER EDUCATION
TOTAL QUALITY CARE

Ronald Barnett

This book provides the first systematic exploration of the topic of quality in higher education. Ronald Barnett examines the meaning of quality and its improvement at the levels of both the institution and the course – contemporary discussion having tended to focus on one or the other, without integrating the two perspectives. He argues against a simple identification of quality assessment with numerical perform-ance indicators *or* with academic audit *or* with the messages of the market. These are the contending definitions of the modern age, but they all contain interests tangen-tial to the main business of higher education.

Dr Barnett offers an alternative approach which begins from a sense of educators attempting to promote an open-ended development in their students. It is this view of higher education which, he argues, should be at the heart of our thinking about quality. Quality cannot be managed, but it can be cared for. Building on the con-ceptual base he establishes, Dr Barnett offers proposals for action in assessing institu-tional performance, in reviewing the quality of course programmes, and in improving the curriculum and the character of the student experience.

Contents
Part 1: The idea of quality – The quality of higher education – Aiming higher – The idea of quality – Can quality be managed? – Part 2: Improving the quality of institutions – Institutional purposes and performance indicators – Inside the black box – What's wrong with quality assurance? – Institutions for learning – Part 3: Improving the quality of courses – Practice makes perfect? – Communication, competence and community – We're all reflective practitioners now – Beyond teaching and learning – Conclusions – Appendix – Notes – Bibliography – Index.

256pp   0 335 09984 X (Paperback)   0 335 09985 8 (Hardback)

THE LIMITS OF COMPETENCE
KNOWLEDGE, HIGHER EDUCATION AND SOCIETY

Ronald Barnett

Competence is a term which is making its entrance in the university. How might it be understood at this level? *The Limits of Competence* takes an uncompromising line, providing a sustained critique of the notion of competence as wholly inadequate for higher education.

Currently, we are seeing the displacement of one limited version of competence by another even more limited interpretation. In the older definition – one of academic competence – notions of disciplines, objectivity and truth have been central. In the new version, competence is given an operational twist and is marked out by know-how, competence and skills. In this operationalism, the key question is not 'What do students understand?' but 'What can students do?'

The book develops an alternative view, suggesting that, for our universities, a third and heretical conception of human being is worth considering. Our curricula might, instead, offer an education for life.

Contents

Introduction – Part 1: Knowledge, higher education and society: The learning society? – A certain way of knowing? – We are all clerks now – Part 2: The new vocabulary: 'Skills' and 'vocationalism' – 'Competence' and 'outcomes' – 'Capability' and 'enterprise' – Part 3: The lost vocabulary: Understanding – Critique – Interdisciplinarity – Wisdom – Part 4: Competence reconsidered: Two rival versions of competence – Beyond competence – Retrospect and coda – Bibliography – Index.

222pp   0 335 19341 2 (Paperback)   0 335 19070 7 (Hardback)

HIGHER EDUCATION: A CRITICAL BUSINESS

Ronald Barnett

Barnett reviews what the academy customarily means when it talks about critical thought, explains why that talk is so often shallow and pessimistic, and holds up for contemplation a positive conception of a 'very wide self' formed through education . . . He breathes completely new life into the dead notion of academic as intellectual.

> Professor Sheldon Rothblatt, University of California,
> Berkley and Royal Institute of Technology, Sweden

Higher Education: A Critical Business is a bold statement about higher education in the modern age. It continues Ronald Barnett's thinking of his earlier books but offers a completely new set of ideas in a challenging but engaging argument.

A defining concept of the Western university is that of critical thinking, but that idea is completely inadequate for the changing and unknowable world facing graduates. Instead, we have to displace the idea of critical thinking with the much broader idea of critical being. In this idea, students reflect critically on knowledge but they also develop their powers of critical self-reflection and critical action. This critique is transformatory. An education for critical being calls for a new approach to the process of higher education. It also has implications for the organization and management of universities, and for the relationship of universities to the wider worlds of work, professionalism and intellectual life.

Anyone interested in understanding how we might develop universities and higher education for the modern world should read this important book.

Contents

Introduction – Part 1: Rethinking critical thinking – Conditions of critical thought – Uncritical theory – Discourse and critical potential – The closing of the critical university? – Part 2: Towards critical being – Critical being in higher education – Critical action – Critical self-reflection – A curriculum for critical being – Part 3: Critique in society – Critical thought in a corporate world – Critical professionalism – Academics as intellectuals – Critical thinking for a learning society – Coda: A critical space – Glossary – Bibliography – Index.

208pp   0 335 19703 5 (Paperback)   0 335 19704 3 (Hardback)